Sri Aurobindo and His Contemporary Thinkers

Sri Aurobindo and His Contemporary Thinkers

Edited by

Indrani Sanyal

Krishna Roy

D.K. Printworld (P) Ltd.
New Delhi

in Association with

Jadavpur University
Kolkata

Cataloging in Publication Data — DK
[Courtesy: D.K. Agencies (P) Ltd. <docinfo@dkagencies.com>]

Sri Aurobindo and his contemporary thinkers /
edited by Indrani Sanyal, Krishna Roy.
p. cm.
Contributed articles and seminar papers.
Sri Aurobindo, 1872-1950, Indian philosopher and nationalist.
Includes bibliographical references.
ISBN 8124604282

1. Sri Aurobindo, 1872–1950. — Contemporaries. 2. Renaissance — India. 3. India — Politics and government — 20th century. 4. Philosophy, Indic — 20th century. I. Sanyal, Indrani, 1950- II. Roy, Krishna, 1941- .

DDC 954.035 22

ISBN 81-246-0428-2
First published in India in 2007

Published by:
D.K. Printworld (P) Ltd.
Regd. Office: 'Sri Kunj', F-52, Bali Nagar
Ramesh Nagar Metro Station
New Delhi-110 015
Phones: (011) 2545-3975; 2546-6019; *Fax*: (011) 2546-5926
E-mail: dkprintworld@vsnl.net
Website: www.dkprintworld.com

in association with
Jadavpur University
Kolkata (West Bengal)

Printed by: D. K. Printworld (P) Ltd., New Delhi

Preface

In the present anthology, *Sri Aurobindo and His Contemporary Thinkers*, an inter-disciplinary approach has been taken to bring to light the position and thoughts of Sri Aurobindo and his contemporaries. This anthology includes many of the deliberations that were presented in the national seminar on "Sri Aurobindo and his Contemporary Thinkers" held in 2006, organized by Centre for Sri Aurobindo Studies, Jadavpur University and the other seminar on "Sri Aurobindo and the Indian Renaissance" held in 2007 and organized by Centre for Sri Aurobindo Studies, Jadavpur University in collaboration with Darsan O Samaj Trust, Kolkata. We are very much grateful to Prahlad Kumar Sarkar, the Founder-Director of Darsan O Samaj Trust for his spontaneous cooperation in organizing the seminar. We are thankful to the authors for their co-operation in bringing out this volume for publication. Our special thanks are due to the University Grants Commission for providing us financial and other assistance for this seminar. We express our deepest gratitude to Jadavpur University. Finally, special thanks are due to Susheel Mittal and his team from D.K. Printworld (P) Ltd., New Delhi for their untiring zeal and productive assistance.

Indrani Sanyal
Krishna Roy

Centre for Sri Aurobindo Studies
Department of Philosophy
Jadavpur University
Kolkata – 700 032

Dedicated to

Professor Arabinda Basu

whose

sound advice and caring support

always encourage us to go ahead

Contents

Introduction

We have learnt from history that there come, in the life of a nation, some stages which are marked by glories and successes as well as stages which are marked by follies and crises. The history of Bengal, and of India in general, is no exception. In course of this journey we notice a period — between the later half of eighteenth century to nineteenth century — which is marked by reawakened national spirit to find self-expression of the passion for reinterpreting and recreating the traditional values in modern light. This is the period which is generally known as the Renaissance in Bengal and also as the Renaissance in India. The word "Renaissance" as it is used in the West primarily implies the reawakening of spirituality. In the case of Indian Renaissance — it is much more comprehensive; it encompasses all the dimensions of human life — social, economic, cultural, spiritual — all at the same time.

There is an eternal message of the *Bhagavad-Gītā* that at the periods of crises there appear on earth some gifted and mighty persons who liberate men from darkness and despair and help in the advancement of the nation. This has happened in India during the Renaissance when many creative, patriotic, powerful luminaries flourished and dedicated their lives for India's emancipation and progress. The history of the period is an account of the thoughts and actions of those illustrious persons, who had faith both in themselves and in their heritage.

The present anthology, *Sri Aurobindo and His Contemporary Thinkers*, is an account of some of those illustrious persons, who by their ideas and actions have enriched our socio-cultural heritage. This is an inter-disciplinary study to deliberate over, and estimate a person extraordinary and a period remarkable. Though in this volume reference to history, politics, sociology and philosophy have been inter-mingled to derive a holistic picture of a period surrounding Sri Aurobindo yet mostly stress is laid on conceptual and analytic approach. We are aware that there is no dearth of account of this glorious period of Indian history, nor that the present anthology could pay attention to the contribution of many of those remarkable personalities. The main purpose of the present work is primarily to look back to those path-makers so that we can carry forward their ideals and messages. The other intention of the present work is to situate Sri Aurobindo's thought in its socio-cultural background, to know the then socio-political milieu, to recapitulate the contributions of his contemporaries, to assess and compare those contributions so that proper evaluation of Sri Aurobindo's distinctiveness can be made.

Kireet Joshi in his article, "Sri Aurobindo's Philosophy of Nationalism, Internationalism and Contemporary Crisis", characterizes Sri Aurobindo "as the most heroic nationalist" and attempts to elaborate his philosophy of nationalism as available mainly in the periodical *Bande Mataram* from the period 1906-08. No doubt that geographical unity, a common past, and a powerful common interest are important factors in developing the spirit of nationality. But these factors were never considered absolutely essential for the nation. Sri Aurobindo maintained that nation is a mighty *śakti*, and it is composed of the *śakti*s of millions of peoples of India. Sri Aurobindo said a nation is a soul, it is immortal. Joshi emphasized that for Sri Aurobindo, preservation, strengthening and enrichment of the nation-soul was very urgent. Further Joshi draws our attention to one of the important distinctions that was maintained by Sri Aurobindo between political unity and real unity. And he calls a nation a real unity and not an empire. Nation will remain so until a greater living unit can be found. The true individual soul and true national soul are characterized by mutuality, interdependence, and inner oneness. This may open the door for the formation of a world unity without interruption. Sri Aurobindo gives us an ideal law of social devėlopment. Sri Aurobindo's philosophy of internationalism has also been elaborated by Joshi. In the book, *The Ideal of Human Unity,* Sri Aurobindo describes the prospect of the coming change in humanity. The most striking outcome of this would be, as believed by Sri Aurobindo, internationalism — the idea of humanity as a single race of beings with a common life and a common general interest. Joshi rightly observes that in the philosophy of Sri Aurobindo this internationalism mingles with the religion of humanity.

D.P. Chattopadhyaya in his article, "The Distinctiveness of Sri Aurobindo's View on Indian Renaissance", highlights Sri Aurobindo's interpretation of Indian Renaissance. Chattopadhyaya suggests that while interpreting the term Renaissance, Sri Aurobindo had in mind meanings of words like *punarjanma,* i.e. re-birth and *navikarana,* i.e. making anew. Sri Aurobindo left behind the then widely popular acceptable thesis that cultural interpretation of the Indian Renaissance was mainly Germanic or Italian. Sri Aurobindo finds similarity between Indian Renaissance and Irish Renaissance and Chattopadhyaya very elaborately brings out similarities between these two countries. Chattopadhyaya makes an interesting observation about how history of all cultures and its underlying civilizations has been interpreted in terms of renewal of the past in the light of the present and addressed to the future. Diverse formulations of different culture and civilization show that facts and ideas lend themselves to different types of formulation, de-formulation and re-formulation. From this it follows, as observed by Chattopadhyaya, that no one should expect to have any unique, unalterable and definite description of any culture or civilization, applicable to it at all times. This accounts for different interpretations of Indian Renaissance and Bengal Renaissance.

Rakhal Chandra Nath dealt with different interpretations of the notion of Renaissance and this is quite obvious from the self-explanatory title of his article entitled, "The Bengal Renaissance : Different Interpretations". Historians are not unanimous in their interpretation of this notion and accordingly that interpretation has coloured their vision of Renaissance. This is the main reason why we see different ways of evaluating Bengal Renaissance among the historians. Naturally a question has also come up regarding finding a parallel of Bengal Renaissance in Italian Renaissance or in English Renaissance. Again some have totally rejected the theory of Bengal Renaissance and have called Renaissance a pseudo event. Till mid-1930s, the attitude towards Bengal Renaissance was one of veneration and uncritical acceptance of it. According to some the real nature of Renaissance is to be discovered from the movement led by Bankim Chandra and Vivekananda. Sri Aurobindo is also another important interpreter of Renaissance. Nath also tries to clarify the position of the Marxists as positive in their understanding of Bengal Renaissance. Among the Marxists, there were also further differences in their reading of Renaissance and assessing its role. Some were of the opinion that Bengal Renaissance was limited in its scope and it was confined only among the middle-class people. A group of scholars associated with American universities and British universities argue that

Bengal renaissance is a British gift. His article provides a very lucid introduction to most of the debates centring around the interpretation and assessment of Renaissance in Bengal.

Dilip Kumar Roy also deals with the concept of Renaissance in his article, "Sri Aurobindo on the Possibility of Renaissance in India". He maintains clearly that pressure of super-imposed European culture has necessitated the reawakening in India referred to as Renaissance. The author analyses the spiritualistic viewpoint of India which believes that behind the universe and even inside man there is a force, by whatever name it is called, and is considered to be the spirit of India and explains its spiritualistic tendency. Sri Aurobindo believed that man has a capacity to extend beyond himself, and he is able to make himself more complete than what he is now. India could excel in science, in philosophy, in literature and in social system because of its unbounded energy and its spiritualistic root. The present author also draws our attention to three factors, as maintained by Sri Aurobindo, that are largely responsible for decline of India. These three retrograding factors are supposed to be decline of vital energy, decline in the functioning of the intuitive mind and scientific mind, and decline in spiritual knowledge.

Dilip Kumar Chatterjee in the article, "Sri Aurobindo and Ireland : A Critical Study of his Response to Ireland's National and Cultural Renaissance" gives particularly an account of Sri Aurobindo's attitude towards Ireland and its comparison with Indian context. The author observes that that course of historical events in Ireland had great influence on colonized India. He gives account of Irish-Indian connections. The Indo-Irish interaction became an interesting phenomenon. From the Indian side, great personalities like Rammohan Roy and Prince Dwarakanath Tagore were in good terms with Ireland, and Irish nationalists and poets like George William Russell, Yeats,

Charles Johnston and James Henry Cousins found deep solace in Indian religious thoughts in times of crisis. Rabindranath and Yeats have developed a unique relation. Sri Aurobindo's poems "Lines on Ireland", "Charles Stewart Parnell", "Hic Jacet" and his article "The Irish Example" in the *Bande Mataram* shows his concern for that country. From Chatterjee's writings we get a vivid description about how these two countries through contacts with each other were trying to reassess their historical identity in different fields. Sri Aurobindo found in Cousins a true friend of India. The author thinks that Sri Aurobindo and other Indian leaders found their model for anti-British agitation from the people of Ireland. Sri Aurobindo along with his Irish counterparts believed that national and cultural resurgence in these countries would initiate a kind of development in human consciousness.

Rama Prasad De in his article "National Education Movement and Satis Chandra" delineated the contribution of Satis Chandra Mukherjee towards the formation and function of National Council of Education, Bengal. Satis Chandra along with Sri Aurobindo and Rabindranath realized the need for having a system of education, based on our culture and tradition. In the context of colonial India, when majority of Indian people, especially the nationalists, were trying to reassert their self-identity, the role of true education became very important. The aspiration for national education is often viewed as closely intertwined with the struggle for national independence. Satis Chandra dedicated his life in pursuance of that mission. As the editor of *The Dawn Magazine* and as the founder of a special institution for providing training to youths, known as Dawn Society (1902) and as the Principal of Bengal National College, Satis Chandra "imperceptibly" and "imperishably" paved the way for national education movement. De refers to these contributions of Satis Chandra

Mukherjee as "exploratory contributions" to the cause of national education. De elaborates Satis Chandra's sincere efforts to tackle three major problems faced by the newly set up Council regarding finance, course content and availability of academicians for implementing the programme. As an administrator and as an educationist, the author observes that Satis Chandra worked with "one purpose, one desire, one goal" for the cause of national education movement of Bengal.

Amal Kumar De in his article, "National Council of Education, Bengal and Sri Aurobindo" gives us a short sketch of the history of National Council of Education, Bengal since its inception to the present day and delineates the role of Sri Aurobindo in the evolution of the Council, which, according to him, is the "trustee to the people of a great instrument of national regeneration." The author primarily focuses on Sri Aurobindo's attitude towards national education. National education, to Sri Aurobindo, was not merely national; it has three levels: individual, national and universal. It further integrates past with the present, East with West. Following this ideal, the Mother also propagated integral education that synthesises the physical, the vital, the mental, the psychic and the spiritual.

Indrani Sanyal in her article, "History As Applied Metaphysics" has engaged herself in a conceptual analysis of the notion of history. In this article Sanyal focuses on the main observations of Pramath Nath Mukhopadhyaya, also known as Swami Pratyagatmananda Saraswati and compares his views with that of other well-known philosophers of history, both Western and Indian. Sri Aurobindo himself was a great scholar of history and the present discussion enables us to have a look at the philosophy of history as espoused by Sri Aurobindo. Sri Aurobindo observes one of the very important distinctions admitted in philosophy of history is between history as description and as an explanation. Pramath Nath also does not subscribe to the view that history is description alone. The author maintains that with regard to any civilization, whatsoever, the question may be raised, "What is it all for?" In this article the author very lucidly explains the new paradigm that was put forward by Pramath Nath and also shows similarities between Pramath Nath and Sri Aurobindo. Sanyal observes that the idea of universal history as understood by Pramath Nath or Sri Aurobindo has much wider connotation than what is ordinarily conveyed by this expression. Sanyal attempts to elaborate the standpoint of Pramath Nath who believed that behind all historical events there is *atman* or consciousness that is trying to reveal itself. In the writings of Pramath Nath the notion of progress occurs as a key concept as it is in the works of Sri Aurobindo. Sri Aurobindo and Pramath Nath do not consider the course of history to be mechanical.

Tirthanath Bandyopadhyaya in his article "Some Renaissance Aspects of Vivekananda's Thoughts", analyses Vivekananda's outlook about morality, caste system and *dharma* and discovers influence of Renaissance on his thoughts. Vivekananda's conviction about universal soul, as shown by Bandyopadhyaya may be projected as the ground for affirming universality of morality. Bandyopadhyaya elaborates in detail Vivekananda's concept of brotherhood and equality in this connection. The main idea of universal morality is contained in the dictum, as clearly pointed out by the author, "not living among others but living with others". Sri Aurobindo strictly rejects casteism. Following Vivekananda's views, the author points out the three-*guṇa* theory of Upaniṣads and makes it clear what it meant for Vivekananda. Bandyopadhyaya observes that Vivekananda does not approve rigidity in caste grouping for he looks upon it more as a human factor than as a social factor. Bandyopadhyaya finally analyses the concept of *dharma* as understood by Vivekananda and shows the most important element in his concept of *dharma* is its this-worldliness. The practical aspect of *dharma* in the view of Vivekananda, as explained clearly by Bandyopadhyaya, consists in providing service to actual living individuals.

Aparna Banerjee in her article entitled "The Western Imperialistic Challenge : Aurobindo, Tilak and Gokhale", explores the differences in political ideals of these three stalwarts of Indian nationalism. The present article tries to bring out the extent of cultural domination by the Western culture even upon our Indian nationalists. This essay is a narration of "pull of Westernization" on the one hand, and the "quest for self-identity and self-respect" on the other. Banerjee is of the opinion that among the three, as specifically mentioned by her, Sri Aurobindo was more successful in getting rid of the influence of the West. Sri Aurobindo, as pointed out by Banerjee, maintained that it was not deplorable that one civilization coming close to another very active civilization often imitates that civilization. But at the same time imitation of one civilization by the other should show tendency towards assimilating some of the good aspects of the other. Banerjee considers Sri Aurobindo to be the most capable person in his endeavour for assimilating two cultures — Western and Indian — by his notion of spiritual transformation.

Sri Aurobindo's appreciation for Tagore's patriotism and creativity continued and this has been the theme of Supriyo Bhattacharya's article "Significance of Tagore's Poetry in the Indian Renaissance : Sri Aurobindonian Perspective". In this article Bhattacharya recapitulates the interpretation of Tagore's poetry from Sri Aurobindo's perspective. In his treatise entitled "Renaïssance in India" Sri Aurobindo analyses the steps which led to Indian Renaissance; the first step being the "reception of the European contact," the second step has been the reaction and partial assimilation of European influence and the third step being the stage of "new creation." According to Sri Aurobindo, Bankim Chandra Chatterjee and Rabindranath Tagore are the two "most distinctive and original geniuses" of such third creative stage. Both in his articles on "Karmayogin" and "The Future Poetry," Sri Aurobindo mentions about Tagore's "new and deeper manner of seeing life" and how Tagore's poetry synthesises the infinite and eternal and the mind and soul with the life of man.

In her article, "The Revolutionary Movement: Rabindranath Tagore and Aurobindo", Manjula Bose has discussed the two different viewpoints of Rabindranath and Aurobindo towards the then revolutionary movement, which was intended to bring back India's independence. Aurobindo, before leaving for Pondicherry, was actively involved in such revolutionary activities. Rabindranath, though not in favour of such violent practices, had great regard for Aurobindo and his followers, for their patriotism, courage and self-sacrifice. Aurobindo felt that armed revolt was the swiftest and most thorough in its results. Through his literary works, poems and plays, Rabindranath wanted to convey his disapproval of such underground violent practices. What is noteworthy is that though both Rabindranath and Aurobindo differed regarding the methods employed for bringing about India's independence, yet both of them were highly appreciative of each other's patriotism and sincerity.

Tara Chatterjea in her article, "Philosophy of Krishna Chandra Bhattacharyya", develops the philosophy of Krishna Chandra Bhattacharyya who was one of the contemporaries of Sri Aurobindo. The author points out that thoughts of Krishna Chandra were very much influenced by Kant and by the philosophy of the Advaita Vedānta school. Krishna Chandra was interested in Indian idealism and has written extensively on the Advaita Vedānta and the Saṁkhya-Yoga philosophy. Chatterjee discusses about the four grades of thoughts, namely, empirical thought, pure objective or contemplative thought, spiritual or subjective thought, and transcendental thought as admitted by Krishna Chandra Bhattacharyya. The present article may provide incentive for future research into the thoughts of Krishna Chandra. A close perusal of the philosophy of Krishna Chandra may throw some light in understanding the philosophy of Sri Aurobindo who was also an idealist and also shares basic tenets of monistic Vedānta.

Tracing the cultural milieu of the period, Sudhir Kumar Nandi in his article, "Acharya Brojendranath Seal : His Aesthetic Ideas," discusses the aesthetic ideas of Acharya Brajendranath Seal in the light of quest for eternal beauty. Seal's philosophy gave us a synoptic view, emphasising on anthropocentricity and interpretation of culture. While formulating his distinctive views on aesthetics, Seal offered constructive criticisms of both Hegelian aesthetics and modern art. Through his ideas of "moral teachings by aesthetic culture," Seal wanted to relate art with morality. In Seal's view on art and poetry, we notice the fusion of mysticism with rationality.

We know that Sri Aurobindo's synoptic vision was directed to all the then social and moral issues and as such he was eager to transform the prevailing attitude towards women in India. In her article, "Change in the Outlook Towards Women : An Influence of Indian Renaissance", Madhumita Chattopadhyay discusses how the spirit of Renaissance, i.e. the spirit of emancipation, is manifested in the attitudes of Sri Aurobindo and other leaders of Indian Renaissance. Most of these thinkers realized that the true Renaissance is dependent on the transformation of the women's condition and without such improvement of the women no lasting development can be possible. In the present article she has focused on the contribution of Sri Aurobindo and Swami Vivekananda. Being respectful of India's ancient tradition, both these thinkers wanted to revive the basic ideals of womanhood as depicted in the Vedas and the Upaniṣads. Both of them believed that the traditional *dharma* was not opposed to women's enlightenment, rather helped to flourish the latent potentialities of the women.

In her article, "Raja Rammohan Roy : The Forerunner of Women's Liberation Movement", Krishna Roy seeks to highlight the contribution of Raja Rammohan Roy for initiating the women's liberation movement in India. Rammohan's effort for abolishing the *satī* practice is well known but his contribution for improving the socio-economic status of women is equally noteworthy. As a non-conformist and a combatant, Rammohan took it as a mission to alter the miserable condition of women at that period. His untiring effort and rational arguments helped the women to regain their lost rights in family property. He emphasised that proper education, liberal attitude and organized efforts would help the women to awaken from inertia and passivity.

Similar attempts to compare the methodologies, pursued by Mahatma Gandhi and Sri Aurobindo can be noticed in the article, "Violence or Non-violence : Interpretations by Sri Aurobindo and Mahatma Gandhi", by Sushmita Bhowmik, who focuses primarily on the interpretation of the concepts of violence and non-violence. While Sri Aurobindo held that violence can be resolved only through violence, Mahatma Gandhi thought that violence can never be resolved except through non-violence.

Tracing the evolution of such patriotic spirit through their biographical accounts, Sujata Mukherjee in her article, "Sri Aurobindo, Mahatma Gandhi and India's Freedom Struggle : From Swadeshi to Non-Cooperation", shows how both Mahatma Gandhi and Sri Aurobindo pursued the common goal of India's freedom following two divergent methods. In spite of such differences both these thinkers wanted to situate India's political struggle on moral and ethical foundations.

Thus to conclude, in the present volume, *Sri Aurobindo and His Contemporary Thinkers,* these are, as discussed above, some of the topics that are mainly touched upon and also from different perspectives. Each individual author has expressed his/her observations on the chosen topic. However, in a volume like this, neither it is possible nor it is expected that an account complete in all respects on the theme, which happens to be so vast and complex, will be provided. We hope this would once again rekindle interest among us for newer analyses, interpretations, debates and discussions centring around Sri Aurobindo, his contemporary thinkers and renaissance in India. This academic pursuit surely would open up avenues for newer research.

Indrani Sanyal
Krishna Roy

Centre for Sri Aurobindo Studies
Department of Philosophy
Jadavpur University
Kolkata – 700 032

1

Sri Aurobindo's Philosophy of Nationalism, Internationalism and Contemporary Crisis

Kireet Joshi

THE central theme in Sri Aurobindo [1872–1950] is that of the contemporary evolutionary crisis of humanity. He was of the view that man is a transitional being, a laboratory, in whose mind contemplation and speculation take place regularly, and with whose conscious co-operation Nature wills to work.

Sri Aurobindo's life was devoted entirely to this laboratory where new evolution could be worked out. In this task, Madame Mirra Alfassa (1878–1973), who was known in India and the world as "The Mother", came from France and collaborated in developing the integral yoga of Sri Aurobindo. The Mother's own experiences and realizations leading up to the supramental transformation and manifestation on the earth are to be found in the 13-volume L'Agenda de Mère.

Sri Aurobindo was a poet par excellence. His most famous poetical work, Savitri, *presented a new kind of poetry, which has been termed as overhead poetry. This is an epic, the longest in English literature, containing about 24,000 lines; a prophetic vision of the future. Sri Aurobindo has written a number of other short and long poems, among which Ilion, extending over 100 pages, is an innovative experimentation in an epic in quantitative hexameters in the history of English literature. Sri Aurobindo has also written five dramas: The Perseus the Deliverer, Rodogune, Viziers of Bassora, Vasavadutta and Eric. He has also translated two plays of Kālidāsa from the original Sanskrit into English. Sri Aurobindo also wrote* The Future Poetry *which is an outstanding interpretation of the meaning of poetry, of the history of English poetry, and the possibilities of that poetry to turn into the higher vehicle of mantric poetry.*

Sri Aurobindo was also in the early part of his life a prominent nationalist leader, and he has rightly been called the "Prophet of Indian Nationalism". Sri Aurobindo had deeply studied and loved India. He had made original research in the Veda, Upaniṣads and the Gītā, the three greatest records of knowledge which have served as the foundations of Indian culture. Apart from his profound knowledge of Sanskrit, he had mastery over Greek and Latin, and he had made a thorough study of Western history. He has, therefore, been rightly regarded as a great synthesiser of the East and the West. His message for human unity is of direct relevance to the contemporary effort that is sweeping all over the world connecting the past with the present and the future. His works have bridged the minds and hearts of the people all over the world.

Sri Aurobindo's Writings Arouse National Spirit

A most luminous and revelatory exposition of philosophy of nationalism, especially of Indian nationalism, is to be found in the writings of Sri Aurobindo. In fact, Sri Aurobindo's own life is a burning example of Indian nationalism, both in its uniqueness and universality. If we study the history of Indian nationalism, we shall find that he stands out as the most heroic nationalist who formulated in the most inspiring terms the true aim of Indian nationalism. During the early period of the national struggle, he accomplished the task of fixing it in the national consciousness within a short period of two years (1906-08) through his electric writings in *Bande Mataram*. This was only a miracle that has remained unparalleled in the history of nationalism of the entire world.

Creation of a new spirit in the country was the greatest achievement. A feeling of ecstasy gripped people all over as they now began to realise the true meaning of nationalism which filled them with enthusiasm. No amount of repressions or depressions could silence the stir. It was only renewed and revived with much vigour and vitality with each passing wave. This wave kept the life's thread of movement for liberation that remained recognizable throughout the nearly 50 years of its struggle. The cry of *Bande Mataram* could be heard on all sides. The people felt glorified and dared to act together with a hope of success. The old apathy and timidity was broken and a force was created which nobody could destroy, and which carried India to the beginning of a complete victory.

Unity in Race, Religion & Language

Sri Aurobindo challenged the contention that unity in race, religion and language is essential for nationalism and its growth. He acknowledged that such elements of unity are very helpful to the growth of nationality, but it is not essential that they, on their own, will assure the country's nationalism. Referring to the example of the Roman Empire, he pointed out that even though it created a common language, a common religion, a common goal and a common life, and did its best to crush out racial diversities under the heavy weight of its uniform system, it failed to make one great nation.

What, then, are the essential elements of nationality? Sri Aurobindo pondered to himself. He then answered:

> We answer that there are certain essential conditions, geographical unity, a common past, a powerful common interest impelling towards unity and certain favourable

> political conditions which enable the impulse to realize itself in an organized government expressing the nationality and perpetuating its single and united existence. This may be provided by a part of the nation, a race or community, uniting the others under its leadership or domination, or by a united resistance to a common pressure from outside or within. A common enthusiasm coalescing with a common interest is the most powerful fosterer of nationality. We believe that the necessary elements are present in India, we believe that the time has come and that by a common resistance to a common pressure in the shape of the boycott, inspired by a common enthusiasm and ideal, that united nationality for which the whole history of India has been a preparation, will be speedily and mightily accomplished.[1]

Love, Both Indian Nationalism and Patriotism

Philosphy of Indian nationalism is also the philosophy of patriotism. In view of this philosophy, patriotism is not limited to the love of the land of the country, *janmabhumi,* but it is also love for the people of the land. This philosophy goes even further and inspires love of the values of the culture that have been nourished and promoted through a long history of 5,000 years and more. And beyond the values of this great culture, patriotism is in its heart, illuminated worship of the smiling and beneficent and strong and powerful *Śakti,* which we call Mother India or Bhārat Mātā. As Sri Aurobindo wrote, a nation is not a piece of earth, nor a figure of spirit, nor a fiction of mind, it is mighty *Śakti* composed of the *Śakti*s of all the millions of units that make up the nation. He further pointed out that the nation is veritably a soul, which is immortal and even when geographically fragmented or divided, it has the power to reunite itself as one unity in diversity.

---

1. Sri Aurobindo: *Bande Mataram,* Centenary Edition, vol. 1, p. 507.

In an inspired article (11 March 1908 in *Bande Mataram*) Sri Aurobindo gave expression to the voices of the martyrs from their cells which cry out to us and give us an imperishable message which we can incorporate in our studies that aim at value-oriented education:

> Work, but aspire, so that your work may be true to the call you have heard and which we have obeyed; labour for great things first and the small will come of themselves. Cherish the might of the spirit, the nobility of the ideal, the grandeur of the dream; the spirit will create the material it needs, the idea will bring the real to its body and self-expression, the dream is the stuff out of which the waking world will be created. It was the strength of the spirit which stood with us before the alien tribunal, it was the force of the ideal which led us to the altar of sacrifice, it is the splendour of the dream which supports us through the dreary months and years of our martyrdom. For these are the truth and the divinity within the movement.[2]

Growth of National Education and National Soul

Sri Aurobindo wrote a series of articles on education in the *Karmayogin* during 1909-10 under the title "A System of National Education" and "The National Value of Art".

In "A System of National Education," Sri Aurobindo points out that the question is not between modernism and antiquity, but between an imported civilization and the greater possibilities of the Indian mind and nature; not between the present and the past, but between the present and the future. He pointed out:

> The living spirit of the demand for national education no more requires a return to the astronomy and mathematics of Bhaskara or the forms of the system of Nalanda than the

2. Sri Aurobindo: *Bande Mataram*, Centenary Edition, vol. 1, p. 745.

> living spirit of Swadeshi, a return from railway and motor traction to the ancient chariot and the bullock-cart.[3]

He, therefore, spoke not of a return to the fifth century but an initiation of the centuries to come, not a reversion but a break forward away from a present artificial falsity to India's own greater innate potentialities, which are demanded by the soul of India.

The major question, he pointed out, is not merely what science we learn, but what we shall do with our science and how, by acquiring the scientific mind and recovering the habit of scientific discovery, we shall relate it to other powers of the human mind. Again, he pointed out that the question is not what language (Sanskrit or any other) should be acquired by whatever method is most natural, efficient and stimulating to the mind, but how we are to learn and make use of Sanskrit and the indigenous languages, so as to get the heart and intimate sense of our own culture and establish a vivid continuity between the still living power of our past and the yet uncreated power of our future, and how we are to learn and use English or any other foreign tongue so as to know helpfully the life, ideas and culture of other countries and establish our right relations with the world around us. He argued that the aim and principle of a true national education is not to ignore modern truth and knowledge, but to take our foundation on India's own being, own mind and own spirit.

Considering that India has always seen in the human being a soul, a portion of the divinity enwrapped in the mind and body, a conscious manifestation in Nature of the universal self and spirit, he concluded that the one central object of the national system of education should be the growth of the soul,

---

3. Sri Aurobindo: *A Preface on National Education*, Centenary Edition, vol. 17, p. 194.

its powers and possibilities, besides the preservation, strengthening and enrichment of the nation-soul and the normative needs of its ascending movements. Not limited to these two, Sri Aurobindo put forth in its aim also the raising of both the individual soul and the national soul into the powers of the life and the ascending mind and the soul of humanity. He added,

> . . . at no time will it lose sight of man's highest object, the awakening and development of his spiritual being.[4]

Three Instruments: Instruction, Example and Influence

There are, according to Sri Aurobindo, three instruments of the teacher: instruction, example and influence. The good teacher will seek to awaken much more than to instruct. He will aim at the growth of the faculties and the experiences by a natural process and free expansion. He will not impose his opinions on the passive acceptance of the receptive minds. He will throw in only what is productive and sure as a seed, which will grow under the benign fostering within. He will know that the example is more powerful than instruction. Actually, the example is not that of the outward acts but of the inner motivation of life and the inner states and inner activities. Finally, he will also acknowledge that influence is more important than example. For, influence proceeds from the power or contact of the teacher with his pupil, from the nearness of his soul to the soul of another, infusing into the pupil, even though in silence, all that which the teacher himself is or possesses. The good teacher is himself a constant student. He is a child leading other children, and a light kindling other lights, a vessel and a channel.

4. Sri Aurobindo: *The Hour of God : A Preface on National Education*, Centenary Edition, vol. 17, p. 200.

Sri Aurobindo's concept of integral education finds its full relevance in the context of what Sri Aurobindo has called the evolutionary crisis; a crisis that occurs in a species at a time when some kind of mutation is imminent.

Integral education would not only aim at the integral development of personality, but it would also embrace all knowledge in its scope. It would pursue physical and psychical sciences, not merely to know the world and Nature in her processes and to use them for material human needs, but to know through them the Spirit in the world and the ways of the Spirit in its appearances. It would study ethics in order not only to search for the good as the mind sees it, but also to perceive the supra-ethical good. Similarly, it would pursue Art not merely to present images of the subjective and the objective world, but to see them with significant and creative vision that goes behind their appearances and to reveal the supra-rational Truth and Beauty. It would encourage the study of humanities, not in order to foster a society as a background for a few luminous figures so that the many necessarily remain for ever on the lower ranges of life, but to inspire the regeneration of the total life of the earth and to encourage voluntary optimism for that regeneration in spite of all previous failures. Finally, it would encourage unity of knowledge and harmony of knowledge, and it would strive to foster the spirit of universality and oneness.

An important characteristic of integral education is its insistence on simultaneous development of knowledge, will, harmony and skill as also various parts of the being to the extent possible from the earliest stages of education. And since each individual child is unique in the composition of its qualities and characteristics, its capacities and propensities, integral education in its practice tends to become increasingly individualized. Again, for this very reason, the methods of education become increasingly dynamic, involving active participation of the child in its own growth.

Developing and Perfecting Integral Yoga

The theme of Indian nationalism occupied Sri Aurobindo throughout his life. He wrote on this subject even when he had left in 1910 active participation in the political activity on account of his total occupation with the future of India and the world, and with the integral yoga that he was developing and perfecting it as an aid to the solution of the evolutionary crisis of humanity. This subject was developed by him in four of his books that he wrote during 1914 and 1921, namely, *The Life Divine, The Foundations of Indian Culture, The Ideal of Human Unity* and *The Human Cycle.* In these books, we find illuminating analysis and exposition of what may be called the philosophical foundations of nationalism and internationalism. These foundations, as we discern them in Sri Aurobindo's writings, are those relating to the philosophy of the individual and the aggregate, philosophy of the national aggregate and national unity, philosophy of nationality and nation-state, and philosophy of nationalism, internationalism, and universality.

There is today much contest in respect of the concept of nation and nationalism, and it is even sometimes suggested that in the coming days of internationalism, globalization and larger aggregation in the formation of a possible world union, nations and nationalities will be overpassed and the world will enter into post-national stage of existence. This debate and conclusion need to be considered seriously in the light of the real truth of the philosophical foundations of nationalism, Indian nationalism in particular, and its possible future.

Political Unity and Real Unity

Sri Aurobindo makes an important distinction between political unity and real unity. In this connection, he refers to the fact that there was in the ancient cycle of development a wide pre-national empire building, which is in contrast to modern cycle of nation-buidling. In other words, empires have been created in the past, indicating the tendency to overshoot nation-units even before they attain any maturity or stability, and that nation is not a final unit of aggregation. But at the same time, Sri Aurobindo points out that although empires have exhibited political unity, they have not shown to have in them the force of real unity. He states:

> Empires exist, but they are as yet only political and not real units; they have to live from within and owe their continuance to a force imposed on their constituent elements or else to a political convenience felt or acquiesced in by the constituents and favoured by the world outside. . . . If the political convenience of an empire of this kind ceases, if the constituent elements no longer acquiesce and are drawn more powerfully by a centrifugal force, if at the same time the world outside no longer favours the combination, then force alone remains as the one agent of an artificial unity.[5]

Empires are, according to Sri Aurobindo, perishable political unities, in contrast to the nation, a real unity, which is immortal and which will remain so until a greater living unit can be found into which national idea can harmonize in obedience to a superior attraction.

Again, dwelling upon the distinction between political unity and real unity, Sri Aurobindo states that this distinction must be made because

> it is of the greatest utility to a true and profound political science and involves the most important consequences. When an empire like Austria, a non-national empire, is

5. Sri Aurobindo: *Social and Political Thought,* Centenary Edition, vol. 15, pp. 285–86.

> broken to pieces, it perishes for good; there is no innate tendency to recover the outward unity, because there is no real inner oneness; there is only a politically manufactured aggregate. On the other hand, a real national unity broken up by circumstances will always preserve a tendency to recover and reassert its oneness.[6]

Sri Aurobindo has given the example of the Greek Empire which has gone the way of all empires. But the Greek nation, after many centuries of political non-existence, again possesses its separate body because it has preserved its separate ego and, therefore, really existed under the covering rule of the Turk. Similar is the example of Italy and the example of Germany. In all these cases, as was in many others — the unification of Saxon England, medieval France, the formation of the United States of America, Sri Aurobindo points out that there was a real unity, a psychological distinct unit which tended at first ignorantly by the subconscious necessity of its being and afterwards with a sudden or gradual awakening to the sense of political oneness, towards an inevitable external unification. It is, Sri Aurobindo concludes, a distinct group-soul which is driven by inward necessity and uses outward circumstances to constitute for itself an organized body.

Arriving at Superficial Unity Ignorantly

Just as the individual is an ontological spirit, and therefore it can never be reduced to become a mere cog in a machine, even so, nation is a living spirit and soul, and therefore it can never permanently be reduced to a status of a mere province of larger and largest aggregates. At the same time, Sri Aurobindo underlines the fact that humanity is turning today towards world unity, and the central problem for the human endeavour in this connection will be as to how the nation will

6. Ibid., pp. 286–87.

adjust itself to the pressure of the forces that are today creating phenomena which are global, world-wide and planetary in character.

In this connection, Sri Aurobindo makes a distinction between national ego and national soul, corresponding to the distinction in regard to the individual life where the superficial ego is seen to be distinct from the true individual soul.

The mark of egoism, according to Sri Aurobindo, is its superficiality and its ignorant attempt to arrive at superficial unity whether that ego is individual or national. The mark of the ego is its sense of division from all the rest, its pretension to be entirely independent in a poise of superiority over all the others. Corresponding to this ego, Sri Aurobindo points out, there is no real reality. There is no ontological superficial reality, there is no independent divided entity which is superior to all the rest. The true individual, on the other hand, has indeed distinctiveness, but is not divided from the others. The true individual and the true nation-soul are characterized by mutuality, interdependence and inner oneness that manifests in diversity. Based upon this philosophical foundation, Sri Aurobindo perceives the future of nations as entities seeking and finding their inner souls by virtue of which they will remain free but mutually interdependent, and this, in turn, will provide the form of world unity that is supportive and not destructive of the nations. Sri Aurobindo speaks of a world union of free nations, each having status of equality, and all contributing through their distinctive capacities to the fund of richness and variety at the global level.

Formulating an Ideal Law of Social Development

Sri Aurobindo formulates an ideal law of social development in which the truths of the individual, of the nations and of humanity are all reconciled and synthesized. This is the law as he has formulated:

> Thus the law for the individual is not only to perfect his individuality by free development from within, but also to respect and to aid and be aided by the same free development in others. His law is to harmonize his life with the life of the social aggregate and to pour himself out as a force for growth and perfection on humanity. The law for the community or nation is equally to perfect its corporate existence by a free development from within, aiding and taking full advantage of that of the individual, but to respect and to aid and be aided by the same free development of other communities and nations. Its law is to harmonize its life with that of the human aggregate and to pour itself out as a force for growth and perfection on humanity. The law for humanity is to pursue its upward evolution towards the finding and expression of the Divine in the type of mankind, taking full advantage of the free development and gains of all individuals and nations and groupings of men, to work towards the day when mankind may be really and not only ideally one divine family, but even then, when it has succeeded in unifying itself, to respect, aid and be aided by the free growth and activity of its individuals and constituent aggregates.[7]

Sri Aurobindo acknowledges that this ideal law has never become operative in the imperfect states through which humankind has so far travelled, and it may be very long before that law can be attained. But Sri Aurobindo maintains that the present is the stage of what he calls *the subjective age of humanity,* when knowledge is increasing and diffusing itself with an unprecedented rapidity, when individuals, societies and nations are attempting to discover their potentialities and their inner subjective states and selves, when capacity is generating itself, when men and nations are drawn close together, and this is the time when we can justifiably develop

7. Sri Aurobindo: *Social and Political Thought*, Centenary Edition, vol. 15, pp. 63–64.

a conscious hope to arrive at a conscious discovery of that ideal law of social development and its conscious application. He finds that the present moment is opportune for an upward march, particularly when people of the entire globe are getting united, although partially and in an inextricable entanglement of chaotic unity. For this is the moment where we are being compelled to know each other and impelled to know more profoundly ourselves, humankind, and the world, and when the idea of self-realization for ourselves and nations is coming consciously to the upper and outer surface. This is the time, according to Sri Aurobindo, for the human being in particular, to know himself, to find the ideal law of his being and his development; and to hold that law before him and to find out gradually the way by which it can become a more and more moulding principle of the individual and social existence.

At the same time, Sri Aurobindo regards the present moment of human history as a moment of acute crisis. For the process of self-realization, both for the individual and the collectivist, is always difficult and it is marked by an acute struggle of groping in the darkness and in the welter of conflicts and uncertain alternatives. In his analysis of the psychology of the process of maturation of self-finding, Sri Aurobindo examines the psychology of barbarism, philistinism, and of the rational, ethical and aesthetic culture, and examines also the means by which the society manages to arrive at some kind of cohesion at different stages of development, namely, through symbolism and later by typal thought, conventional thought and, still later, by subjective self-awakening both of the individual and collectivity.

Ideals of Liberty, Equality and Fraternity

In the subjective age, which is marked by preponderance of Reason as also by a revolt against conventions, customs and traditions, Sri Aurobindo perceives the possibility of a true flowering of the inner spirit, which can harmonize the individual good and the social good and in the context of which a form of world unity could be invented whereby human beings of the entire globe can live together in durable peace and progressive harmony as in one united family. In this context, Sri Aurobindo finds those three great ideals which were put forward explicitly and forcefully during the French Revolution to be most significant, namely the ideals of liberty, equality and fraternity. He finds that these three ideals served the purpose of motivating the great experiments that humankind conducted during the curve of the Rational Age, the age which was ushered in by Renaissance in Europe, the age through which humankind is at present passing, and which has now reached a kind of an end and which has the possibility of opening the gates of a beginning of a new age, which he calls the "Spiritual Age."

It is when Reason explores its possibilities and brings into operation its capabilities that the human race can arrive at a critical point of its self-realization and self-perfection. For it is then, as it has now become clearer, that it is found that the role of Reason is not to govern but to become a medium and an intermediate power that can lift human life from the levels of blind impulse to the realms of light of the Spirit. For the real governor can be only that light and knowledge, which is integral and which unites the individual with the universal without requiring the individual to be abolished and which shows both to the individual and to the universal that their source is in the same transcendental that is the foundation of oneness and unity of existence.

Age of Reason and Ideal of Anarchism

The Age of Reason, according to Sri Aurobindo, has shown that when the ideal of liberty is emphasized and sought to be implemented, the ideal of equality is required to be sacrificed; and when the ideal of equality is emphasized and sought to be implemented, the ideal of liberty is required to be strangulated. Towards the end of the Age of Reason, there emerges, therefore, the ideal of anarchism and the question arises whether anarchist thought can any more successfully find a satisfying social principle.

Sri Aurobindo points out that the anarchist thought, although it is not yet formed in its assured form, cannot develop any appropriate basis or form of harmony as long as it relies on the powers of the intellect. He points out that a rational satisfaction cannot give to humanity safety from the pull from below nor deliver it from the attraction from above. It is true that the more the outer law is replaced by the inner law, the nearer will man be to his natural perfection, and the perfect State must be one in which governmental compulsion is abolished and man is able to live with his fellowmen by free agreement and co-operation. But this can truly be secured by a power greater than that of reason. According to Sri Aurobindo, it is not intellectual anarchism but a spiritual or spiritualized anarchism that will bring us nearer to the solution or at least touch something of it from afar.

Arrival of Spiritual Age

According to Sri Aurobindo, the present stage of human development can become a gate for the arrival of a spiritual age in which the ideal of brotherhood can come to be practised and it is only in that condition that a new form of human unity can be forged in which the individual and the collectivity, even on a global scale or organization, can come to be harmonized. In the meantime, however, the transition from the end of the curve of Reason to the advent and progress of the spiritual age is a stage of crisis, which needs to be examined in a greater depth, since it is that crisis which has become accentuated today by the latest developments with which we are besieged today.

Sri Aurobindo considers the present stage of crisis as an evolutionary crisis in which human will is called upon to make a free choice. This is the crisis where evolution of human Reason is increasingly compelled to yield to the pressure that impels the creation of a life of universalized rule of economic barbarism. At the same time, Reason is increasingly obliged also to exercise its role in lifting up humanity to create a life of unity, mutuality and harmony born of a deeper and wider truth of our being. In fact, there are three forces that work today upon humanity. On the one hand, there is a force that is striving to assert the barbarism within the civilized man. For it is possible to utilize the present scientific and technical knowledge to create an order of existence in which physical and vital wants of the human being can greatly, if not fully, be satisfied, and this order of existence can be maintained by mechanical devices and application of the power of machines that can imprison the human spirit. There is also a second alternative in which human reason can continue to spin into larger or narrower circles propounding great dreams but never fulfilling them. And there is a third alternative in which the human being consents to rise to the higher levels than those of the Reason and consents to be spiritualized.

The question, therefore, is whether the human being will choose to remain arrested in some kind of intermediary typal perfection like earlier animal kinds, or whether he will consent to rise to a higher level of evolution. The necessity to make the choice has created a state of a crisis, since the choice to pursue a higher level is not only difficult but appears at first sight to be almost impossible. Sri Aurobindo describes this crisis as follows:

> At present mankind is undergoing an evolutionary crisis in which is concealed a choice of its destiny; for a stage has

> been reached in which the human mind has achieved in certain directions an enormous development while in others it stands arrested and bewildered and can no longer find its way. A structure of the external life has been raised up by man's ever-active mind and life-will, a structure of an unmanageable hugeness and complexity, for the service of his mental, vital, physical claims and urges, a complex political, social, administrative, economic, cultural machinery, an organized collective means for his intellectual, sensational, aesthetic and material satisfaction. Man has created a system of civilization which has become too big for his limited mental capacity and understanding and his still more limited spiritual and moral capacity to utilize and manage, a too dangerous servant of his blundering ego and its appetites. . . . A greater whole-being, whole-knowledge, whole-power is needed to weld all into a greater unity of whole-life.[8]

Important Development : Change in Humanity

In his book *The Ideal of Human Unity,* Sri Aurobindo refers to two important developments which indicate a prospect of the coming change in humanity. The first of these is internationalism, the idea of humanity as a single race of beings with a common life and a common general interest. Sri Aurobindo identifies those tendencies in human life at present which are favourable to the progress of the international idea.

But internationalism, according to Sri Aurobindo, is not enough; there is a need of a religion of humanity or an equivalent sentiment which recognizes a single soul in humanity of which each human being and each people is an incarnation and soul form. This religion has already expressed itself in the philosophy of humanitarianism, which itself is a most prominent emotional result of the Age of Reason.

---

8. Sri Aurobindo: *The Life Divine,* Centenary Edition, vol. 19, pp. 1053–55.

Sri Aurobindo, however, contends that the religion of humanity must be a spiritual religion of humanity, not an institutional religion, not an intellectual religion, not a sentimental religion. That humanity is pressing forward towards this spiritual religion of humanity is of great significance for all of us who are keen to find the solution to the contemporary crisis. And it is here that Sri Aurobindo's perception of the significance of the contemporary crisis and his philosophy and yoga of supramental transformation come to us as the needed light and guidance.

Yoga of Supramental Manifestation

For an adequate understanding of the yoga of supramental manifestation, which is expounded in his *Synthesis of Yoga,* we need to study also three big volumes containing Sri Aurobindo's letters on yoga, which throw illuminating light not only on the principles of the integral yoga but also on multitudes of difficulties that are encountered during the process of yoga, as also on experiences and realizations. But, above all, we need to study *Savitri,* that great epic of the adventure of the Spirit. For it is through *Savitri* that one gains a ready access to the concreteness of psychic, spiritual and supramental experiences as also their impact on all parts and planes of the being through the magic of the rhythmic word and vision in their highest intensities. To study *Savitri* is to enter into the realm of experiences and into a veritable process of yogic transformation.

Whether humanity will respond to the need of this new turn will depend upon its increasing perception of the necessity of spiritual transformation. Sri Aurobindo points out that a change from the vital and mental to the spiritual order of life must necessarily be accomplished in the individual and in a greater number of individuals before it can come to have an effective hold upon community. What is necessary is that the common human mind begins to admit the ideas proper to the higher order that is in the end to be, and the heart of man begins to be stirred by aspirations born of these ideas. Sri Aurobindo concludes that if this condition is fulfilled then there is hope of some advance in the not distant future.

In spite of the difficulties and critical trials through which humanity may be required to pass, Sri Aurobindo underlines the need of understanding the inevitability of the spiritual solution. Indeed, in presenting this solution, Sri Aurobindo is aware that it may be objected that it puts off the consummation of a better human society to a far off date in the future evolution of the race. But Sri Aurobindo affirms forcefully:

> . . . if this is not the solution, then there is no solution; if this is not the way, then there is no way for the human kind. Then the terrestrial evolution must pass beyond man as it has passed beyond the animal and a greater race must come that will be capable of the spiritual change, a form of life must be born that is nearer to the divine. After all there is no logical necessity for the conclusion that the change cannot begin at all because its perfection is not immediately possible. A decisive turn of mankind to the spiritual ideal, the beginning of a constant ascent and guidance towards the heights may not be altogether impossible, even if the summits are attainable at first only by the pioneer few and far-off to the tread of the race. And that beginning may mean the descent of an influence that will alter at once the whole life of mankind in its orientation and enlarge for ever, as did the development of his reason and more than any development of the reason, its potentialities and all its structure.[9]

According to Sri Aurobindo, the world is a mutable world and uncertainties and dangers cannot be avoided. Much will

---

9. Sri Aurobindo: *The Human Cycle*, Centenary Edition, vol. 15, p. 207.

depend, according to Sri Aurobindo, on the intellectual and moral capacity of humanity to carry out what is evidently the one thing needful, namely, a concentrated effort at the spiritual change that can sustain a global and untied human family.

2

The Distinctiveness of Sri Aurobindo's View on Indian Renaissance

D.P. Chattopadhyaya

SRI AUROBINDO'S view on the Renaissance in India needs to be situated in its historical perspective. He started writing on the subject in response to the illuminating essays written by Mr James Henry Cousins who has been described as poet, subtle critic and thinker who studied the movement called the Renaissance of India and wrote on it in the early decades of the last century. Taking cues from James' view, but substantially departing from the same, Sri Aurobindo developed his own views, keeping in mind the then unfolding scenario of the colonial Indian polity and its different trends of future development.

The initial question he raised and tried to answer was: Was there really a renaissance in India? The Indian mind of the time, mainly under the influence of the colonial education and culture, was trying to understand the question against the backdrop of European culture and its different forms like Christian, Tutonic, and the Old Graeco-Latin. The Tutonic version of the Latin spirit, as developed by the influential historians like Jacob Burckhardt, in particular, excessively moulded the Indian thinkers and political leaders of the time. In contrast, Sri Aurobindo was against this obsessive preoccupation of the colonial attitude of the fellow Indian thinkers and writers. The term *renaissance* is basically a modern one and that owes its currency in the nineteenth century in the work of the historians like Burckhardt. The word literally means rebirth, or renewal or restoration of a former state of socio-cultural life. When Nietzsche coined the expression "trans-valuation of value", he had perhaps the Italian word, *Rinascimento,* in mind. Sri Aurobindo's use of the term suggests that he had the Indian words like *punarjanma* and *navinikarana* in the back of his mind. What is really original in his view[1] is his own critico-creative view on the subject. He substantially left behind the then widely popular acceptable thesis that cultural inspiration of the Indian renaissance was mainly Germanic[2] and Italian.[3] It may be mentioned here that the movements of Italian unification under the influence of Mazzini and Garibaldi and that of German unification under the power of Bismarck caught the imagination of the social reformers and political thinkers of India in the second half of the nineteenth century. The Italian renaissance with its humanist label emerged out of the medieval Italy, particularly Tuscany, Florence and Siena. The ideas and ideals of the Italian Renaissance gradually spread into the rest of Europe, triggering off the Northern Renaissance centred around the Netherlands and England.

---

1. Sri Aurobindo, 1972 *The Foundations of Indian Culture and the Renaissance in India,* Sri Aurobindo the Birth Century Library, vol. 14, Pondicherry: Sri Aurobindo Ashram Trust.
2. J.R. Hale, 1971, *Renaissance Europe* 1480–1520, London: Collins: *The Fontana History of Europe.*
3. Jacob Burckhardt, 1960, *The Civilization of the Renaissance in Italy,* ed. and intro., Irene Gordon, New York: A Mentor Book.

Indian and European Renaissance

Basically a student of history, literature and political thought, Sri Aurobindo was deeply aware of a difference between the Italian paradigm of Renaissance together with its background and ramifications from the Indian renaissance which was in progress under the shadows of colonial education and culture. His perceptive mind, exposed to the ideas and ideals of the then England and Ireland, was deeply impressed by the similarity between the Indian renaissance and its Celtic, basically Irish, counterpart. It is to be remembered here that from 1801 to 1922 the whole island of Ireland was a reluctant constituent part of the United Kingdom of Great Britain and Ireland. During this period, or at least the most phases of it, Ireland was under the direct rule of the Parliament of the United Kingdom in London. During the nineteeenth century the economic problems of Ireland, particularly the great famine of 1840s, antagonized and alienated most of the Irish people from their British rulers. In this respect the case of India, ravished by several famines as documented in the works of economic historians like Dadabhai Naoroji and Ramesh Chander Dutt deserves serious attention. The literary reflections of the same are found in the writings, among others, of Bankim Chandra Chattopadhyay and Dinabandhu Mitra. In both Indian and Irish cases economic factors were deeply dyed in religious ideas as evident from the works like *Ānandamaṭh,* against the backdrop of *Sannyasi Bidroha* and *Nil (Indigo) Bidroha.* That the peasants' unrest contributed to political unrest was common both to India and Ireland under the colonial yoke of the British Government.

Renaissance Interpreted Differently

History of all cultures and that of their underlying civilizations exhibit or/and have been interpreted in terms of renewal of the past in the light of the present and addressed to the future. The basic concept of dialectic and its surrogates of different forms and times, viz. Indian, Hellenic, Hegelian, and Marxist are well known and have been discussed and criticized extensively. In the Indian traditions it is observed that many streams of thought owing their origin to the Vedic and the pre-Vedic times differ between themselves. The phases of differences have been followed by those who attempted synthesis. The concepts of Thesis or *Pūrvapakṣa,* Anti-Thesis or *Uttarapakṣa, Pūrvamīmāṁsā* or the Previous (terms of) Settlement, and *Uttaramīmāṁsā* or the Later (terms of) Settlement are well known in the history of Indian thought and culture. In this connection the names of Gauḍapada and Śaṅkara, in the context of *Uttaramīmāṁsā* , and those of Jaiminī, Kumārila and Prabhākara, in the context of *Pūrvamīmāṁsā* are well known. The operation of dialectic never reaches a stage of permanent and conclusive end. In different forms and in different names these creative and critical developments, or modifications thereof, continue. In the context of European thought the concepts of (i) Pre-modern or Pre-Cartesian, Modern or Post-Cartesian and Post-modern or Post-Derridan; (ii) totalization, de-totalization and re-totalization; and (iii) pre-structuralism, structuralism and post-structuralism are among the well-known rhythms of thought. This diverse formulation of different forms of culture and civilization show, among other things, the concerns, facts and ideas that lend themselves to different types of formulations, de-formulations and re-formulations. This historical view of thought makes it abundantly clear that no culture or its underpinned civilization, nor any phase of it has a unique, unalterable and definitive formulation holding good for all time to come.

Euro-centric Accounts of Italian Renaissance

Every renaissance whether it is Indian or European, has been understandably interpreted in very many ways. Like the European Renaissance, the Indian renaissance, has its different forms and formulations. Most writers on the Indian renaissance, under the influence of colonial education in general, and the Euro-centric accounts of the Italian Renaissance in particular, had been trying to present it as what happened to Europe, or rather what was supposed to happen there after the Middle Ages in the fifteenth century — between the downfall of the classical Hellenic-Roman world and its rediscovery in the wake of decline and fall of the Roman Catholic Church and the Holy Roman Empire. Originally, it was known as the Carolingian Empire allegedly founded by the Frankish aristocrats and dynasty (CE 750–887). Later on, it became widely known as Holy Roman Empire and Charlemagne (CE 800-14) is claimed to be the main architect and founder of this long lasting Empire. Notionally this Empire lasted from 802–1806, the time of Napoleon Bonaparte. This Empire comprised, at different periods, west Europe, north Europe, central Europe and a major part of southern Europe. After the fall of Napoleon it was Bismarck [Otto von Bismarck] (1815-98) who became the Head of the German Empire. About the last and waning phase of the Holy Roman Empire, Bismarck is reported to have observed that "it is neither Holy nor Roman, nor Empire."

The hallmark of the European Renaissance is said to be humanism resting on the philosophico-religious culture of Catholicism, new forms of art and literature associated with the names of Dante (1265–1321), Petrarch (1304-74), Leonardo de Vinci (1452–1519), Michelangelo (1475–1564) and Raphael (1483–1520).

While most Indian writers accepted, almost uncritically, the model of Italian Renaissance for their understanding and interpretation of the Indian renaissance, Sri Aurobindo (1872–1950), unlike them and departing from them, found it more akin to the facts and spirits of the Irish Renaissance. It was believed to be the acme of the Celtic renaissance with which the famous names, among others, of Richard Sheridan (1751–1816), Parnell (1846–1891), George Barnard Shaw (1856–1950), and Eamon de Valera (1882–1975) were attached. Like de Valera, Sri Aurobindo, to start with, was a teacher at Baroda. Educated in London and Cambridge he, by nature, was fiercely patriotic right from his student life, and later on followed the same track as an influential member of the Radical Wing of the Indian National Congress led by Bal Gangadhar Tilak, Lala Lajpat Rai and Bipin Chandra Pal who are collectively designated as a radical troika of the then Congress politics. The other side of Aurobindo's character which deserves special mention is his strong and strict feeling of spirituality in his personal life and equally strong spirit of patriotism in political life. Though he studied the famous European thinkers of the eighteenth and nineteenth centuries, but what influenced most was the classical spirit of the European culture, marked by its languages like Greek, Latin, German and French. Only later on he learned Sanskrit, and various other Indian languages, including Bengali, which together with Sanskrit was learnt by him around the early 30s of his life. Strongly influenced by Ramakrishna and Vivekananda, Aurobindo preferred to describe himself as a politician and poet and not as a philosopher. These background informations about him are extremely relevant to understand his thought and life.[4]

4. Several books authored by Sri Aurobindo himself are extremely helpful to understand his view on his political thought, religious thought and the nationalist movement of his time. Among those Volumes I find some particularly important, viz. *A System of National Education*: *Bankim-Tilak-Dayananda* and The works of A.B. Purani, *Life of Sri Aurobindo;* Sisir Kumar Mitra, *Resurgent India;* K.R. Srinivasa Iyengar, *Sri Aurobindo;* Haridas Mukherjee and Uma Mukherjee, *Bande Mataram and Indian Nationalism;* Karan Singh, *The Prophet of Indian Nationalism;* Dinendrakumar Roy, *Aravinda Prasanga* (Bengali); Promod Kumar Sen, Sri Aurobindo — Jiban-O-Yoga (Bengali).

Indo-Irish Struggle : A Similarity

The points on which the history of India and Ireland resembled and differed in the nineteenth century and the earlier part of the twentieth century should be advisedly borne in mind so that the renaissance of these two countries[5] may be better understood in the light of those like the Hindu-Muslim divide in India, and the Catholic and Protestant in Ireland. The religious difference between the Catholic majority in the Southern Ireland and the Protestant majority in the Northern Ireland gave rise to some similar and comparable problems and which were fully utilized by the United Kingdom, the common ruler of these countries during this period. For example, under the leadership of Daniel O'Connell, the Catholics of Ireland wanted to achieve independence according to their own terms. O'Connell, somewhat like Gandhi was in favour of a peaceful method of struggle for independence in which he wanted that both Catholics and Protestants might co-operate. Secondly, with the change of Government in the UK, alternatively between the Whig (Liberal) under the leadership of Gladstone and Tory (Conservative party), under the leadership of Palmerstone, their changing policies towards Ireland defined differently their relation between the concerned peoples, the ruler and the ruled. Thirdly, both these colonies or countries under the UK Parliament witnessed several land agitations for securing better rights for tenant farmers and less oppressive turns for their tenancy. Fourthly, and very importantly, the culture of Ireland, like that of India had undergone significant change

5. Comprehensive Overviews of Ireland History can be found in Christopher Haigh, ed., 1985, *The Cambridge Historical Encyclopedia of Great Britain and Ireland,* Cambridge: Cambridge University Press.

during the nineteenth century. The devastated famines,[6] which proved very severe in the Irish-speaking rural and relatively more poverty-stricken areas of the country, cast their dark shadows on the life of the people. Consequently, the same was reflected in their language and literature. It gave rise to what is known as Gaelic Revival. It may be mentioned here that the ancient history of the Irish language bears closer family resemblance to their Indic counterparts as members of the Indo-European family of languages. Also to be noted is that the English language used in Ireland, known as Hiberno-English was somewhat updated compared to the older Elizabethan-English. Many Irish writers like J.M. Synge (1871–1909), George Barnard Shaw (1856–1950), Sean O'Casey (1880–1964) and Oscar Wild (1854–1900), and some of the most famous Anglo-Irish writers, preferred a style which had a distinct Irish flavour and therefore somewhat jeered and caricatured by the more modern English writers and readers of the urban orientation. Fifthly, like in India, in Ireland also there were two different approaches to independence. Pro-Home Rule Liberal Party led one of the approaches. Charles Stewart Parnell was leading this party and it was in favour of an autonomous Ireland within the framework of the UK Government. But the other party, more radical in character, was being led by O'Connell and demanded a complete repeal of the act of Union and complete independence for the country. The difference between these two parties and their approaches is likely to remind us between the moderate wing of Congress Party under the leadership of Gokhale, Ranade, Lord S.P. Sinha and S.N. Banerjea and the radical wing led by Tilak, Bipin

6. Cecil Woodham-Smith, *The Great Hunger: Ireland* 1845-49 (1962, Reissued 1987). It is one of the worst disasters which influenced the course of Irish history. As a companion volume the reader may consult Robert Dudley Edwards and T. Desmond Williams, eds. *The Great Famine Studies in Irish History*, 1845–52, (1956, Reissued 1976).

Chandra Pal and Aurobindo Ghosh. Sixthly and finally, the Irish War of Independence (1919-21) and the Civil War (1922-23) ended up with the partition[7] of Catholic-dominated Southern Ireland, with its capital in Dublin, and the Protestant-dominated Northern Ireland, with its capital at Belfast. While the former achieved full freedom, the latter continued to remain within the UK Parliamentary framework. Here also one cannot miss the parallelism between the Partition in Ireland on the basis of religion[8] and the Partition of India (India/Pakistan). Importance of this political ups and downs had their discernable bearing on economic and cultural development of the pre-partitioned and the post-partitioned countries. The parallelism breaks down when on the basis of language, Bangladesh achieved its independence and India witnessed its second partition.

Renaissance and the Role of Language, Literature and Religion

Reverting to the theme of cultural renaissance it may be observed here that in the life of every country, language, literature and religion are bound to play a very important role. The discourse of Indian nationalism and that of Irish nationalism are no exception to this general rule. It must be stated here that Sri Aurobindo's political thought was closely related to India's cultural history but not its "religious" history in the received sense.

The qualifying expression "in the received sense" has to be taken with deep attention. It is true that in his thought and

7. For the twentieth century developments of Ireland the reader may consult Dorothy Macardle, *The Irish Republic: A Documented Chronicle of the Anglo-Irish Conflict and the Partitioned Ireland, with a detailed account of the period* 1916-23 (1937, Reissued 1965).
8. Terence Brown, *Ireland: A Social and Cultural History*, 1922 to the Present (1985).

action programme one finds frequently two terms, *śakti* and *surrender*, receiving special emphasis. The cult of *śakti* is associated with the Tantric tradition of India and it was highlighted by Ramakrishna and Vivekananda, who influenced him much. Ramakrishna, the recognized *guru* of Vivekananda was also a devoted worshipper of Kālī or *śakti*.

Life and facts of Ramakrishna show that he followed the religious paths and realized the truth of each of these apparently diverse paths prescribed by various religions — Christianity, Islam, Vedānta, Vaiṣṇava. His conclusion was: Every individual's spiritual quest needs to be freely shaped by his/her inner spiritual craving. A substantially similar approach is evident in the teaching of Vivekananda. But it is undeniable that actual practices of the followers of these two very influential religious teachers of India in the nineteenth century, mainly because of the practices like *puja* and chanted hymns in Hindu temples of their followers, their religious views are understandbly believed to be basically aligned to Hinduism. But in the case of Aurobindo this description does not apply. Because, first, he had no acknowledged *guru*. Secondly, he did not believe in idol worship, although in his philosophical discourse he explicitly mentions that the Supreme Reality God or *Brahman* may be worshipped both in his indeterminate form and determinate form. In every religion this symbolic approach is recognized, directly, or indirectly. For example, the followers of those religions who, formally speaking, do not believe in idol worship, have their own symbolic and specially sacred places of worship like Church, Synagogue and Masjid. Thirdly, the followers of different religions have their own sacred days and, in many cases, their own different calendars and places of pilgrimage. If one takes a scientific view of space and time, one has no compelling reason to attach special importance to some places and some days or nights, to the exclusion of other places and times.

Fourthly and finally, ritualism available in different religions is widely different. Many other considerations can be offered suggesting the weaknesses of traditional or denominational approaches to religions.

Sri Aurobindo was Opposed to Violence

Sri Aurobindo, to start with, was simply Aurobindo Ghosh, his family name and "Sri Aurobindo" is his self-given name. Unlike Ramakrishna and Vivekananda, he was not particularly inclined to his self-description as Hindu, notwithstanding his deep appreciation of the Vedic tradition and Tantric cult. Like many other nationalist leaders of his time he allowed to figure the cult of *śakti* in his early religious and political writings. After the Surat Congress of 1907 when the Indian National Congress had undergone a formal split into two factions, "moderates" and "radicals", Sri Aurobindo virtually left active politics and lent his support to some political groups which were not opposed to the use of violence as one of the means for achieving national independence. It may be mentioned here that after his imprisonment at Alipore Jail and subsequent release he had completely withdrawn himself from party politics. Also he left behind denominational Hinduism. Even after he moved to Pondicherry in 1909, and devoted most of his time and activities to yoga and writings, he never disclaimed his political identity. In spite of his practical withdrawal from the public life, he started writing on a variety of subjects like Metaphysics, Spiritualism, Social Philosophy, Indian Culture, Aesthetics, Poetics, the Vedic and Upaniṣadic themes, and particularly Yoga. He continued to describe himself as "poet and politician".

In politics, Sri Aurobindo differed from Gandhi's principle of non-violence. In the struggle for national freedom he was more inclined to the radical approach represented by the terrorist groups like Anusilan Samiti, Yugantar and various other regional groups of Maharashtra and Madras (now Tamil Nadu). It is interesting to recall that from 1907, the year of Surat Congress, to the Rising of the Naval Ratings [*Nau Bidroha*] at Bombay (now Mumbai) and Karachi in 1944, expressing solidarity with the cause of Indian National Army (INA) led by Netaji Subhas Chandra Bose, indicates a pro-violence approach to the cause of national liberation. Undoubtedly, the mainstream was represented by Gandhi who returned to India from South Africa in the second decade of the twentieth century.

Sri Aurobindo's Concept of Indian Renaissance

To understand correctly and clearly Sri Aurobindo's concept of renaissance one has to look back into his philosophy of history, in general, and that of Indian history, in particular. Every civilization, according to him, exhibits at least three rhythms of phases in history — symbolic, typal-conventional and subjective. He finds systematization and best blossoming of the richness of the Indian culture that took place during this period. He thinks that the last three centuries of the first millennia, marked by the consolidation of the Vedāntic mode of thought and the beginning of the Islamic incursion in north-west India, e.g. Dahir in Sind, should be regarded as the beginning of the typal-conventional period.

To Sri Aurobindo, from that time to the beginning of the nineteenth century, characterized by the arrival of the European powers, e.g. British, French and Dutch, in India should be understood as "a long lingering Indian summer." The vitality of the second rhythm of the Indian history, according to him, came to its end, but the creativity of the Indian psyche was yet to come up. It is clear here that Sri Aurobindo does not adequately recognize the positive aspects of the periods of the Sultanate and the Mughal period. Though here and there he has some good words to say about this period, his account of this period is not adequately reflective of internal weaknesses, and internal and internecine wars of the Hindu rulers of India.

But the very use of the metaphor "long lingering Indian summer" suggests that some light of earlier creativity was still at work, and that seems to explain Sri Aurobindo's sagacity and astuteness of not using the typical expression "dark age" which has been extensively used in the context of the Renaissance studies in Europe. One gets the impression that this long period, nearly 900 years of Indian history, was not entirely sterile or suppressive of all that was good and bright before the arrival and continued presence of the Central Asian forces in the Indian sub-continent. He gives a mixed picture of the period and recognizes the importance of the arrival and contribution of the European ideas triggering off a new phase of the Indian history.

What Sri Aurobindo calls the subjective period of the Indian history is symbolic of the beginning of the Indian mind's relook at its partly forgotten and partly suppressed inner excellence of the past in the fields of thought, administration and creativity. Sri Aurobindo's tri-rhythmic — symbolic-typal-subjective, was borrowed from the German historian Karl Lamprecht (1856–1915), who wrote, among several other books, *Deutsche Geschichte,* 14 vols., and *What is History*? It may be mentioned here that Sri Aurobindo's mastery of classical languages like Greek and Latin, supplemented by his knowledge of other European languages like French and German provided him the necessary insights into the history of European civilization and culture.

Curiously enough, in spite of his philosophical bent of mind he did not take seriously the writings of the famous European philosophers like Kant and Hegel. The only reference which I find in his studies in European intellectual history, besides classical writers, poets and famous historians, are mainly Nietzsche and Goethe. It must be mentioned here that Sri Aurobindo was a prolific writer of poems, drama and other forms of literature. It is amazing to recall that all his major philosophical writings, viz. *The Human Cycle, The Foundations of Indian Culture, The Ideal of Human Unity, The Synthesis of Yoga, The Future of Poetry, The Secrets of Veda, The Upaniṣads, The Gītā,* and *The Indian Renaissance,* were all written within a span of eight years, 1914-22. Most of these writings appeared in the journal, *Aryan,* which he himself used to edit. Thereafter, from 1924-48, for long 24 years, he kept himself creatively busy in writing the epic poem, *Savitri,* the only work which he agreed to revise, while the other books he wrote in, to use his own words, "aeroplanic speed". He was a prolific writer of letters, only a part of which is available in the 30 vols. Birth Centenary Edition, 1870–1972, followed up by 4 subsequent volumes. This shows his yogic power and extraordinary creative capacity.

Some Limitations to Sri Aurobindo's Views

While I do appreciate many positive points of Sri Aurobindo's views on the Indian renaissance, I find some limitations of the same as well. The limitations I have in mind are of two types, personal and academic. His writings should be taken in totality, inclusive of his historical time and socio-political place. Secondly, the writers like Sri Aurobindo who have their own philosophy, notwithstanding his disclaimer, and to which they are somewhat strongly attached, gets reflected in their writings.

Most of Sri Aurobindo's social, political and philosophical writings, as noted before, were articulated against the backdrop of his English education, exposure to his experience of his stay and study in England, and the turbulent period of the last decade of nineteenth century and the first decade of the twentieth century when the partition of Bengal, mainly due to Lord Curzon, the then Governor-General of India, took place. The partition of Bengal gave rise to a widespread revolutionary fervour as was evident from the events of the time and writings of the nationalist leaders and literary figures like Rabindranath Tagore.

Also that was the time when the Muslim League was established in Dacca under the leadership of the Nawab of Dacca, the Agha Khan and others who favoured not only the said partition but also started preparing the ground for the future partition of the country as a whole. Besides, Sri Aurobindo and some other nationalist leaders like Satish Chandra Mukhopadhyay, Subodh Chandra Basu Mallik and Rabindranath Tagore, realized the importance of reviving and introducing a kind of education which would be genuinely nationalist and clearly distinguishable from the colonial kind of education that was in vogue at that time.

Sri Aurobindo, like several other nationalist leaders of the time, clearly realized that without a nationalist agenda of education which could correctly motivate the young minds of the time, to talk of the renaissance in India would not be correct and fruitful. In the contemplated agenda of education they thought of introducing the young minds to the rationalist and spiritualist elements of the Indian heritage which were either suppressed or marginalized by the colonial rulers. Secondly, they attached much importance to *technical* education as preparatory to the necessity of industrialization of India's economy. In effect they wanted to erase the baneful effects of the colonial education which proved contrary to the interest of the country. It is to be noted that Sri Aurobindo and other like-minded people thought the renaissance to be favourably responsive to the positive side of modern and scientific Western education. Only the attempts of debunking Indian tradition was being opposed, pointed out and criticized.

In this case, as mentioned before, Sri Aurobindo was deeply influenced by the intellectual part of Irish freedom movement. In the process I, for one, feel that he partially underestimated the Greeko-Roman contribution to the European Renaissance. We need not overemphasize the Burckhardt model of understanding the European Renaissance. At the same time, the norms of academic fairness and historical objectivity demand of us to try to get to the bottom of the real state of affairs. While we must be careful to avoid the negative side of colonial rule, we should be equally alert in the matter of ensuring objectivity and fairness to facts. Our patriotism, if allowed to be dyed by deep emotivism that will not give a correct picture of the modern education for the young students and scholars of the emerging India.

In general terms Sri Aurobindo and his colleagues might have been persuaded of the truth of this approach but situated as they were in the emotionally surcharged atmosphere of nationalism generated by the freedom movement and the partition of Bengal, at times, some of their writings apparently fail to betray the spirit clearly and correctly. In this context we have to remind ourselves, the point already referred to before, that Sri Aurobindo belonged to the radical fringe of the freedom movement.

3

The Bengal Renaissance
Different Interpretations

Rakhal Chandra Nath

THE awakening in Bengal witnessed in the nineteenth century mainly due to the creative response to the stimulus of Western thought and culture has often been described as "renaissance," obviously keeping in mind the Italian Renaissance of the fifteenth and sixteenth centuries. But the validity of the term "renaissance" as applied to nineteenth century Bengal has recently been critically examined. Modern Indian historians are becoming more and more aware of the necessity of a scientific analysis of the historiographic concept of "renaissance" for a critical study of nineteenth century Bengal. It is interesting to note that the Bengal renaissance as viewed by successive generations varied from glorification to cautious reconsideration and even to ultra-left rejection. Actually, historians differ in their interpretations of the nature of this renaissance and particularly on the positive aspect. Earlier debates were raised on the comparative and relative importance of the different trends of this renaissance. Some attached more importance on the Brahmo movement and some on "New Hinduism" propounded by Bankim Chandra and Swami Vivekananda; but none ignoring the role of this renaissance in modernizing Bengal. But, of late, this debate has been intensified since some historians give stress more on its limitations and find no positive aspect. Differences of opinion among historians on this question are natural due to the fact that this awakening in Bengal suffers from much contradictions and limitations as compared to the Italian Renaissance. Usually all thought movements, however high-minded, have a few minuses as well as a majority of pluses and we are to enquire whether despite limitations, this cultural efflorescence in Bengal had any glory.

Process of Modernisation in Bengal

Time was when it was thought that the changes brought about in the nineteenth century in the realm of thoughts in religion, social reform, education, literature, etc. initiated the process of modernization in Bengal headed by the newly born "middle class" and Calcutta served as its nerve-centre. It was the polyglot Madhusudan Dutt who established our first contact with the Renaissance Italy. He read Tasso in original[1] and imitated the Petrarcan measure in his Sonnets.[2] Bankim Chandra Chatterjee was impressed by the civilization of the Italian Renaissance and hoped for a "new birth" of Bengal à la Media Florence.[3] In describing the Bengal of his time Keshab Chandra Sen used the term "renaissance" as well as the adjective of its Bengal equivalent: *Nabajāgarita*. In the writings of other contemporary thinkers like Pyarichand Mitra, Kishorichand Mitra, Rajnarain Bose, etc., we can easily discern a conscious attempt on their part to portray the civilization that was obtaining in India.

1. Nagendra Nath Shome, *Madhu Smṛti*, p. 612.
2. Ibid., p. 276.
3. Haraprasad Shastri, "Bankim Chandra Kānthālipārāya," Nārāyan, Bankim, Smṛti Saṅkhya, Vaisakh, 1322 B.S. He found its parallel in the revival of philosophy, logic and literature in the fifteenth century Bengal (*Bangla Itihas Sambandhe Kayekti Katha*, Bangadarshan, Agrahayan, 1287 B.S.).

The young Rabindranath wrote essays on Dante and Petrarch for *Bharati* (1878) but he considered Western literature and thought to be more intoxicating than nourishing for our appetite.[4] In Rabindranath Tagore we are in the presence of the full-bloom of this renaissance. The impact of Western ideas had evoked various responses in the nineteenth century. Some had attempted a synthesis between the East and the West in the field of learning, some in the field of social reforms and some again in the field of religion. In Tagore we see all these strands of thought merging into a creative whole. Tagore not only inherited their traditions but blended them to effect another synthesis — in the realm of beauty. By way of portraying the characters of Rammohan and Vidyasagar, he discovered the main purport of this renaissance. He discerned in it the mainspring of modernization in India. He described renaissance as: "An all-consuming torrent of ideology, with its irrepressible influence, creating a beautiful mental frame to the basic and deep-seated laws of the unified humanity's all-pervasive mind, expressing itself all over the world in its kaleidoscope of beauty, style and movements." He had hailed Rammohan as the inaugurator of the new stream of ideas in our country. Addressing Rammohan as "Bharat Pathik," Tagore wrote, "when Rammohan was born, India had been plunged in the darkness of destruction. What a critical time it was! On one side the shores of Hindu society was degenerated into ruins, and on the other, the terrific flood of foreign civilization was approaching at a high speed. Rammohan came and stood at the centre with his undaunted supremacy. With the help of his magnanimous heart and free intellect, he succeeded in accepting the occident without rejecting the orient."

About Vidyasagar, the unforgettable figure in the history of our renaissance, Tagore wrote, "Vidyasagar by sheer dynamic personality smashed through the pettiness of rural

4. *Jiban Smṛti*, 1318-19 B.S.

life and the torpor of Bengali society; (he) directed the course of his solitary but firmly integrated life not towards narrow sectarian Hinduism, but towards the broad ocean of humanity filled with tear of compassion. . . . Vidyasagar stood alone in this Bengal . . . he was always an exile for want of comrades of equal stature."

Bengal's Cultural Activities and the Renaissance of Europe

The conscious comparison between Bengal's cultural activities in the nineteenth century and the Italian or the English Renaissance began with the emergence of militant nationalism in politics. Bipin Chandra Pal's estimate of Rammohan as its pioneer (1901) was followed by Sibnath Sastri's *Ramtanu Lahiri O Tatkalin Banga Samaj* (1903). Sibnath Sastri's book gives an overall picture of this awakening. It may be recalled that in a seminar on the occasion of Rammohan's death centenary in 1933, speakers like Rabindranath Tagore, Brojendranath Seal, Ramananda Chattopadhyay, etc. discussed the glorious character of this renaissance by way of estimating Rammohan's role in it.[5] The concept received unqualified blessings of Acharya Jadunath Sarkar. "It was truly a renaissance, wider, deeper and more revolutionary than that of Europe after the fall of Constantinople." Acknowledging that this statement is an exaggeration, we can conclude that up to mid-1930s, the prevalent view and attitude towards the Bengal renaissance was one of glorification and uncritical acceptance of it.

Parallel to this interpretation, we can trace another trend which upheld that the real nature of this renaissance can be

5. Discussions in the seminar were published in a book form entitled *The Father of Modern India*, Commemoration volume of the Rammohan Roy Centenary Celebration, 1933, compiled and edited by Satis Chandra Chakraborty, 1935.

found in the movement led by Bankim Chandra and Swami Vivekananda. This view apparently influenced by nationalist sentiment intends to establish that the Brahmo movement alone did not bring about the awakening in the nineteenth century. The Hindus also played significant roles in the process. The writings of Girija Sankar Raychaudhuri strongly advocated the case.[6] Sri Aurobindo approached the question of renaissance from an idealistic perspective and discussed the phenomenon with deep insight.[7] Ramesh Chandra Majumdar in his book *On Rammohan Roy* published from the Asiatic Society in 1972 made a thorough study on Rammohan Roy's contributions to the renaissance of Bengal in the nineteenth century. Majumdar argues — it almost always happens in the case of a great personality — that myths and legends grow around him and it becomes difficult to separate the truth from the fiction by which it is enveloped. So it has been also with Rammohan, and his admiring followers assert, and have sought to prove, that practically all that was good or great in the nineteenth century and made the renaissance possible, must be traced to Rammohan. Majumdar, after a critical analysis of Rammohan's contributions, concluded that Rammohan did not create the New Age, but he was one of the greatest representatives of that age and reflected in himself many distinguished features that heralded renaissance in Bengal. In protest, Brahmo intellectuals also took their pen and as a result, the debate on the nature of this renaissance was clouded and turned into a quarrel between the Brahmos and the Hindus.

---

6. Girija Sankar Raychaudhuri, *Swami Vivekananda O Banglay Unabinsa Unabinsa Satabdi*. (1334 B.S.)
7. Sri Aurobindo's views expressed in "The Renaissance in India, (Chandannagore, 1927), Bankim–Tilak–Dayananda, Bankim Chandra Chatterjee (Pondicherry).

Bengal's Renaissance Awakens the Marxists

Curiosity of the Marxists about this awakening in Bengal in the nineteenth century arose in the wake of the rise of Fascism and the World War II. Marxists of all countries tried to discover the cultural identity of their countries. It may be recalled that in 1935 at the seventh Congress of Comintern, George Dimitrov submitted a report regarding anti-Fascist struggle. His contention was that Marxism, in a particular country must be modified in keeping with regional variations; it must be harmonized with local peculiarities. This report encouraged the Marxists to look behind in search of traditions of their countries. This type of interpretation has tended to give the Bengal renaissance its due importance taking into account the objective and subjective constraints that operated in nineteenth century colonial India. This point needs illustration. There occurred bourgeois democratic awakening in India, China and other Asiatic countries through a complex process. Western countries, advanced in capitalistic development, began to use the above-mentioned countries as suppliers of raw materials. As a result, by virtue of the law of uneven development of capitalism, these oppressed countries did lose not only political freedom, but also, in the economic and cultural sphere, an underdeveloped cursed life that remained as their companion.

Against this background, in the fight against colonialism and its associate feudalism, the question of initiating the country to the doctrine of modernism (i.e. to master the ingredients of modern machine civilization and establishment of contact with scientific thought) was marked as essential pre-condition of national awakening. Considered from this angle, Bengal's awakening was an inseparable part of bourgeois democratic movement. It is to be remembered at the same time that there existed objective and subjective difficulties in Bengal's awakening in the historical situation.

The objective conditions that were created in Europe were absent in India. Rather colonial rule created constant obstacles in the way of developing similar objective pre-condition by joining hands with indigenous feudalism. An inner obstacle was the English-educated middle-class who proceeded to develop the modernizing process. They were government employees in professions and jobs. Their livelihood depended on foreign and indigenous feudalism in many ways. So, a hesitation was always present in their attitude of anti-colonialism and anti-feudalism. But Dimitrov's contention was that though it was an imperfect movement, it was a movement of some consequences. The concept of perfection remained always as a motto and every movement should be geared to attain it.

Written at this time, Amit Sen's (Professor Susobhan Sarkar) book *Notes on the Bengal Renaissance* (1946) acknowledges the bright aspects of this renaissance and at the same time points out its inner contradictions.[8] According to him, renascent Bengal was moulded by Westernism or liberalism and orientalism or traditionalism — two opposite thought movements, two logical concepts, battling over the minds of men. To him, there was no synthesis since synthesis takes place only when the two opposites are sublated into a third higher thing. There was rather a compromise — a co-existence or eclectic combination in certain minds of fundamentally opposite ideas. So, not a synthesis; such a mixture of ideas may more aptly be called an "interpenetration of opposites." Still, he held, "The role played by Bengal in the modern awakening of India is thus comparable to the position occupied by Italy in the story of the Italian Renaissance." This

---

8. "Notes on the Bengal Renaissance" was not written to give a marxist interpretation of the Bengal renaissance. To know Prof. Sarkar's own views, please read "Bengal Renaissance and other Essays" by Sushoran Sarkar.

clearly shows that Marxists acknowledge the positive aspect of this renaissance and take pride in the tradition of their country.

Marxists Interpretation of Bengal Renaissance

Gradually, necessity was felt for a Marxist interpretation of the Bengal renaissance. Rabindra Gupta (Bhabani Sen — Marxist intellectual) reached the conclusion that the trend which Rammohan–Bankim Chandra–Rabindranath fostered was not a progressive trend, rather it was opposite. He proceeded further to assert that, if it is true to say that the British rule inaugurated progressivism in India, then this trend can be called the progressive trend. His attitude towards the renaissance as an anti-people movement has culminated in the total rejection of any such renaissance. To him, with English establishing itself as imperialism's intellectual weapon for consolidating the empire, and with the elite's preserve resolute to speak and think in it only, emerged the most harmful constraint to the fulfilment of India's renaissance — alienation, consequent upon the loss of language and of the means of communication with the people. So, according to Rabindra Gupta, a renaissance which assured the people neither a recognition nor a place in the manifestation of its will was from its very inception, from both qualitative and quantitative considerations, a distorted, sapless renaissance.

But this interpretation of Rabindra Gupta was rejected by the Marxist intellectuals. They opined that this was not a Marxist interpretation, it was rather a distortion. Amit Sen,[9] despite having personal attachment to Marxist ideas, approached the renaissance from the viewpoint of nineteenth century European liberalism. According to him, although compared to its European counterpart, Bengal renaissance was a thing of limited, partial and somewhat artificial dimensions,

9. Ibid.

its historical value cannot be neglected. Actually, the value of any cultural efflorescence has to be judged with reference to the background provided by the immediately preceding age. The standards of eighteenth century intellectual and social life in Bengal certainly do not warrant a contemptuous attitude towards our nineteenth century renaissance. Uncritical glorification and scornful rejection of Bengal's awakening both violate alike the canons of historical objectivity. The achievement of an age is never absolute; its relative value, therefore, must not be ignored. Considering that, it was a movement of intensions distinct from performances. Amit Sen specifically mentions "Derozians" as ardent patriots, the first flower of contemporary patriots.

The above interpretations have been challenged by another interpretation whose basis was a criticism of colonialism. One of the propounders of the interpretation was Sri Benoy Ghosh who earlier was an appreciator of the Bengal renaissance, but later refused to accept its far-reaching significances. This group of historians criticizes the social evolution in the nineteenth century and concluded that this awakening was limited and the Bengali middle-class society had never been transformed into a modern one. Its main reason was that in the economic field, there was no other trend excepting colonialism. Sri Ghosh, by way of explaining his argument[10] asserted that the spirit of money-making which dominated the field of commerce, also brought a significant change in the texture of human relations in rural society. This was made possible by a change in the attitude to landed property, from "paternal" to "contractual." The paternalism of the benevolent despots of feudal days was largely replaced by cash-nexus in social relationships, and this was done by the new class of money-minded land-speculators and land-revenue contractors and

10. *Renascent Bengal*, Published from the Asiatic Society, Calcutta, article by Benoy Ghosh.

sub-contractors, whose socio-economic position was firmly stabilized by the enactment of the Permanent Settlement and the subsequent legalization of intermediate tenures. This means, the old feudal aristocracy was ruined and replaced by a more dehumanized new feudal aristocracy. The latter were more dependable as political allies of the British rulers, more oriented to monetary gains, and who would not press for any progressive economic development in the main subsistence sector of rural economy, for serving the economic interest of their colonial masters. This was not a change of the feudal framework of society, but a reorientation of the feudal set-up to make it more subservient and accommodating to the capitalist-imperialist ethos of the British rulers.

Distorted Process of Urbanisation

The same policy of economic strangulation of a colonial country led to a distorted process of urbanization and to the consequent growth of a semi-feudal urban social hierarchy. The social division between the city and the village stood on the level of class-division between the capitalist and the proletariat, the landlord and the peasant. This happened in Bengal, in the historic city of Calcutta. The city of Calcutta, under colonial conditions, steadily grew as a commercial and administrative rather than an industrial centre, in which the so-called "services" were the only broad category of employment showing any general increase with urbanization. Sri Ghosh further asserts that even the social mobility induced by education, especially by English education, proved ineffective in removing caste-ascriptions. The history of education in Hindu College from 1817, or of our university education from 1857-58, will affirm this statement.

Not more than five per cent till 1857, and ten per cent till the end of the nineteenth century, belonged to castes other than the three upper caste Hindus (Brahmins, Kayasthas and

Vaisyas), who could get the benefit of English education in Bengal. Sri Ghosh concludes that none of the two new criteria of social mobility — money and new English education — could effectively erode the feudal institutional structures of Bengali society. In the field of agriculture, new Zamindari System was strong and there was no perceptable change in industry. Bengal's overwhelmed agrarian economy was dented here and there by British capitalist activities, more commercial than industrial in nature. Bengali society failed to develop mercantile and industrial capitalism and what is more important "modern" science. It is a historical fact that the renaissance cannot be thought of without the reformation, the reformation cannot be thought of without the rise of modern science, and none of them can be thought of without the rise of capitalism, capitalist society and the disappearance of feudalism. It is a kind of organic whole, a well-integrated cluster of changes. The impact of Western liberal ideas was confined within a section of upper-class and middle-class caste-Hindus and English-educated elite, and as such the socio-religious reform movements emanating from it in urban areas, had very little spread effect, vertical and horizontal. Naturally, the common people were denied desired fruits. Moreover the small middle-class also was dependant on colonial economy. This limitation was also reflected at the turn of the century in the relation between the two major communities in India. So, this group of historians concluded, there was no genuine renaissance in Bengal or in India.

Some scholars[11] approach the Bengal renaissance from two perspectives: re-birth of Hinduism and re-vitalization of Bengali letters. They, however, accept the term "renaissance" for Bengal's overall development which could be viewed as a global process of historic consciousness of a people. Needless

11. Muhammad Shah Qureshi, etc.

to say, this constitutes a recent factor of modern history, to re-discover oneself on the basis of one's remote and immediate past. According to them, this has been an exclusive affair of the Hindus for the first fifty years or so of the nineteenth century.

Actually, this was Prof. S.C. Sarkar's warning that worship of past glory, to which the nineteenth century harked back, was a predominantly Hindu past and the "awakening" in Bengal also happens to be almost Hindu by origin. This factor created a new element in our traditionalism — a consciousness of Hindu superiority. As a defence mechanism against the alien impact, Hindu cousciousness may have some justification, but its basic weakness can never be slurred over. The majority of Indians are, of course, Hindus, but non-Hindus also form a sizeable part of the population. If it hurts the feelings of non-Hindus, the awakening itself could be frustrated by bitterness. It is surely the special responsibility of the dominant community to guard against the danger as history is full of failures on this count. The cool assumption that minorities do not matter, or that it is their duty to identify themselves with the majority, cannot but irritate such groups. Saifuddin Joardar, in a monograph has condemned the Bengali middle-class of the nineteenth century for veering more and more towards tradition, orthodoxy and exclusiveness rather than towards reason, humanism and scientific attitude to life.

Branding Bengal Renaissance Differently

Branding the resurgence of Bengal as an elitist movement is not a new phenomenon. According to the proponents of this interpretation, very few intellectuals were prepared to accede to the people a legitimate share in the life of the nation. Rammohan undoubtedly was keenly aware of his involvement in the affairs of the people, but his preferences for Western style of living and eclecticism could not be reconciled to his sense of involvement. The Hindu College elite were totally estranged beings, suffering from a built-in dread of the given situation. The only glorious exception was Vidyasagar, but there emerged no second Vidyasagar to emulate his example. As such, the elite community's talk of freedom or of love of the country remained mostly a mere intellectual concept, an empty cliche. The nature of their alienation did not only block their way back to the people, but it also prevented the latter from having an entry into the periphery of their mental life or world view.

In recent years attack on Bengal renaissance has been concentrated from another direction. A group of scholars associated with American Universities and Cambridge University has raised various questions on the issue. The main purport of their argument is that the Bengal renaissance is a gift of British rule. David Kopf,[12] for example, argued that the history of British rule in India was not the history of exploitation, it is an exaggeration or half-truth. According to him, East India Company and the British Orientalists took the responsibility of spreading light of civilization in India. He attributed the renaissance to the contact between a group of "accultured" civil, military and judicial officials and missionaries on the one hand and Bengali intelligentsia on the other. To him, Warren Hastings and Lord Wellesley were the inaugurators of cultural evolution in India. His intention is clear: he wants to ignore the prevalent idea that Rammohan, Derozio, Bankim Chandra or Swami Vivekananda were the leaders of this renaissance.

Another American scholar J.H. Broomfield[13] contended that the movement launched in Bengal at the beginning of the

---

12. *British Orientalism and the Bengal Renaissance*, University of California, 1969.

13. *Elite Conflict in a Plural Society*, Universtity of California, p. 1968.

nineteenth century by the English-educated middle-class cannot be called a national awakening. To him, it was a movement by the self-seeker, "bhadraloks" who fought for the realization of their own interests. It was more anti-people than anti-British. Following this model, Anil Seal[14] also upheld that co-operation with the Indians was the basis of British rule in India. Upper caste elite with firm financial roots pressed for various concessions. They had no contact with the people; they were exploiters and hence they had no right to represent the common people. So, it is clear, these writers try to ignore the importance of the Bengal renaissance and its bright flower — the birth of nationalism in India.

This imported concept of "bhadralok" received attention from some of our contemporary scholars who concluded that the so-called renaissance is a myth, a historical hoax, since it was the accomplishment of the agents of the British. This group criticizes David Kopf, Broomfield, and Anil Seal here and there but lend support to their main thesis indirectly. As for example, Prof. Barun De prefers to call the leaders of this renaissance "comprador intelligentsia" and argues that it was a renaissance created by collaboration with British imperialism.[15] Professor Ashoke Sen writes, "the new Bengali middle-class came to be a participant in the building up of the structure of colonial political economy." Prof. Sumit Sarkar's analysis of this renaissance resembles closely with Broomfield's. The only comment we want to make here is that these scholars blindly rejected tradition of this country and subjected their analysis to Marxian class standpoint. To what extent it is consonant with Marxian analysis becomes clear when we remember that

14. *The Emergence of Indian Nationalism*, Cambridge University Press, 1968.

15. Barun De, A critique of the Historiography of the Trend entitled Renaissance in the Nineteenth Century; Barun De, Some stray thoughts on the colonial context of nineteenth-century Bengal.

Karl Marx himself considered the birth of an English-educated middle-class in Bengal to be significant and Lenin drew our attention to the role of the intellectuals in the bourgeois democratic awakening in Asian countries. Karl Marx discerned a regenerative role of British rule in India. British rule, he observed, broke down the historical economic structure of India, i.e. myriads of industrious patriarchal and unoffensive social orgnizations, which although appeared unoffensive became the solid foundation of Oriental despotism restraining the human mind within the smallest possible compass, making it the unresisting tool of superstition, enslaving it beneath traditional rules, depriving it of all grandeur and historical energies. These little communities, Marx noticed, subjected man to internal circumstances instead of elevating him to be the sovereign of circumstances and thus they transformed a self-developing social state into a never changing natural destiny. But it did not elude his notice that while causing a "social revolution" in Hindustan, England was actuated only by the "vilest interests" and was stupid in her manner of enforcing them. But Marx concluded by saying that whatever might have been the crimes of England, she was the "unconscious tool of history" in bringing about that revolution.

Ultra-left Condemns Bengal Renaissance

Ultra-left denunciation of the "renaissance myth" resembling Rabindragupta's interpretation began to express itself from the late 1960s in a series of leftist journals edited by Samar Sen. Seeking to evaluate the regeneration in terms of its special context, i.e. colonialism, they found it only as a retrograde movement. Bengal renaissance was criticized as a pro-colonial movement, an act of sinister conspiracy between upper Indian society and colonial English society.

No easy solution to this debate on the nature of Bengal renaissance is possible. As we have seen above, critics are not tired of pointing out its limitations. Prof. Amales Tripathi approached the issue with deep insight and from his writings,[16] we find a balanced appreciation of Bengal renaissance. He warned against blind application of Burckhardt's interpretation of the Italian Renaissance to an altogether different phenomenon in India. The scenes were so different. He pointed out the parallelisms as well as the differences between the Italian Renaissance and the Bengal renaissance. In his analysis of the development of nineteenth century culture in Bengal, he stressed on conflict between tradition and modernity and showed how the actual creators of the nineteenth century culture, instead of abandoning and rejecting tradition, employed the same in modernizing various aspects of our society and culture.

So, we should pause for a while before dismissing the cultural efflorescence of the nineteenth century. Certain considerations demand our attention. True, no fundamental economic changes took place in the nineteenth century, but this does not mean that Bengal did not experience significant changes in the realm of society and culture. In poetry, literature, art and science there had been definite beginnings. As Sri Aurobindo puts it, "Bengal in these, as in many other directions, has been recently the chief testing crucible or the first workshop of the Shakti of India; it is there she has chosen to cast in the greatest vivacity of new influences and develop her initial forms and aspirations!"[17]

---

16. Amales Tripathi : "Itali Renaissance Bangalir Sanskriti" (in Bengali). Article "Bengali Literature in the Nineteenth Century" in *History of Bengal*, ed. N.K. Sinha from the Calcutta University.

17. Sri Aurobindo: "The Renaissance in India." Pondicherry, 1973 (first published in 1920), p. 35.

One should take note of the magical efflorescence of vernacular literature in myriad forms and glory and the appearance of a host of remarkable individuals in different walks of life within the short span of a century. We can easily discern traits of modernism in the evolution of society and culture in Bengal from Rammohan to Rabindranath. That this was an age of modernization is acknowledged, although limits of modernization are pointed out. Again, Bengal witnessed in the nineteenth century the birth of an urban and civic society which differed fundamentally from the society of the immediately preceding centuries which was predominantly rural.

Calcutta initiated the process of urbanization and sophistication. Even as a colonial city, Calcutta experienced the impact of international influences. These influences might not fundamentally change the structure of its society but the impact went a long way in influencing the mental horizon. It will not be an exaggeration to say that Calcutta became the ground of union between the civilizations of the East and the West. Fort William College and Hindu College were centres of such union. Even if one refuses to accept it as union of two civilizations, none can deny that in the nineteenth century certain objective conditions created a new environment which gave birth to new attitudes towards society and culture. The whole spectacle provided a background which helped the emergence of Rammohan, Vidyasagar, Bankim Chandra, Rabindranath and a host of brilliant individuals. It is not difficult to trace in them the birth of a secular ideal, and individualist and amoral urbanity and a spirit of enquiry, criticism and realism (which are the traits of the Italian Renaissance).

But this renaissance suffers in comparison[18] with the Italian or West European Renaissance. Basic differences exist between them. The horizon of European Renaissance was well-spread and with it were associated geographical discoveries, a profound revolution in religion, the rise of centralized states, the beginning of the break-up of the old social system, the re-organization of trade, industry and agriculture, development of natural science and above all, recovery of classical culture. Our renaissance cannot possibly claim any such tremendous sweep. In Bengal, the role of the Greek and Latin classics has been given not to the old Sanskrit literature but to the Western arts and sciences taught through the medium of English. Bengal went to the school not at Athens of Pericles nor at Rome of Augustus but at England of Shakespeare, Milton, Spencer and Mill. Renaissance Italy was the grave of the empire and the playground of small well-knit independent princely or republican states, while Bengal's (and India's) heterogenous anarchy was being brought under one centralized bureaucratic sway of a foreign power which left no scopes like the Sforza Milan or the Medici–Florence, for the development of unusual talents. The social and economic matrices of the twelfth and the thirteenth century Italy, which contributed to the magnificence of the Quattrocento and the Cinquecento, were wholly wanting in the nineteenth century Bengal whose overwhelming agrarian economy was dented here and there by British capitalist activities, more commercial than industrial in nature. Calcutta, no doubt, dwarfed everything in the landscape, but it never had any productive life like Florence, nor a trading empire like Venice, which "held the gorgeous East in fee." It was hardly a century old while the others hailed back to the Roman times.

---

18. Amales Tripathi, "Bengali Literature in the Nineteenth Century", in N.K. Sinha, ed. *History of Bengal.*

The patrons and appreciators of the Italian Renaissance were bourgeoisie with firm roots in industry, commerce and high finance, while those in India were the middle-classes created by the Cornwallis Settlement with limited employment opportunities in the Company's courts and commissariat. The first source of income, land, was speculative; the second, commerce, was controlled by the Company (till 1833) and the private British capitalists. There were not many doctors and engineers. Banks did not provide much opportunity as there were only 15 in Bengal in 1901. These people, half urban and half rural (for many were dependent on income from land), were not a fit vessel to receive the Protean gift of the Renaissance. It is idle to seek for a Lorenzo dé Medici among the banians or a Federigo of urbino among the Zamindars.

Revival of Dharma in Bengal Renaissance

The Bengal renaissance witnessed the revival of *dharma* in the ancient sense of an ethical way of life and an intense awareness of God. Herein lies the most marked difference between the Italian Renaissance and our nineteenth century cultural efflorescence. In the former the ferment of new life exploded the accepted code of morality and men reverted to nature and the free play of instinct and experience. In the latter a new code of morality was fashioned and the claim of society set up against the liberated individual. Where the Italian Renaissance preserved its triumphs in art, the nineteenth century Bengal preserved its triumphs in its spiritual story from Rammohan to Rabindranath. In Italy artistic glory was accompanied by moral misery and social disintegration. In Bengal, the artistic glory was one-sided and limited but the moral victory was unmistakable and, instead of political and social disruption, we find the beginning of a new integration after an initial setback in the first phase of Westernization.

Two points are relevant in understanding the real nature of the Bengal renaissance: (a) Impact of the West, and (b) Role of Indian civilization and culture. On the first, Sri Aurobindo very aptly remarked, "For whatever temporary rotting and destruction the crude impact of European life and culture has caused, it gave three needed impulses. It revived the dormant intellectual and critical impulse; it rehabilitated life and awakened the desire of new creation; it put the reviving Indian spirit face to face with novel conditions and ideals and the urgent necessity of understanding, assimilating and conquering them. The national mind turned a new eye in its past culture, reawoke to its sense and import, but also, at the same time, saw it in relation to modern knowledge and ideas. Out of this awakening vision and impulse the Indian Renaissance is arising."[19] Jadunath Sarkar, while emphasizing the impact of the West and English education, reminded us of the role of ancient Indian civilization in this context. He writes, "The Indian renaissance was possible only because a principle was discovered by which India could throw herself into the full current of modern civilization in the outer world without totally discarding her past. She could approach the temple of modern art and science not as a naked beggar, not as an utter alien, but as a backward and at present impoverished country cousin of Europe. She had a special and intellectual heritage of which she need not be ashamed before the world. In fact India was not called upon to plume herself in the borrowed feathers of European civilization, she had only to assimilate modern thought and modern arts into her inner life without any loss of what she had long possesed."[20] Modern-day historians could do well to give due importance to this aspect,

19. Sri Aurobindo: "The Renaissance in India", pp. 18-19.

20. Jadunath Sarkar: *Fall of the Mughal Empire*, vol. IV, Calcutta, 1950, p. 348.

for the vision of an ancient Indian civilization and culture made us turn our look upon all that our past contains with new eyes which have not only enabled us to recover something of their ancient sense and spirit, long embedded and lost in the unintelligent practice of received forms, but to bring out of them a new light which gives to the old truths fresh aspects and therefore novel potentialities of creation and evolution." Our contemporay historians being influenced by personal ideology and writings of foreign authors discard this aspect. They fail to understand that any discussion on the nature of Bengal renaissance ignoring this would be incomplete.

Conclusion

Now, finally, the question comes — whether at all there was really a Renaissance in Bengal. That depends a good deal on what we mean by the word . . .. "The word carries the mind back to the turning point of European culture to which it was first applied; that was not so much a reawakening as an overturn and reversal, a seizure of Christianized, Teutonized, feudalized Europe by the old Graeco-Latin spirit and form with all the complex and momentous results which came from it."[21] That is certainly not a type of renaissance that is at all possible in India or Bengal. For as we know, the objective conditions in Italy and Bengal were different and hence the nature would also differ. And that is why Bengal renaissance was not a carbon-copy of the Italian Renaissance. It is futile to seek affinities in all aspects. Differences were there. It is agreed on common consent that though Bengal renaissance suffers in companion with Italian Renaissance, the former was not without merit; it had positive and illuminating directions. It is to be understood that the term "Renaissance" should not be used strictly on the basis of similarities with the Italian

21. Sri Aurobindo: "The Renaissance in India", pp. 1-2.

Renaissance. History recognizes Carolingian Renaissance, Ottonian Renaissance and twelfth century Renaissance and this shows the epithet "Renaissance" has been loosely used denoting significant changes. So, acknowledging the fact that the thought movement in the nineteenth century served as passport to modernization, we can very well apply the term "Renaissance" to the cultural efflorescence in Bengal in the nineteenth century.

4

Sri Aurobindo on the Possibility of Renaissance in India

Dilip Kumar Roy

THE question of the possibility of renaissance in India was discussed by Sri Aurobindo in great detail in his article *The Renaissance in India* published serially in his English monthly "*Arya*" from August to November in the year 1918. While discussing about Indian civilization and its rebirth, he suggests that in every sphere there is a necessity of an effectual new creation. This rebirth is signigicant in respect of India because of the meaning signified in the regaining or change of the old Indian spirit and national ideal. We are to understand first what India means by its life and then what meaning the word "renaissance" conveys to the human race. Without this understanding our discussion about the renaissance in India would be inane.

The Reawakening in India

The question that is often raised is whether at all the Renaissance had taken place in India. The answer to this question depends largely on the meaning of the word "renaissance" and also on the future as it is only in an early stage of development, and hence it is not possible to say beforehand what results it will lead to. The word "renaissance" was first applied at a time of important change of European culture; but what will be worth saying is that, instead of naming this change a renaissance, it should be rather termed as a change of what prevailed before, as "a seizure of Christianised, Teutonised, feudalised Europe by the old Graeco-Latin spirit and form,"[1] with all the results, at once complex and significant. Hence it would be better not to relate renaissance that is possible in India to the change in European culture. Rather, it can be said that a reawakening which stands out as a possibility in India is almost alike the recent Celtic movement in Ireland. In Celtic movement in Ireland we find an upsurge of a reawakened national spirit in a vigorous impulse supplying a spiritual power for the rebuilding and remoulding of a nation on a solid rock. A similar movement, to some extent, is noticed in India — the movement which takes a turn marked by the sudden emotional expression in the political field in 1905. But here also the analogy is not expressive of the whole truth.

As India always remains in an awakened state and does not wait for being reawakened, so a question arises as to whether at all the word "reawakening" (or renaissance) is applicable in the case of India. This query was practically made by an Irish poet James Henry Cousins (1873–1956) who was also a theologian, a social worker as well as an educationist. No doubt, his query contains a grain of truth, since any person coming to India from outside may think that there exists a living continuity between India of the past and India as seen in the present. But the Indians do not agree to this. There was a time, however short, when India had to endure pains and sufferings, and this happened for political turmoil which gave the Europeans an opportune moment to create pressure on

1. *Sri Aurobindo Birth Centenary Library (SABCL), vol. 14 : The Foundations of Indian Culture,* p. 397.

the Indians. This plight of India is also due to some internal cause, say, our inertia in the fields of religion and arts and with this inertial attitude was attended our incapability to adjust overselves with the changing states. Science, philosophy and intellectual knowledge had long been in dying condition or replaced by scholasticism — all suggesting the lowest point of energy — the point which marks the beginning of a new age. The pressure of a super-imposed European culture followed by that momentous beginning has necessitated the reawakening.

Indian Spirit is the Root Cause of Her Reawakening

Cousins turns his attention to Indian spirituality which has always been able to maintain its existence even when the national life-force was at the point of stagnation. It is true that this spirituality has saved India at the ultimate moment of its destiny. If there be any starting-point of reawakening in India, that point is what has been called its spirituality.

Every race has a basic support which serves the main source of its strength. Any race may face an acute crisis for any reason or other, but if the main source of its strength remains unperturbed and unhurt, that race, although it may be in a living-dying condition for the time being, is not fully extinguished. As for example, it can be said that the main source of strength of the French lies in its political independence. The French may endure torture and injustice timelessly, but they will not tolerate any foreign interference into the jurisdiction of their political independence or liberty which seems to be their birthright. To protect this right, they can go to any length. No human race wants to lose what is their own, since this race is quite aware of the main source of its own, and the seat of this mentality is spirituality. In the past India had to go through much suffering and agony; but, in spite of all that, she was able to maintain her identity because the main source of her strength has not yet received any blow, causing a harmful or damaging effect. If we look at the past glorious history of India, we shall see that Indian spiritualism is present at the root of her unbounded energy expressed in every domain of life — in science, in philosophy, in literature, in social system and so on. If any question arises as to whether there will be reawakening in India, to this question there is only one answer which is : reawakening is sure to come in India since India still finds her locus in the main source of her strength, in her spiritualistic tendency. Generally speaking, the cause of our downfall can be traced to the fact that we have traversed quite a distance away from our national spirit, or the fact that under the spreading influence of ignorance we have forgotten the main source of our strength.

European writers depict the picture of India as a mind, abstract and metaphysical, with a religious attitude which is of no use in practical life and hence is unreal. They also think that the Indian mind is possessed of the sense of the infinite to such an extent that exceeds what is normal and usual. Later, of course, Europeans have seen in Indian art the presence of remarkable power and beauty; but at the same time it is true that they have failed to apprehend much of the significance as suggested by Indian art. European writers' view of India stands unjustified from the Sri Aurobindonian point of view. We shall see that shortly.

Spirituality is the Key-note of Indian Mind

Sri Aurobindo strikes on the head of the nail when he says that spirituality and no other thing, is "the master-key of the Indian mind."[2] Such a mind is naturally inclined towards the infinite. It has that insight which leads it to know that a life cannot be truly lived by attending to its external sides. India

2. Ibid., p. 400.

has never expressed doubt as to the importance of natural science, physical laws and forces; she knows how to organize the ways of ordinary life; she comes to notice that the complexity of the universe cannot be explained from a superficial point of view, as the sense of the natural can never be complete without relating it to what is called supra-natural. Behind the universe, even inside man, there is a force, naturally unknown to him. Man himself is not aware, rather ignorant, of his own complete being. He does not know that surrounding the natural or the sensible there is the supra-natural or the supra-sensible, that the invisible centres round the visible, and that the infinite surrounds the finite. This also has been noticed by India with her insight that man has a capacity to extend beyond himself, that he is capable of making himself more complete than what he is now. These are the insights flashed into the Indian mind. Although modern Europe has begun to catch the glimpses of those insights, it seems that they remain far from being completely sensed by its ordinary intellect.

The Indian mind, when put to analysis, shows itself to be unique in this respect that its deep curiosity to know leads it to the idea of the One from the idea of the Many. Thus it makes a steady progress from the idea of many gods to the idea of one God, from the latter to the idea of the Supreme Being, beyond which there is still a Beyond.

Spirituality, the key-note of the Indian mind, does not take its rise from the void. If we turn our eyes towards the past of India, what strikes our mind with wonder is that her life-force is inexhaustible, and her creativeness prolific and unimaginable. If we make a survey of the history of about last 3000 years, we come to see how India has been able to spread her creative power in many directions, in what are called "republics and kingdoms and empires, philosophies and cosmogonies and sciences and creeds and arts and poems and all kinds of monuments, palaces and temples and public works, communities and societies and religious orders, laws and codes and rituals, physical sciences, psychic sciences, systems of Yoga, systems of politics and administration, arts spiritual, arts worldly, trades, industries, fine crafts,"[3] these are the few items, to the list of which many more can be added, and in each item there is an excess of activity. The main objection posed by European critics is that the ancient India has not shown any reticence in her architecture, sculpture and art — in each of them there is more than is needed. But whether this excess of activity is her defect or not, what needs to be said is that here everything comes up necessarily from the fullness of her life.

Strong Intellectuality is another Main Feature of Indian Mentality

Apart from its extreme spiritualism and fullness of life, another feature of Indian mentality is its "strong intellectuality, at once austere and rich, robust and minute, powerful and delicate, massive in principle and curious in detail."[4] This mentality has a strong propensity towards maintaining order and arrangement; it gives stress on the possibility of practising anything conscientiously or from a sense of duty; the order it is prone to maintain is based on the finding out of the inner law and truth of things. India proves her superiority to all other countries in respect of her *dharma* and *śāstra*. To find out the inner truth, to search for the law of each human or cosmic activity is her *dharma*; after that she labours to apply it in fact and rule of life into elaborate form and detailed law of arrangement.

Thus India's life is spread over three periods. In the first period of her life, she discovers the Spirit; her second period ends with the discovery of the *dharma*; and in her third period,

3. Ibid., p. 401.
4. Ibid., p. 402.

she applies the *dharma* into the rule of life and that into elaborate form, maintaining the law of arrangement. The third period of her life is dedicated to the detailed elaboration of "the first simpler formulation of the *śāstra*."[5] These three elements of the three periods are never missed from the life of India and herein lies her uniqueness or superiority in excellence.

Caste System of Ancient India

A question arises here: Is it not true that the *varṇa* (or caste) system prevalent in ancient India is not in accord with her mentality so far sketched? Here Sri Aurobindo says that the caste system was formalized by the ancient Indian mind for the simple reason that it should be treated as the symbol of the social order; but the one idea that makes its room in the Indian mind is that the soul of man is above all caste or race. It thinks that the divine nature or divinity belongs to men of all types — from the human being of the highest stature like the king to the human being of the lowest stature like the poor and the downtrodden. The idea of *Nara-Nārayaṇa* has never slipped the Indian mind; it continues down the ages.

The ideal followed by the ancient India is that of spiritual anarchism. Here the word "anarchism," though widely misused, has received a lofty sense, the sense of "a spiritual, an inner freedom,"[6] without which a perfect human order cannot be possible. Out of this inner freedom is born a "deeper brotherhood, a yet unfound law of love."[7] This brotherhood is something different from any vital or mental sense of brotherhood; it means "spiritual comradeship which is the expression of an inner realisation of oneness."[8] Spiritual

5. Ibid., p. 403.
6. *SABCL*, vol. 15 : *Social and Political Thought*, p. 206.
7. Ibid.
8. Ibid., p. 207.

brotherhood or comradeship, or "the love, which is founded upon a deeper truth of our being,"[9] is "the only sure foundation possible for a perfect social evolution."[10]

As there is, on the one side, extreme spiritualism of the Indian mind, so, on the other, there is the life of the senses and its enjoyments. It may seem to us that the one is opposite to the other, but actually they are not so. The Indian mind is not merely spiritual and ethical; it is intellectual and artistic also. In every extreme it is in search of a law and sees whether its application is in accordance with a rule. There is a thoroughly fixed characteristic of the Indian mind, and that is its synthetical tendency by which it establishes a balance and harmony in action and institution. "Balance and rhythm which the Greeks arrived at by self-limitation, India arrived at by its sense of intellectual, ethical and aesthetic order and the synthetic impulse of its mind and life."[11]

The Tendency of Spiritual Realisation

Sri Aurobindo deals with the above-mentioned facets of the Indian spirit with a view to showing that these facets are not accepted by the European critics. Even at a time of fall, the glorious past has a residual lingering effect. This residuum will serve as a starting-point of the future. Every bit of the past found in India lies dormant in the present residue; it has not been destroyed; it awaits the opportune moment when it will begin to unfold itself. The decline means the ebbing away of the creative spirit towards creation, and the renascence means a tide of creation caused by the same spirit, although the forms it takes may be quite new.

---

9. Ibid.
10. Ibid., p. 206.
11. *SABCL*, vol. 14 : *The Foundations of Indian Culture*, p. 406.

The tendency of spiritual realization is the central principle of the Indian mind. The history of this tendency means its progression through the different ages.

The age that comes first is the spiritual age. This age is marked by India's seeking for the truth of existence through the intuitive mind and through the inner experience and interpretation of both the psychic and the physical existence. But this spiritual tendency is not that of metaphysical abstraction merely, since the Indian mind does not tend to go upwards towards "the abstract, the hidden and the intangible"[12] to the exclusion of what is objective. Its spiritual tendency is not to proceed by way of bracketing "the multiplicities of thought and the richness of life."[13]

The second long era of India's greatness is what is called the "age of the intellect." In this age what is noticed is a strong ethical sense assisted by a dynamic will in action to build and regularize life in the light of spiritual truth. The curiosity of the intellect, in this age, helps in gaining, in detail, new ideas in the fields of art, science, literature, politics, sociology, mundane life, etc. This probing of the intellect into different areas of life results in the great classical age of Sanskrit culture. This age is found to be replete with rich experiences of objects relating to beauty, emotion, even sensuous pleasure. But behind all these mental and vital acts the old spirituality remains dominant. The age that follows the great classical age is the age of the Purāṇic and Tantric systems and the religions of *bhakti*. Later comes Vaiṣṇavism. In Vaiṣṇavism the whole of the aesthetic, emotional and sensuous being is absorbed into the service of the spiritual. Thus, the curve of the cycle or a period of time in which the above events occur at regular intervals comes to be complete.

---

12. Ibid., p. 407.
13. Ibid.

Three Movements Responsible for the Waning of India's Career

The ebbing away of the glorious past of India starts after the completion of the said curve. Three retrograde movements are responsible for the waning career of India. First, the superabundant vital energy begins to decline; a wan look appears on the face of life because of the lacking of its vitality and the fading of its joy. Even in the period of the decline the vital energy is not totally lost: it "is still something splendid and extraordinary."[14] Of course, if we compare its present state with its past greatness, we come to notice its marked decadence in spirit and action. This comparison shows that it is almost in a state of torpor. This is one movement of retrogression.

Another retrograde movement starts with the cessation of the "free intellectual activity." The functioning of the scientific and the critical mind comes to a halt; the intuitive mind ceases to play its role: all are in a state of slumber, so to speak.

The third movement of retrogression places spirituality in a jeopardized condition which can be described thus: "spirituality remains but burns no longer with the large and clear flame of knowledge of former times, but in intense jets and in a dispersed action which replaces the old magnificent synthesis and in which certain spiritual truths are emphasised to the neglect of others."[15] This reduction in the spiritual knowledge appears as a bar thwarting "the progress towards the perfect spiritualisation of the mind and the life."[16] But, in spite of all this, the essential of spirituality "still remains in the heart of the race," although it is "covered up in a great smoke of confusion."[17]

14. Ibid.
15. Ibid., p. 408.
16. Ibid.
17. Ibid.

This plight of India becomes worsened when the wave of an opposite current, an opposite type of civilization, strikes the shore of the Indian mind. The first impact of European life and culture on such a mind is not at all healthy to it. India faces her peril from two sides: on the one side a rapid diminution of her past glory; and on the other, a slavish imitation of foreign ideas and habits. Such a situation is surely disastrous to any nation and civilization.

The crude impact of European life and culture, however disastrous and destructive it may be, renders three impulses needed for the revival of India from her deadening condition: the impulse to revive the dormant intellectual and critical activity of the mind; the impulse to rehabilitate life and to awaken the desire of new creation; and the impulse to encounter new alien ideas and ideals and to make them reconcilable with one's own ideas and ideals, valuable for a new statement of life. By the force of these impulses, the national mind will turn its attention to its past glory, its past rich culture and try to apprehend anew the meaning and the significance of this culture; not only that, it should also try to see it in relation to modern knowledge and ideas. The Indian renaissance is arising out of this awakening vision and impulse, and its future tendency will be determined by the same vision and impulse.

Conclusion

Sri Aurobindo, from his integral and yogic point of view, says clearly that three most essential works are to be done by the Indian mind for bringing in the renaissance in India and for determining the future of humanity. "The recovery of the old spiritual knowledge and experience in all its splendour, depth and fullness is its first, most essential work; the flowing of this spirituality into new forms of philosophy, literature, art, science and critical knowledge is the second; an original dealing with modern problems in the light of Indian spirit and the endeavour to formulate a greater synthesis of a spiritualised society is the third and most difficult."[18] The future of humanity will depend on the successful carrying of those works in accordance with the lines as suggested by Sri Aurobindo.

18. Ibid., p. 409.

5

Sri Aurobindo and Ireland
A Critical Study

Dilip Kumar Chatterjee

After six hundred years did Fate intend
Her perfect perseverance thus should end?
So many years she strove, so many years,
Enduring toil, enduring bitter tears,
She waged religious war, with sword and song
Insurgent against fate and numbers, strong
To inflict as to sustain; her weak estate
Could not conceal the goddess in her gait;
Goddess her mood. Therefore that light was she
In whom races of weaker destiny
Their beauteous image of rebellion saw;
Treason could not unnerve, violence overawe —
A mirror to enslaved nations, never
O'ercome, though in the field defeated ever.
O mutability of human merit!
How changed, how fallen from her ancient spirit!
She that was Ireland, Ireland now no more . . .[1]

1. Collected Poems of Sri Aurobindo, Pondicherry.

Aurobindo's Response to Ireland's National and Cultural Renaissance

THE above excerpt of Sri Aurobindo's early poem, *Lines on Ireland* (1896) is undoubtedly an important document to suggest how an Indian poet in English draws our attention to the bottomless misery of colonization of Ireland as well as its glorified past. Sri Aurobindo is the first poet of India to instill into our minds his sympathy and respect for Ireland, a country which had been under British domination for several centuries and struggling hard against it with "sword and song". Sri Aurobindo imaginatively constructed the image of Ireland as of his own country India as a goddess, "goddess in her gait and goddess her mood" and affirmed significantly that Ireland's national and cultural insurgence over the centuries against the British colonization hold "a mirror to enslaved nations" like India, his native land.

As the poem was written during his early youth, 1890s, this impassioned address to Ireland is here by no means a mere effusion of an adolescent sensibility. It foreshadows the maturer Sri Aurobindo, the avid reader of history, who had always a penchant for getting himself informed of revolutions and rebellions of countries leading to their national liberations. Sri Aurobindo's heroes were the heroes who went on fighting uncompromisingly against foreign domination and he was of course, keeping in mind the martyrdom of Robert Emmet, the great Irish leader who was hanged to death in 1803 in Ireland. Emmet's speech from the gallows echoes the great Indian martyr Khudiram : "I acted as an Irishman, determined to delivering my country from this doubly-riveted despotism, I wished to place her independence beyond the reach of any power on earth."[2] Sri Aurobindo exclaims in great admiration

2. Curtis Edmund, 1951, *A History of Ireland,* (sixth ed., London), ch. XIX.

to Ireland "O nurse and mother of heroic men" and affirms that no alien oppression can ruin, can discourage, no disease and famine could "abate a nation" like Ireland. Sri Aurobindo concludes this 140 lines poem in a prophetic vein and his prophecy came true in the next century:

In time's full ripeness and the date of men
Alien oppression maddened has the wise, —
For ever thus preparing Nemesis
In ruling nations unjust power has borne
Insolence, injustice, madness, outrage, scorn,
Its natural children, then, by high disdain
And brave example, pushed to meet their pain,
The pupils of thy greatness shall appear,
Souls regale to the mould divine most near,
And reign, or rise on throne-intending wings,
Making the father to a line of kings.[3]

The British colonizers who denigrated the Irish as well as the Indians' glorious past and heritage and treated them by their insolence and injustice are scathingly criticized in this illuminating poem where Sri Aurobindo's love for Ireland registers an unmistakable authenticity, an overwhelming and ennobling sense of commitment. The poem expresses not only his love and admiration for Ireland but an anxiety as well. While celebrating the glorious past of Ireland the poet expresses his wound because of the country's fallen, miserable plight under the alien rulers.

Aurobindo's Heart Beats for Ireland

Sri Aurobindo was genuinely gripped by the march of events in Ireland and he was certainly thinking in the hinterland of his consciousness of his own country where the oppressor's

3. Collected Poems of Sri Aurobindo, Pondicherry.

wrong, the proud man's contumely, the insolence of office and the pangs of subjection torment every citizen of India. A powerful feeling began to grow in the young Aurobindo that a period of general upheaval and revolutionary changes was about to dawn in the world and he was destined to play a part in it. Sri Aurobindo's attention was now drawn not only to Ireland but also to India and this feeling soon developed into the idea of India's national and cultural resurgence in which he wholeheartedly participated since his return to India.

Probably no country in the world exercised greater influence on the course of India's national and cultural resurgence than Ireland. Educated Indians after Rammohan — quite long before Sri Aurobindo, showed a great interest in Ireland. The suffering of Ireland and her heroic struggle against heavy odds to preserve her religion, culture and nationality struck a responsive chord in the hearts of the leading figures of India's renaissance.

Rammohan Supports Irish Cause

It is worth remembering that it was Rammohan who first drew our attention to the deprivation and humiliation of the people of Ireland in an essay, "Ireland : The Causes of Its Distress and Discontents." This was published on 11th October, 1822 in the journal *Mirat Ul Akhbar*, of which Rammohan himself was the editor. Here Rammohan was sharply critical about the inhuman treatment of the people of Ireland by its British rulers. He defended the Catholic Emancipation as a democratic right of the Irish which their alien rulers kept pending with a divisive intent to disrupt the unity of the country.

Just after five years (1827), while writing a letter of protest to John Crawford, Rammohan was vehemently attacking the British Parliament for their not including the Hindus as well as Muslims in their grand Jury as they had done it in Ireland by isolating the Catholics from the Protestants. In this connection, Rammohan significantly remarked on the similarity of the Irish and the Indian situation:

> Were India to share one-fourth of the knowledge and energy of that country (Ireland), she would prove from her remote situation, her riches and her vast population, either useful and profitable as a willing province, an ally of the British Empire or *troublesome and annoying as a determined enemy* (18 August, 1828). (Emphasis mine)

It is in this letter that Rammohan made a prophetic hint at the anti-British attitude and the possibility of India's liberation from the British rule.

Rammohan did not even spare the British when the "Coercion Bill" was executed in Ireland and hundreds of Irish protesters were arrested and imprisoned by the British police. In one of his letters to an anonymous friend Rammohan wrote: "In justice to my conscience and feelings I cannot express approbation of the Irish Coercion Bill and its authors and supporters"[4] (19th May, 1833).

Rammohan's friend Prince Dwarakanath, another great figure of the nineteenth century Bengal renaissance, and Rabindranath's grandfather, showed a considerable interest in Ireland. He went to England in 1845 and in August of that year he visited Ireland. He met and talked to O'Donnell (1775–1847), brilliant successful Irish barrister, who dedicated himself to the cause of the Irish nationalism. During the great famine in Ireland in 1845-48 which reduced 250,000 people to death and 2 lakhs immigrant to America, it was Prince Dwarakanath who came forward to offer immense financial help to the famine stricken people of Ireland. O'Donnell's close friendship with Gyanendramohan Tagore, a patriotic and wealthy Bengali residing in London, enabled him not only to

---

4. See S.D. Collet, *The Life and Letters of Raja Rammohan Roy*, 1900.

appreciate Indians' political aspirations better, but also to establish contacts with Indian visitors to the United Kingdom and with the British Indian Association in Calcutta.[5]

Indo-Irish Relations Flourish

Rabindranath Tagore went to England to his brother for higher studies and he described in his autobiography (*Jibansmriti*), how he was witnessing O'Donnell's Parliamentary address in the British Parliament in London in favour of the colonized people of India.

Thus, the Indo-Irish national and cultural interaction became an interesting phenomenon during the closing decades of the nineteenth and in the beginning of the twentieth century. The Irish nationalists and writers turned to India because of similarities they noticed in their social, cultural and political aspirations with those of India. In fact a strong feeling was cultivated among the poets and writers of Ireland's literary Renaissance that spiritually Ireland belonged to the East. Hence the Irish nationalist and poets like AE (George William Russell), Yeats, Charles Johnston and James Henry Cousins developed a bond of spiritual kinship with their Indian counterparts like Sri Aurobindo and Rabindranath.

AE (George William Russell, 1867–1935) believed that Indian religious thought could provide an answer to the contemporary religious problems for its all-inclusiveness. He built his ideas of a new Renaissance on the discovery of the wisdom religion of India. In his spiritual autobiography, he says:

> If Europe is to have a Renaissance comparable with that which came from the wedding of Christianity with the Greek

5. S.R., Mehrotra, 1971, *The Birth of the Indian National Congress*, ch. "The Rising Tide," p. 326.

> and Latin cultures, it must, I think come from a second wedding of Christianity with the culture of the East.[6]

By this kind of "Renaissance" AE meant what the discovery of ancient India did to Europe. Raymond Schawb in his book *The Oriental Renaissance* argues that the Europeans had two, not one Renaissance — one was the Florentine Renaissance in Italy and the other was the impact on Europe of the discovery of Indian wisdom.[7] AE's autobiography *The Candle of Vision* (1916) draws our attention to this discovery of Indian thought by the west. Its title is revelatory: wisdom religion of India is the candle which led the Irish poet through the dark passages of his own Celtic past. In chapter "Intuition" of this autobiography, he expresses his desire to feel akin to his Indian brothers:

> I came to feel akin to those ancestors of the Aryan in remote spiritual dawns when earth first extended its consciousness into humanity. In that primal ecstasy and golden age was born that grand spiritual tradition which still remains embodied in Veda and Upaniṣads, in Persian and Egyptian myth and which trails glimmering with colour and romance over our own Celtic legends.[8]

In one of his essays "The Legend of Ancient Eire" published in the *Irish Theosophist* in March and April 1895, AE was welcoming the spiritual character of the Irish Literary Renaissance. This essay contains the germs of AE's rapidly growing belief that his own country Ireland was as sacred as India or Tibet, and that it was one of the pivots on which mankind's spiritual destiny was to turn. It is this same pattern

---

6. AE (George William Russell) : *The Candle of Vision*, 1916.
7. See Majeed Javad, 1992, *Ungoverned Imaginings*, Oxford Clarendon Press.
8. *The Candle of Vision*.

of thought or vision envisaged by AE that found a kindred echo in Sri Aurobindo and AE's younger contemporary Irish poet James Henry Cousins who finally settled in India since 1915. In one of his poems called *OM,* AE was trying to put himself in the place of his Aryan ancestors affirming thus that his Celtic ancestors and the Aryan were one.[9]

Irish Poet AE Receives Indian Accolades

Sri Aurobindo, Rabindranath as well as Gandhi were fascinated by AE, the Irish mystic poet and social reformer, and everyone of these Indian thinkers appreciated AE's social and political philosophy that the Irish visionary presented in his book *The National Being: Some Thoughts on an Irish Polity* (1916). AE's vision of a co-operative commonwealth in this book certainly influenced Gandhi and Tagore — in their rural reconstruction programme. AE's aim is:

> To bring the primitive economic cave-man out into the wider arena of universe so that the former could make exchanges with all other members of the world.[10]

Tagore's idea of rural reconstruction and nationality to pave the way for a wider resurgence in Bengal for which he built up his Sriniketan in 1922, is similar to that of AE.

In *The National Being* what AE observes about the conflicts in contemporary Europe is quite similar to the observations of Rabindranath as well as Sri Aurobindo. AE says:

---

9. See mine, *The Renaissance in India,* ed. with Introduction and Bibliographical Notes, 2005, Kolkata: Standard Book Agency. This is the first re-print of Cousins' *The Renaissance in India.* Interested researchers may find relevant discussion on AE and Cousins and the interaction of the Irish Renaissance with the Indian Renaissance in the introductory notes in this book.

10. *The National Being,* Dublin: Maunsel & Co., 1916.

> Europe by its conflicts today is reducing itself to barbarism and powerlessness, and these conflicts arose out of the internal conflicts in society, for individuals and nations act outside themselves as they act inside themselves. The problem for Europe is to create a harmonious life and the creation of a harmonious life among a people must come from within.[11]

Sri Aurobindo and Rabindranath both wanted to develop this harmony in the social, political and spiritual life of the Indians and they knew that any kind of resurgence or awakening is impossible without the integration of the three and it must come from within. AE who believed in this philosophy of harmony, expressed his genuine interest in the Indo-Irish socio-cultural understanding in one of his letters that he wrote to an Indian correspondent Mr B.P. Wadia on October 17, 1922. We see the nature of AE's concern with India in the following line of this letter:

> I have watched with interest so far I could the economic and spiritual movements in India, the country which I regard as a kind of spiritual fatherland and whose influence on the thought of the world must, I think, grow greater because in no literature is there such a reservoir of divine truth as in the Indian.[12]

Irish Poets' Interest in India

Among the advanced Irish writers of this period Yeats and AE's interest in Indian thought was widely known. Charles Johnston (1867–1931), another key figure of this movement, came to India by the end of the nineteenth century as a member of the Indian Civil Service. But he had to leave India because of his suspected political sympathies for Indian nationalists.

11. Ibid.
12. See Alan Denson, 1961, ed., *The Letters of A.E.*, New York, p. 167.

Johnston's deep interest in Indian religious thought is revealed in various works he did after his retirement from India. His translation of Śaṅkara's philosophy called *The Awakening of the Self* (1897), *Bhagavad-Gītā, The Songs of the Master* (1908), and *The System of the Vedānta* (1912) were remarkable contributions to the study of Indian thought in the west.

The Irish writers' sympathy for India was further strengthened through Yeats' relationship with Rabindranath whom he introduced to the Western world in the beginning of the twentieth century. In his introduction to Tagore's self-translated *Gitanjali* (1912), Yeats is seen searching for terms that will at once evoke and effect the stirring encounter with Indian culture that Tagore's poetry seems to invite. The wholeness of Tagore's poetic vision, its unification of the spiritual and sensual aspects of being and its reciprocity between the elite and the "unlearned" led Yeats to reflections on the lack of integration, the self-deprecating "continual warfare" that marks public life in Europe, and more specifically in Ireland, his own country.

What is striking to note is that in the contrast between the Indian renaissance, to be more precise, the Bengal renaissance, and the warfare that is aesthetic and political life in Ireland, we see Yeats, AE and their contemporary Irish poets James Henry Cousins beginning (within a context of shared colonization) to project their own images upon Tagore, Sri Aurobindo and upon Bengal. Yeats' celebrated poem *Leda and the Swan* dramatizes the highly complex idea of the allegorical relationship between the imperializing power of a god and the subjugation of the mortal Leda. The god's possession of and rape of the etherized Leda is at one level the story of colonial conquest and subjugation. Yeats believed that Ireland as a colony of the empire was possessed and raped and that the consequences of such a colonization, rather conquest, must be tragic. Yeats' poetization of his feelings is redolent of the feelings of Tagore and Aurobindo. Leda the mortal woman is like the effeminate figure of India that was possessed, raped and abandoned.[13]

Beginning of the Literary Nationalist Movement

Like all artists of the decolonizing world since their time Yeats, AE, Sri Aurobindo and Tagore confronted the question of how to give form to a national culture emerging out of a history of dispossession. Yeats was drawn to the cultural idealism of the Bengali nationalist like Tagore because of the latter's attempt to reclaim local language and traditions. Yeats, AE, Sri Aurobindo and Tagore were all in part formed by the powerful national resurgence in Ireland and India from the 1880s onwards. Thus in 1912 Tagore came to Yeats in the form of another colonial's mystical lyricism and revealed to his own image. In his Introduction to Tagore's *Gitanjali* what Yeats attempts is to establish some sort of connection with India and here he calls the literary nationalist movement of which Tagore is a part a "new Renaissance."[14]

Yeats, AE and James Cousins' apparent identification with Tagore as a cultural nationalist working against the effects of colonial occupation is important to note in connection with our study of Sri Aurobindo's response to Ireland. This bond of spiritual kinship between the Irish and their Indian counterparts is revealed in the writings of some Indian nationalists and thinkers. Sri Aurobindo for instance, showed a great interest in Ireland. We have already mentioned that his early poem *Lines on Ireland* reveals a reciprocal interest in

---

13. K.D. Verma, 2001, *The Indian Imagination,* New Delhi: Macmillan India Ltd.
14. See *Modernism and Empire,* 2001 ed., Booth and Rigby, U.K.: Manchester University Press. See chapter, C.L. Innes, "Modernism, Ireland and Empire : Yeats Joyce and their implied audiences" in this book. See also Gregory Castle, 2001, *Modernism and the Celtic Revival,* U.K.: Cambridge University Press, p. 41.

the political situation in Ireland. In the last decade of the nineteenth century, Ireland captured the imagination of most young radicals and the rise and fall of the great Irish leader Parnell, which was a sensation in that period, stirred the mind of young Aurobindo. His poems *Charles Stewart Parnell* (1891), *Lines on Ireland* (1896) and *Hic Jacet* — these three poems are testimonies to his imaginative attraction of Ireland. In these poems we note the same tone with which the poets of Ireland lamented the lot of Ireland and suggested her political, national and cultural resurgence. It is this interest in Ireland which manifests even when Sri Aurobindo edited the *Bande Mataram* since 1906 to set forth ideals of extremism — Sri Aurobindo referred to Robert Emmet, O' Connel and Parnell whose glorious struggle for a separate nationality with its own culture, language and government made history. Under the caption "The Irish Example" Sri Aurobindo wrote in the *Bande Mataram* (16 April, 1907) about these great Irish heroes to set forth the ideals of Extremism.

Indo-Irish Culture Sharing Develops

The affinity of the Irish with the Indians seem so natural that even at popular level it seems to be reflected. Tagore's Gora and Kipling's Kim, for instance, are presented with the Irish connections. Gora who turns out to be a Hindu revivalist was led towards universalism after his discovery that he was born of Irish parents who were killed in the war. India's national and cultural resurgence and the Irish national resurgence of the later phase were almost contemporaneous and there were striking parallels between the two in the way the national self images were created through a shared culture. In James Cousins' view the interweaving of Irish and Indian culture led the two countries to their common struggle against British colonialism, Cousins says:

> *So subtly, however had the Aryan influence intermingled with the culture of Ireland that when, once again, at the beginning of the twentieth century, the ancient Asian spirit touched Ireland through the philosophy of India,* as conveyed to it through the works of Edwin Arnold and the Theosophical Society, there was an immediate response. Two poets (AE and Yeats) found their inmost nature expressed in the Indian modes. They found also *the spiritual truths that Asia had given to the world reflected in the old myths and legends of Ireland, and out of their illuminations and enthusiastic response arose the Irish literary and dramatic revival whose influence at its height was purely spiritual.*[15] (Emphasis mine)

Here what is important to note is Cousins' description of the influence of Indian thought on the Celtic Renaissance and his affirmation that there exists a religio-racial mixture of Celt and Aryan which was also emphasized by Dwarakanath in his meeting with O'Donnell. This unique mixture he argues, prepared the ground for the "discovery" of Asia's spiritual truths. His perceptive remark on the intermingling of the Irish-Indian cultural influences on the Celtic Renaissance can be distinguished from the so-called Orientalist scholarship of his day. He argues that Celtic Renaissance and the "renaissance" in Indian art and literature, both are attempts to create an "authentic" self-liberating national identity and history in the face of colonialist and Orientalist literary strategies of containment. In fact, both Cousins and his contemporary Irish poets and nationalists as well as Sri Aurobindo, wanted to assert the uniqueness of their national identity, a rebirth of their culture, without which renaissance is impossible. But before we discuss Sri Aurobindo and James Cousins'

---

15. James Henry Cousins, 1918, *The Renaissance in India,* Madras: Ganesh & Co. For a new interpretation of this vol., see mine "J.H. Cousins *The Renaissance in India* : An Anti-colonial Discourse and the Vision of a Great Renaissance of Humanity" in the *Journal of the Asiatic Society,* vol. xliv, no. 3, 2002.

expositions of this great phenomenon in their book, *The Renaissance in India,* let us see striking parallels between the Irish and the Indian national and cultural resurgence during the last quarter of the nineteenth and the beginning of the twentieth century.

Striking Parallels of Indo-Irish Cultural Resurgence

The first stirrings of Irish nationalism as in India (especially Bengal), were articulated in literature, art and education. Douglas Hyde's Gaelic League in Ireland and Bangiya Sahitya Parishad (the Bengal Akademy of Literature), both were founded in 1893. Both had the same objectives to revitalize native literature. The Bengali intelligentsia from Rajnarain Bose to Rabindranath, began to speak of "renaissance" in Bengali literary arts since the close of the nineteenth century and we find an increasing use of the idioms of "awakening", "revival" and "rebirth" in their works to describe the new development of Bengali literature as the Irish did in their own context during this time. Douglas Hyde's *The Story of Early Gaelic Literature* (1895), *The History of Irish Literature* (1899) and the Bengali professor and nationalist Dinesh Chandra Sen's *Maiman Singh's Geetika* (Folk Songs and Ballads of Maiman Singh) and *Folk Songs of East Bengal* were published in the same year. As Gaelic League pioneered in bringing out the first grammars of Irish language and anthologies of Irish folk literature, so in Bengal, the writers and scholars associated with the Bangiya Sahitya Parishad, devoted themselves in writing and editing Bengali grammars, dictionaries and bringing out various anthologies of Bengal literature.

Parallelism of this kind may also be seen in the establishments of national education in India and Ireland in the beginning of the twentieth century. National Council of Education, Bengal was founded in Calcutta in 1906 and the first National University was set-up in Dublin in 1908. Gaelic was to be included as compulsory language in the curriculum in the matriculation level and this was Hyde's important issue. He won over this issue as Sir Ashutosh did in Bengal — Bengali was made compulsory since 1906 in Bengal. Thus, both the countries like all other colonies of the British Empire had been trying to reassert their historic identity through literary, cultural and educational organizations to pave the way for renaissance.

Politics Through Poetry and Indo-Irish Relations

In the political level this Indo-Irish interaction is quite clear during this period. The Home Rule League of Annie Besant and Tilak was essentially inspired by the Irish Sinn Fein Movement. The Sinn Fein idea of relying on oneself and not looking to Great Britain for succour or charity readily appealed to the militant Indian nationalists. The Indian nationalists in 1906 passed a resolution urging the people to set up educational institutions on national lines and under national control. They were certainly inspired by Arthur Griffith, the founder of the Irish Sinn Fein Organization in Ireland. He was the main organizer editing a weekly journal *United Irishman* since 1899, introduced passive resistance and the boycott of all British goods which was later adopted by Sri Aurobindo and Gandhi in India's freedom struggle. In 1905 during the first conference of the "Sinn Fein" ("we ourselves alone"), A. Griffith said: "Our policy, in a word, is to lead our people to reliance in themselves and to establish in Ireland a capital, a national legislature endowed with the moral authority of the Irish nation. If we place our duty to our country before our personal interests, and live not each for himself but each for all, the might of England cannot prevent our ultimate victory." He also said that because Irish schools were controlled by the British Government, the "language of Ireland, the history of Ireland, the economics of Ireland, the possibilities of Ireland, the rights of Ireland . . . found no place in their curriculum." Many Indian leaders felt that when Griffith was speaking about Ireland, he was in some measure, "unconsciously speaking of India also."[16] Margaret Noble, Swami Vivekananda's Irish disciple later known as Sister Nivedita, Annie Besant and James and Margaret Cousins — all from Irish descent, made India their "spiritual home" fighting against British colonialism and dedicating themselves to the cause of India's national and cultural resurgence. Their wholehearted participation in the revitalization movement of India underlined not only the cultural and educational concerns but political concern to free India from the British rule as well. While studying the nature of Sri Aurobindo's response to Ireland's Renaissance, one cannot but refer to Sri Aurobindo's interaction with Cousins, the contemporary Irish poet who settled in India.

Sri Aurobindo found in Cousins, the Irish poet, a true friend of India, a person who was able to grasp the soul of Indian culture and who was prepared to help in the process of its resuscitation. Cousins appeared to him not only as a powerful writer of philosophical and critical insight but also as a poet and a visionary. Quite naturally a friendship and a philosophical understanding developed between them and Sri Aurobindo was generous enough to admit that several of Cousins' books and essays influenced his understanding of literature of the West.

Sri Aurobindo remarks that it was Cousins' *New Ways in English Literature* which originally prompted him to write a series of articles in the *Arya* under the title of "The Future Poetry". Sri Aurobindo's essays were written between 1917 and 1920 and were published in book form only in 1953. Cousins' book was published in November 1917. Both of them

16. Sankar Ghose, 1969, *The Renaissance to Militant Nationalism in India*, Calcutta: Allied Publishers.

like many nineteenth century thinkers spiritualized the theory of evolution and emphasized the evolutionary process of human consciousness which would bring about new modes of poetry and art with a decisive drift away from the egoistic or merely individualistic states of mind to the universal or cosmic consciousness. It is from this standpoint that Cousins and Sri Aurobindo view the trends of developments in literature and art of the late nineteenth and early twentieth century. Cousins' *New Ways in English Literature* (1917) and *The Renaissance in India* (1918), both were written during this transitional period and were marked by new hopes and aspirations.

Sri Aurobindo, Tagore, Sarojini Naidu, Harindranath Chattopadhyay and all the writers of Indian avant-garde, appreciated Cousins as a critic of art and literature. Sri Aurobindo specially commanded Cousins' genuineness of scholarship of Indian art and philosophy in an essay, "A Rationalistic Critic of Indian Culture" (1920). Here he said that for the definitive view of Indian culture and civilization one should turn to those who can speak with some authority. He dismissed the works of many so-called authorities on Indian culture as basically anti-Indian. He said:

> It matters very little to me what Mr Archer, Dr Gough or Sir John Woodroffe's unnamed English professor may say about Indian philosophy; it is enough for me to know what Emerson or Schopenhauer or Nietzsche or *What thinkers like Cousins and Schlegel have to say about it.*[17] (Emphasis mine)

---

17. Sri Aurobindo, *Collected Works,* vol. 9. Centenary Library Edition. Sri Aurobindo's long appreciative Review article on Cousins' *New Ways of English Literature* which was "abandoned" since the first edition of *The Future Poetry*" (1953), has now been included in its new edition published form Pondicherry in 2005, see the Appendix 1 of this volume, pp. 310-12. For more details on Sri Aurobindo's interaction with Cousins, see mine "Cousins and Sri Aurobindo : A Study in Literary →

It is clear from this statement that Sri Aurobindo had great admiration for Cousins, the Irish poet and critic, who like Nivedita came to serve India, and he did not hesitate to include him among the most celebrated thinkers of the West.

No wonder that Cousins' subsequent book, *The Renaissance in India* immediately caught Sri Aurobindo's attention. Sri Aurobindo's book of the same title was written in appreciation of Cousins. In the opening of his book Sri Aurobindo thus mentions Cousins for his "illuminating" focus on the subject of "renaissance" in contemporary India. He says:

> There has been recently some talk of a Renaissance in India. A number of illuminating essays with that general title and subject have been given to us *by a poet and a subtle critic and thinker Mr James Henry Cousins* and others have touched suggestively various sides of the growing movement towards a new life and a new thought that may well seem to justify the description.[18] (Emphasis mine)

Term "Renaissance" Gets Focus in Books

The word "Renaissance" is commonly used by historians to indicate the rather spectacular phenomenon which took place first in Italy and then in other parts of West Europe from the fourteenth to the sixteenth century and which ushered in what is called the modern age. The term Renaissance was first consciously used by the Florentine writers of fifteenth century who saw in this phenomenon the rebirth of the human spirit that had virtually died or fallen into deep slumber after the fall of Rome. The great outburst of creativity which was taking place all around them — in painting, sculpture and architecture,

→ Influence" in *The Journal of South Asian Literature,* vol. 24, no. 1 (1989): Michigan State University, Asian Study Centre, USA. Prof. K.S. Shastri in his outstanding book, *Hindu Culture and the Modern Age* (1956) spoke highly of Cousins' role in Modern India, see chapter XXI.

18. Sri Aurobindo, *The Renaissance in India,* Pondicherry: Sri Aurobindo Ashram, p. 2.

in vernacular literature and natural philosophy, in printing and other invention struck them as marking the end of the long dark night of Europe.

During the first quarter of the twentieth century, Cousins and Aurobindo both noted similar outburst of creativity all around them — in painting, poetry and in vernacular literature as well. Thus Sri Aurobindo is in perfect agreement with Cousins when he speaks about his perception of a new dawn in the field of literature, art and culture calling it a "Renaissance in India". He said:

> The word (Renaissance) carries the mind back to the turning point of European culture to which it was first applied . . . that is certainly not a type of renaissance that is at all possible in India. *There is a closer resemblance to the recent Celtic movement in Ireland, the attempt of a reawakened national spirit to find a new impulse of self-expression which shall give the spiritual force for a great reshaping and rebuilding: in Ireland this was discovered by a return to the Celtic spirit and culture after a long period of eclipsing English influences, and in India something of the same kind of movement is appearing and has especially taken a pronounced turn since the political outburst of 1905.*[19] (Emphasis mine)

In fact, except the revival of classical learning, that too under a very dissimilar politico-economic circumstance, there seems to be no substantive analogy between the Italian Renaissance and what happened in India. The point of disanalogy may be highlighted by referring to two very important areas of life, viz. science and religion. The character of the Indian renaissance was, in many respects unlike the European one. It had no political or economical impetus. Another important aspect of the Indian renaissance was the non-participation of

---

19. Ibid.

the common people and its being limited especially to the educated and affluent sections of the urban community.

Indian Renaissance Similar to Celtic Renaissance

There is an important point in Sri Aurobindo's observation that the Indian renaissance was more kindred to the Celtic Renaissance, not the European one and that it was primarily based on language and literature, art and culture. Indian renaissance of which Cousins and Sri Aurobindo speak was the outcome of the social consciousness generated by intellectual and cultural endeavours of the Indian poets, artists and thinkers who have created through their cumulative effort an appropriate political and cultural climate for the emergence of a new India in the beginning of the twentieth century just as the Irish poets and writers of the Celtic revival had been doing for the emergence of a New Ireland since the last decade of the nineteenth century. It is against this national, cultural and political background that one can see the flickers of the Renaissance in Ireland and India.

Thus, the original notion of Renaissance that referred to a definite period in the history of Italian civilization or to the pre-Reformation humanist movements of northern Europe has been expanded considerably by Sri Aurobindo and Cousins as this has been done by historians during recent years to include a range of new culture patterns in non-Western countries like China, India, Arab and Africa. For their being representatives of the Indian intelligentsia Sri Aurobindo and Irish writers like Cousins employed the term "renaissance" as revitalization or awakening and they did it largely with the aim of legitimizing India's and Ireland's national and cultural awakening in the context of British colonialism. As Hu Shih's modernizing movement in China in 1917–18 and the rise of national consciousness or nationalism in colonial Africa have come to be accepted as the Chinese renaissance and Harlem renaissance so India's encounter with the West, her entrance into modernity and her being awakened of her cultural uniqueness is called "renaissance".

David Kopf in his *British Orientalism and the Bengal Renaissance* (1969) while referring to the revitalization movements of the non-Western countries like Arab, Africa, China and India observed that historically-minded intellectuals in the non-Western world have freely reinterpreted the European model or models of Renaissance to suit the values implicit in their self-image as a culture.

Cousins and Aurobindo, who are by-products of this national and cultural awakening of their countries, interpret the term "renaissance" as revitalization movement stimulated by India's encounter with the West during the colonial period and in their interpretation they seek to promote a universalist morality and culture taking a global view of mankind.

The Celtic Renaissance and the Indian Awakening both were anti-imperial in its general orientation. Edward Said has justly argued that many Third World nationalist writers like Sri Aurobindo, Tagore, Senghor, Neruda, Vallejo, Cessaire Faize, Darwise and others saw in the Irish literary and cultural Renaissance a model for their own cultural and nationalist movements. For the poets of the Irish Renaissance like Yeats and AE the way in which the Irish might overcome the debilitating effects of their colonization was "to awaken the national idea" through culture. For their part they had worked since 1890s in support of Ireland's "war" to affirm her own individuality and to oppose materialism.[20]

In their books of the same title *The Renaissance in India*, Cousins and Sri Aurobindo both sought to redeem India from

20. Edward Said, 1990, "Yeats and Decolonisation" in *Nationalism and Colonialism and Literature*, Minneapolis: University of Minnesota Press, p. 71.

colonialist misrepresentation "affirming her own individuality" expressd through her literature, art, culture and religion. Both of their expositions are anti-imperialist discourses providing a nationalist defence against the ideological pressures exerted by imperialist critiques and propaganda on India's fitness for self-governance. Cousins and Sri Aurobindo's books were written against imperial attempt at cultural domination — against its onslaught on Indian art, culture and religion. Sri Aurobindo and Cousins both realized that Indian culture was in need of defence against the so-called Western criticism. Their books provide a much needed corrective to the colonialists' misrepresentation of India.

Conclusion

Sri Aurobindo and Cousins, the Indian sage and the Irish poet and savant, both affirm in their books on the renaissance in India that Ireland's national and cultural Renaissance and the Indian awakening constituted the dynamic principle of literary and cultural change and their struggle would precipitate the move to an essential unity of them and their liberation from the colonial rule.

Both of these twentieth century thinkers emphasized on the one hand "the recovery of the old spiritual knowledge and experience in all its splendour, depth and fullness" but on the other, "the endeavour to formulate a greater synthesis of a spiritualized society." Both of them firmly believe that poets and artists of India's renaissance and their spirituality are akin to those of the poets of the Ireland's Renaissance and they consider both these movements a new world phenomenon ushering a new age of the "Great Renaissance of Humanity" including those who are yet under the colonial bondage.

Different manifestations of India's renaissance have been worthily treated by Indian scholars but the cultural interaction between the Irish literary Renaissance and the Indian renaissance missed their critical attention. In this limited space I have therefore, endeavoured to focus on this subject in brief emphasizing the fact that Sri Aurobindo and Cousins' expositions of India's renaissance though begin as a nationalistic project serving the Indian nationalist enterprise, ends with a larger vision keeping India in the nodal point establishing a spiritual kinship with all humanity. Sri Aurobindo strongly believed like the Irish poets AE and Cousins that national and cultural resurgences in Ireland, India and other subject nations, signify a great change in human consciousness. Through the national and cultural awakening of Ireland and India they saw the promises of a new development in human consciousness as imminent. Sri Aurobindo, a strong believer in this kind of development of spiritual life, thought that the inspiration derived from the Celtic or Irish Renaissance along with the spread of the wisdom religion of India, would provide the base for a new spiritual hope in the world, a new renaissance. Their espousal of the values inherent in this type of renaissance embodied in their books of the same title, are in need of recovery in a new form today.

6

National Education Movement and Satis Chandra

Rama Prasad De

THE year 1793 stands marked in history as a black-letter year. The great French Revolution overshot itself when the extreme Republican Jacobins under the leadership of Maximilien Francois Robespierre established the Reign of Terror and in the name of "public safety" sent to the guillotine hundreds of people — kings, queens, aristocrats, officials, priests and ordinary citizens, many of whom were absolutely innocent.

Exactly a century later, the year 1893 presented an auspiciously pleasant contrast. It was a year of discoveries and inventions, explorations and creations — apparently small beginnings, which, however, were destined to be recorded in history as great memorabilia. In 1893 Rudolph Diesel made the first diesel engine. Otto Lilienthal, another German inventor, demonstrated a heavier-than-air flying machine, a glide, resembling the birdman, designed by Leonardo da Vinci about four hundred years ago. Fridtjof Nansen, a Norwegian explorer, set out on his spectacular voyage to the North Pole. In the same year, Antonin Dvorak, a Czech composer residing in New York, wrote the world-thrilling ninth symphony and called it ***From the New World***.

A New World! The events involving these inventors, explorers, composers and creators crystallize man's eternal yearning for a new world — a world alternative to, and certainly newer and better than the existing one. For India, too, the year 1893 proved to be graciously auspicious. The nineteenth century Bengal renaissance had already visioned a more or less clear picture of the New World, which started giving the people of India the first strong feeling of nationhood. The year 1893 itself witnessed and recorded several incidents which were apparently uneventful but eventually proved to be profoundly significant.

February 1893, A ship arrived at the Apollo Bunder off Bombay with Aurobindo Ghosh as one of its passengers. Aurobindo who had left India for England when he was a boy of seven, now returned to his motherland as a young man — a symbol of limitless energy and divine splendour sparkling through the veil of a "vast calm".

May 1893, Another ship left the port of Bombay for Vancouver with Swami Vivekananda who was going to attend the World's Parliament of Religions at Chicago.

Thus in 1893, at an interval of some three months, India got back from the West a son of Bengal and sent off to the West another son, and we are aware of the providential nature of the blessings of these two arrival and departure. But we do not generally care to be aware of another event — the event of another journey — not, of course, a physical journey as such but a spiritual one, but it is this event which has to be considered as one of the most powerful contributory factors in the history of national education movements in India.

In the late 1880s Bejoy Krishna Goswami was a towering spiritual personality and a dynamic social force in Bengal. He had already drawn to himself a band of devoted and enlightened followers. On 26 September, 1893, Satis Chandra

Mukherjee who had been a teacher (1886-88) and a lawyer (1890-92) received a message from Bejoy Krishna Goswami, quite surprisingly, asking Mukherjee to accept Goswami as his guru and get spiritual initiation from him. As if under a hypnotic spell, Satis Chandra went and got initiated on September 27, 1893. The day is certainly a red-letter day not only in the life of Satis Chandra but in the history of national education in India.

In the 1870s and 1880s positivism developed as a powerful movement in Bengal. Satis Chandra's father Krishna Nath Mukherjee joined the movement as a steadfast devotee of Auguste Comte and became a staunch positivist. In his early life, Satis Chandra, quite naturally, came under the influence of positivism. His spiritual initiation at the hands of Bejoy Krishna transported Satis Chandra to a revised model of positivism, when he shrugged off the atheistic aspect of positivism and clung closer to the positivist ideal of social service and the religion of humanity. As advised by his guru, Satis Chandra resolved to dedicate his life to the cause of education and make an all-out effort to inaugurate a new system of education in the country. He started looking back at the roots of India's religious and cultural heritage. Spiritual doubts and questionings which were disturbing him in the late 1880s were all gone. Once secure in his moral moorings, he could outline, though somewhat dimly then, his intellectual missions. He surrendered himself completely to his *sad-guru* and vowed to be guided by the instructions he received from him either directly or, as he believed all his life, telepathically. Vivekananda, his classmate, had Ramakrishna to guide him; Satis Chandra had *Prabhupāda* Bejoy Krishna Goswami.

II

In their book *The Origins of the National Education Movement*, Prof. Haridas Mukherjee and Prof. Uma Mukherjee made their survey of Satis Chandra's life in three phases; the first phase (1865, the year of his birth to 1892,) the second phase (1893, the year of his spiritual initiation to 1913, the year of the publication of the last volume of *The Dawn Magazine*) and the last phase (1914–1948).

It is the second phase of twenty years (1893–1913) that was undoubtedly the most productive and, therefore, the most memorable period of Satis Chandra's life when we see him emerging and establishing himself as the noblest educator of the nation at that particular point of time.

Long before the boycott movement triggered by Lord Curzon's sinister design to partition the province, Bengal had started protesting against the system of education introduced by the British rulers and controlled by the Department of Public Instruction (DPI) and the University of Calcutta. Gooroodas Banerji, the first Indian Vice-Chancellor of the Calcutta University, pointed out the deficiencies of the prevailing system in the convocation addresses he delivered in 1890, 1891 and 1892. In 1892, in his article "Sikhsar Herfer", Rabindranath made a scathing criticism of the prevailing system which, he said sarcastically, gave the needy people of our country winter garments in summer and summer garments in winter. There were several other voices decrying the existing system as having no connection with our national life.

It was, however, Satis Chandra who took the first bold step to envisage and implement an alternative system of education. In 1895, more than six years before Rabindranath founded his model school at Santiniketan, Satis Chandra established at Calcutta the Bhagavat Chatuspathi as the first specimen of his creative imagination and organizing ability. Although the primary mission of the Chatuspathi was to stimulate the study of Hindu religion and philosophy and Sanskrit literature in general, Satis Chandra saw to it that his new system catered to some other essential needs of the students, by helping them acquire healthy habits, both physical and moral, and offering them industrial and technical training which was being grossly neglected in the prevailing system followed by the DPI and the Calcutta University.

The next two exploratory contributions of Satis Chandra made to the cause of national education were the publication of *The Dawn Magazine* in 1897 and the foundation of the Dawn Society in 1902. The foundation of the Dawn Society reveals the dynamic originality of Satis Chandra as a thinker and organizer, capable of doing the right thing at the right moment when a crisis precipitated. In January 1902, Lord Curzon constituted the Indian University Commission. In spite of the strong dissenting note from Gooroodas Banerji, the Commission published its report. Bengal's intelligentsia and popular sentiment found in the report a conspiracy to constrict the scope of higher education and to bring education completely under government control. There were protest-meetings, protest-rallies, speeches and newspaper-articles condemning the report. But it was Satis Chandra who silently did what the nation exactly needed at the time. The report was published in June 1902; within a month Satis Chandra founded the Dawn Society.

Satis Chandra started publishing *The Dawn Magazine* to disseminate knowledge — knowledge that he considered to be most important both as the means and the end of the alternative system of education he was experimenting with. Two years after founding the Bhagavat Chatuspathi, Satis Chandra brought out *The Dawn Magazine* and made it the organ of the Chatuspathi. Significantly, just two years after founding the Dawn Society, Satis Chandra made his magazine an organ of the Society and renamed it as *The Dawn and the Dawn Society's Magazine* (1904).

There were obvious changes in the objectives of the magazine as well. As an organ of the Bhagavat Chatuspathi, *The Dawn Magazine* published some 300 articles, and of these, as many as 77 dealt with Hindu religion and Hindu philosophy. In the very first issue of the magazine, Satis Chandra had emphasized on the "need of covering the whole field of human activity within the fold of an all-embracing religion" and as a devout and enlightened Hindu, he proposed "to make a special study of Hindu life, thought and faith in a spirit of appreciation, while remaining fully alive to the usefulness and necessity of the existence of all other systems."

It is quite significant to note that the overtly religious articles which thronged the pages of the early volumes of *The Dawn Magazine* practically disappeared from the subsequent volumes (1904–1913) after the magazine became an organ of the Dawn Society.

Then again, the subtitle of the first volume of *The Dawn Magazine* was: "A Monthly Magazine Devoted to Religion, Philosophy and Science". But after the magazine had become the organ of the Dawn Society, Satis Chandra changed the subtitle and declared that it was "An Organ of the Dawn Society Educational Movement"; and the slogan of that movement was "To love one's country, one must know one's country".

Satis Chandra of the Bhagavat Chatuspathi was first and last an educationist and a teacher — never a religious preacher. The be-all and end-all of his life's missions was to prepare model students for the country. Satis Chandra of the Dawn Society too had the same mission. But Satis Chandra had the foresight and the prudence to realize that it was now time for him to expand his activities and channelize his energies into constructive and responsible tasks of founding educational institutions capable of producing ideal students for the country.

III

In every sense the Dawn Society was the precursor of the National Council of Education, the foundation of which was the fourth and the greatest achievement of Satis Chandra. We need not waste time recounting the history of the foundation of the National Council in the wake of the partition of Bengal. The history is known to all of us. But I feel I should boldly underline two observations in connection with this history. It has always to be remembered that the National Education Movement, an offspring of the wider Swadeshi Movement in the first decade of the twentieth century, received a concrete shape in the National Council of Education, Bengal, the foundation of which was certainly the first glorious assertion of national self-respect in the field of education. Secondly, it should never be forgotten that it was Satis Chandra who made the greatest sacrifice and rendered the greatest service in connection with this foundation. The moment the National Council came into existence, Satis Chandra vowed himself body and soul to the sacred cause of the Council.

There was an unprecedented assemblage of luminaries including Rabindranath and Aurobindo who intimately associated themselves with the inauguration of the National Council. But even then, the weather was never all fair for the new-born Council which had to face and solve three major problems before it could really start sailing at all. The problems were:

1. The problem of securing financial support;
2. The problem of settling a controversy over the exact nature of education to be imparted by the Council; and
3. The problem of finding a group of academicians to implement the curricular programmes and to look after the day-to-day activities of the proposed college.

To cut a long story short, it was Satis Chandra who readily accepted the challenging assignments and became the most effective instrument in finding solutions for all those three problems.

IV

The first problem was the problem of financial support. We all know that the National Council could overcome the financial hurdle as huge donations came, first from Subodh Chandra Mallik and then from the two Rajas of Mymensingh, Brojendra Kishore Roy Choudhury and Surya Kanta Acharya. As regards the donation promised by Subodh Chandra Mallik, there is a background story. Yes, we may dismisss it as a mere story or hearsay, since it is not confirmed by the biographers of Satis Chandra.

Yet I feel I should tell you the story since I personally believe that the account is quite likely to be true. You have it on pages 59, 60 and 61 of Adinath Chatterjee's book *Troyee: Acharya Satishchandra, Gandhiji o Krishnadas.* Adinath Babu had it from Subodh Ganguly, son of Matilal Ganguly who was a nephew and a close associate of Satis Chandra.

On his way to Nasik from Nepal sometime in October 1945, Subodh Ganguly spent a couple of days at Benares, during which he had talks on various topics with his grandfather Satis Chandra whom he called "*Sejodadababu.*" This is the relevant portion:

"One day the name of Subodh Mallik came up in our talks. Sejodadababu said that he was once holding a meeting of the National Council of Education; the purpose was to raise funds. Subodh Mallik was present in that meeting and reacting to Satis Chandra's appeal, made a public declaration that he would donate a sum of one lakh for the work. Members present greeted the offer with a huge applause.

". . . Subodhbabu's proposal naturally made Satis Chandra feel very happy and he hoped that he would get the money in a short while. But days passed and there was no sign of the money coming from Subodh Mallik. Then one day he himself went to Subodhbabu's residence and reminded him of the promise he had made at the meeting. Looking greatly embarrassed, Subodh Mallik said 'My promise does stand. I am quite eager to give you the money; but something has happened in the meanwhile. After hearing the news, Aurobindobabu (Aurobindo Ghosh) called me one day and wanted to know what purpose I would serve by giving so much money to Satis Chandra. He would only arrange for some education for the students. Instead, if the money is given to me, I can accelerate the revolutionary movement. Our country will reap a much greater benefit through it . . .. This has made me feel hesitant. Please find me a solution for the problem.' You know how deeply cordial the relation between Sri Aurobindo and Satis Chandra was. It was on Sejodadababu's initiative that Sri Aurobindo became the Principal of National College. So on that day he (Satis Chandra) requested Subodh Mallik to arrange for a face-to-face talk with Sri Aurobindo.

"As arranged by Subodh Mallik, Satis Chandra called on Sri Aurobindo on the appointed day. The moment they met, Sri Aurobindo said that he had got from Subodh Mallik the substance of their talk and now he wanted Satis Chandra himself to say what he had to say. In a speech, neither very short nor very long, Satis Chandra presented his views about the benefit that could be derived if the money was spent on education.

"Sri Aurobindo patiently listened to Satis Chandra's speech. He never interrupted the talk, nor raised a single question. After Satis Chandra completed his speech, Sri Aurobindo only said, 'I approve your views. The money will be most appropriately spent through you. I am lifting the objection I had.'

"Satis Chandra did not have to wait for the money any more and as soon as he got it, he invested it in promoting national education."

V

Let us now come to the second problem — the controversy that jolted the Council on the very first day of its birth, 11 March 1906. The controversy centred around the question: Whether the Council should impart **only** technical education or whether it should prepare and implement an integrated system of education — Literary and Scientific as well as Technical and Professional. Tarak Nath Palit and some others who stuck to the slogan: "Technical education only," left the Council and formed another society, "Society for the Promotion of Technical Education." Satis Chandra along with Aurobindo, Rabindranath, Gooroodas Banerji and several others insisted on, prepared and implemented the integrated curriculum. Going through the objectives of this programme as declared in about thirty paragraphs incorporated in the Council's Memorandum of Association, we cannot but conclude that perhaps, in that particular phase of national crisis, no other programme could have been more rational than the one prepared by the National Council.

There must have been numerous consultations and discussions before the academic programme to be adopted by the National Council could be finalized. But when we recall Rabindranath's assessment of Satis Chandra's role in the national education movement and Aurobindo's observation on Satis Chandra's contribution to the foundation of the National Council and as we go through the articles on the activities of the National Council, which were being regularly published in the 1906 issues of *The Dawn*, we can at once identify the main brain and the energy behind the formulation of the National Council's concept of national education. Benoy Kumar Sarkar has clearly stated in his book *Education for Industrialization* that "It was almost exclusively by him (Satis Chandra) that the burden of moulding the new ideology into a concrete pattern was shouldered."

VI

As regards the third problem, namely the problem of finding someone to take in his hands the total responsibility of running the Bengal National College, the first institution established by the National Council, the unanimous choice was again Satis Chandra, and he readily volunteered himself. The Bengal National College started functioning from 15 August 1906 with Aurobindo Ghosh as its first Principal and Satis Chandra as Superintendent. Just ten days before, Aurobindo had joined *The Bande Mataram* as its Assistant Editor. Moreover, he had other thoughts, other political agenda of great national importance. It was not possible for him to come to the college everyday and attend to diverse problems, both academic and administrative.

The load of work fell mainly on the shoulders of Satis Chandra and during the three years (1905-08) when Satis Chandra was in the Council, he carried the load most gladly, most silently and most effectively. In return — the Savant of *Ākāś-Vr̥tti* expected and received practically nothing. As the spearhead of the National Council, Satis Chandra did indeed work, as Aurobindo observed, as the "disciple of a Sannyasin" and "a Sannyasin himself."

VII

Satis Chandra was the central figure in the national education movement in the first decade of the twentieth century. Like Rabindranath, Satis Chandra firmly believed that education should be rooted in the soil of the country, in its cultural heritage. They were both utterly disgusted with the prevailing system of education and deeply felt the need to change the system. In the February 1898 issue of *The Dawn Magazine,* Satis Chandra wrote: "Foreign education has failed to produce original men among us. Must then the same system be still persisted in? Foreign education has not enabled us to be self-reliant, self-dependent, self-sacrificing and patriotic." When it was time to act, both Rabindranath and Satis Chandra acted. In 1901, Rabindranath founded the Brahmacaryāśram at Santiniketan; the next year in 1902 Satis Chandra founded the Dawn Society at Calcutta.

What distinguished, however, Satis Chandra from Rabindranath was that his approach to the problem was much less emotive than the poet's and much more pragmatic and technically thorough. Before embarking on any project, Satis Chandra made elaborate preparations applying managerial methods which are surprisingly modern. Satis Chandra founded the Dawn Society in July 1902. In the April, May and June issues of *The Dawn Magazine,* he brought out a series of articles under the common caption "An Examination into the Present System of University Education in India and a Scheme of Reforms." In the articles presented in 15 sections covering about 52 pages,* Satis Chandra studied everything — admission system; examination system; tutorial system; relations and conditions of work between the university and the affiliated colleges; qualifications and trainings of teachers and students; courses in English, Sanskrit and History — scrutinizing every deficiency and suggesting reform. Thus, before taking up a mission, Satis Chandra prepared himself

---

* The reference is to the pages of the edition being reprinted under the editorship of Professor Madhabendra Nath Mitra and published by the Jadavpur University and the National Council of Education, Bengal.

dispassionately, methodically and thoroughly so that once in the job, he never looked back, never hesitated and never felt helpless or uncertain.

Rabindranath was somewhat sceptic about the success of the mission the National Council proposed to carry out. The poet wrote two articles directly relating to the activities of the Council. National Council had requested the poet to prepare for it a comprehensive syllabus. In reply, in a long article captioned *Śikṣā Samasyā,* he advised the Council to make up its mind first as to the purpose the Council sought to fulfil through its academic programme. The poet harped on the ideals he cherished all his life — imaging a school or college as an *āśram* or *gurūgṛha* and emphasizing on the need of students living in close communion with nature and natural social environment and practising *brahmacarya* for attaining patience, power and purity. The poet seemed to be somewhat depressed and apprehensive that the National Council might not live up to his ideals.

The next article *Jātiya Vidyālayā,* written a few months later, breathes, however, a warmer, happier note. The poet read the article at the Town Hall on 14 August 1906 when the Bengal National College was inaugurated. He welcomed the new-born college as a *Sajib Mangal,* as a blessing for the nation. But strangely enough, in that long article Rabindranath mentioned practically nothing about the National Council which brought the *Sajib Mangal* (that is, the Bengal National College) into existence. A blessing for the child but no congratulations for the mother!

With all his doubts and reservations, however, Rabindranath actively involved himself in the academic programmes of the Council as long as Satis Chandra was there at the helm of its affairs. He had the highest regards for Satis Chandra. In course of his speech on Swadeshi Movement, delivered at the Dawn Society on 25 February 1906, just a couple of weeks before the National Council was founded, Rabindranath observed: "Satis Babu is one of the main props of the movement for national education which is now going on in our country; in fact it is he who has inspired it." The poet never changed that opinion.

VIII

Briefly recalling Aurobindo's assessment of the National Council and of Satis Chandra's connection with it, we note that Aurobindo himself explained why he had joined the Bengal National College as its Principal. To spare his college from unnecessary police harassment, Aurobindo had to resign his Principalship when he was accused of seditious activities in connection with certain writings in the *Bande Mataram.* In his farewell address to the students on 23 August 1907, Aurobindo said: "When we established this college and left other occupations, other chances of life, to devote our lives to this institution, we did so because we hoped to see in it the foundation, the nucleus of a nation, of the new India which is to begin its career after this night of sorrow and trouble on that day of glory and greatness when India will work for the world." This hope — Aurobindo felt a couple of years later — was belied.

Apart from the tug-of-war between liberal education and technical education for getting priority in the Council's programme, what particularly disappointed Aurobindo was the decision taken by some office-bearers of the Council to discourage students from political activism. In an article captioned "The Apostasy of the National Council", an apparently frustrated Aurobindo observed: "All that we can now accept of the Council is to be a centre of scientific and technical education; it can no longer be a workshop in which national spirit and energy are to be forged and shaped."

Like Rabindranath, however, Aurobindo did not change his opinion about Satis Chandra's contribution to the cause of national education. In a speech delivered before the Bombay National Union on 19 January 1908, Aurobindo said: "I spoke to you the other day about National Education and I spoke of a man who had given his life to that work, the man really organized the National College in Calcutta — and that man also is a disciple of a Sannyāsin, that man also — though he lives in the world — lives like a Sannyāsin."

IX

We can very well appreciate that it was never possible for either Rabindranath or even Aurobindo to pay full-time attention to the National Education Movement or to the National Council spearheading that movement in the first decade of the twentieth century. While giving leadership to the Swadeshi Movement, Rabindranath — well, very fortunately for us — never stopped writing his verse and prose, his songs, his short stories and plays. His first love was his creative writing. And, during the period, Aurobindo, again fortunately for us, remained involved in active politics, studying the work of revolutionary organizations, contacting and joining secret societies, writing and distributing revolutionary pamphlets, supervising revolutionary journals like the *Jugantar* and the *Bande Mataram,* controlling the Nationalist Party in Bengal, attending and often presiding over sessions of the Indian National Congress, delivering speeches at Surat, Poona, Bombay, Nasik, Dhulia, Amaroti, Nagpur and many other places.

But as a leader of the Swadeshi Movement, Satis Chandra had made up his mind to play only one role — the role of an educator, an educationist. As the founder and the guiding force of the Bhagavat Chatuspathi and the Dawn Society, as Superintendent and later Principal of the Bengal National

College and as the editor of *The Dawn,* Satis Chandra was just a teacher, perhaps the noblest, the most dedicated and enlightened teacher Bengal had ever produced. His only mission was to organize and popularize national education. Satis Chandra firmly believed that, if properly implemented by the National Council, the new system of education would equip the students of our country with a panoply of knowledge and power which the existing system of colonial education had failed to provide but which it was essential for them to cultivate if a new India was to be built up.

As the anti-partition agitation and the boycott movement peaked in October-November 1905, while Aurobindo was writing his revolutionary pamphlets — *Bhawani Mandir* and *No Compromise* and Rabindranath was composing his songs of patriotism to foster and keep up the fire of the agitation, Satis Chandra was busy formulating his scheme of the new education to be imparted to the students.

In November 1905, in an article captioned "The Birth of the National Idea," Satis Chandra crystallized his concept of the inseparably close relation between national consciousness and national education. In the very next issue of *The Dawn* (January 1906), he wrote another long article, outlining in detail his scheme of this national education. In that article, he meticulously laid down the objects and ideals which the two proposed different departments of the Council — the General Department and the Technical Department — should follow; he detailed his lists of the subjects to be taught in the two departments; he explained how the students were to be exposed to the best Oriental ideals of life and thought and to the best assimilable ideals of the West; how, again, the students were to be trained up as efficient workers and managers of mills, factories and workshops so that they could earn a livelihood and serve the nation at the same time.

In the next issue (March 1906) Satis Chandra printed the entire Report of the Ways and Means Committee on the basis of which the National Council of Education, Bengal was formally established on 11 March 1906; he also published the entire list of the founding members of the Council, some 92 in number.

The Dawn Magazine had been an organ first of the Bhagavat Chatuspathi and then of the Dawn Society. Though there was no formal announcement, immediately after the National Council came into existence, Satis Chandra made his magazine — *The Great Dawn* — virtually an organ of the Council. In the issues of *The Dawn* (1906-07), he minuted down the important activities of the Council, explained the why's and how's of these activities and offered suggestions for further improvement.

In this at least, Satis Chandra reminds us of the legendary figure of the Oxford Scholar, immortalized by Matthew Arnold in his pastoral elegy "The Scholar Gipsy". He never allowed himself to be affected by, what Arnold called, "the strange disease of sick hurry and divided aims." During the three years of his association with the National Council, he had, like Arnold's scholar, one purpose, one desire and one goal, and Satis Chandra pursued that goal with the conviction and faith of a *sannyāsin* and with a scholarly tranquillity that is simply amazing.

X

As the founder of the Dawn Society and of *The Dawn Magazine,* Satis Chandra was highly regarded by almost all his great contemporaries; and as such, his name came to stand almost inseparably coupled with the word "dawn". Even today, the few of us who occasionally remember him refer to him as "*dawn-er* Satis Chandra" or "*dawn-er* Satis Babu." "*Dawn-er*", a hybrid of an English word with a Bengali suffix, is an epithet which, more than any other word, English or Bengali, conjures up the most faithful image of the man who led the national education movement in the last decade of the nineteenth century and first of the twentieth.

Each dawn pronounces the end of a night and heralds a new day. All their life Rabindranath, Sri Aurobindo and their great contemporaries hoped for, worked for the dawn of a new age in India. The word "dawn," the symbol "dawn" recur again and again in the speeches and writings of Rabindranath and Aurobindo.

Bengali equivalents of the English "dawn" appear in captivating abundance in the writings of Tagore, particularly his songs and poems. In 1907 — Rabindranath was then intimately associated with the activities of the National Council — the poet wrote a poem captioned *Suprobhāt* for a magazine which also bore the same caption. *Suprobhāt* means "an auspicious dawn" and the poem is remarkable as an announcement of the advent of a dawn after the night of sorrows and sufferings in the life of the nation. In 1939, two years before his death, Rabindranath composed a song with the throbbing opening: *orey, nutan juger bhorey* (. . . at the dawn of a new era).

Aurobindo, too, was a poet and prophet of the dawn. In his farewell address to the students of the National Council on 23 August 1907 Aurobindo unveiled the portrait of a dawn which, he hoped, would come. He wanted the students to note that the foundation of the National Council was, in a sense, "the foundation of the new India which is to begin its career, after this night of sorrow and trouble, on that day of glory and greatness when India will work for the world." Years later, he wrote his divine epic *Savitri* and captioned the very first canto of the first book — *The Symbol Dawn.*

In his zeal to introduce a new system of education that, he believed, would dispel the prevailing darkness and bring the nation the promise of a new light, Satis Chandra perhaps wanted to keep his mind's eye glued on the image of a daybreak. Both for the educational journal and for the educational society he chose the word "dawn" to christen them. The National Council of Education does not have the word "dawn" in its name; but its emblem portraits a rising sun. Dawn again. In the absence of any other evidence to the contrary, I am almost certain that the emblem was designed by Satis Chandra or else, by somebody who simply planted Satis Chandra's vision of a dawn in the emblem of the National Council.

In a recent article, Professor Rabindra Kumar Dasgupta has called Satis Chandra "Hero with a noiseless step." It is this "Hero," more than anybody else, who noiselessly, imperceptibly and imperishably injected into the tissues of the National Council a faith and a strength which enabled the Council to overcome numerous hurdles in the fifty years of its existence till it founded the Jadavpur University in 1955. The irony is that posterity has not cared much to remember this hero, this dreamer of the dawn of a new era.

On the 13th of July 2006, in the presence of His Excellency the President of India, at a golden jubilee function of the Jadavpur University, Vice-Chancellor A.N. Bose observed: "We are a self-oblivious people; we do not bother to remember Satis Chandra." Our Vice-Chancellor is, I strongly feel, absolutely correct.

7

National Council of Education, Bengal and Sri Aurobindo

Amal Kumar De

SRI AUROBINDO was one of the most illustrious and noblest founding fathers of the National Council of Education, Bengal and a great exponent of what true and living education should be like. Just as the 15th of August is an eventful day being our country's Independence Day, similarly the 15th of August is also the birthday of Sri Aurobindo. The Bengal National College, which was established by the National Council of Education, Bengal and of which Sri Aurobindo was the first Principal, was brought into existence at a historic meeting at the Town Hall, Calcutta on the 14th of August, 1906 and the College started functioning at 191/1 Bowbazar Street with effect from the 15th of August, 1906.

The National Council of Education, Bengal, which stepped into its hundred years of existence on 11 March 2005, may certainly be considered as the originator of a system of education, which has never lost its significance. Let us revert to the first decade of the twentieth century to have a retrospective view of what Tagore observed as the *Golden Foundation on which the National Council of Education, Bengal has been built.*[1] Already in the nineteenth century, the Bengal renaissance had visioned a new India agog with activity that engendered the first feeling of nationhood. After Vidyasagar, Bankim Chandra and Vivekananda, a new generation of leaders rose to accelerate the spirit of nationalism. As Russian philosopher I. Frolov writes:

> It was Swami Vivekananda who condemned the Indian liberals' policy of appealing to the British authorities[2] and also . . . condemned imperialist oppression of nations, racism and militarism . . ..[3]

Swamiji was one of the predecessors of the nationalist movement that raised its head in the first decade of the twentieth century.

This growing nationalistic spirit posed a positive threat to the then imperialist British rulers who, in order to stifle the growth of this spirit, under the leadership of Lord Curzon resorted to a number of repressive measures such as the Indian Universities Act (1904) brought to restrict the area of higher education, the Pedlar letter, the Carlyle Circular (1905) barring students' participation in politics, and the partition of Bengal designed evilly to frighten, fracture, and handicap Bengal socially, politically and culturally.

Bengal Takes on Swadeshi Challenge

Bengal took up the gauntlet thus thrown down by the British administration. The magic incantation that clicked and cast a spell was *Swadeshi.* Rabindranath composed his patriotic songs, which ignited the fire of the anti-partition upsurge. People

1. Haridas Mukherjee and Uma Mukherjee, *The Origins of the National Education Movement*, National Council of Education, Bengal, 2nd revised edition, 2000, p. 115.
2. Frolov, I., 1984, *Dictionary of Philosophy,* Moscow: Progress Publishers, 2nd revised edition.
3. Ibid.

felt inspired to boycott British goods in favour of indigenous products. It so happened that, on the cultural front, the movement created a demand for revival of Indian art, music and literature. Besides, a demand for a national university and a thorough overhauling of the prevailing system of education was voiced in no uncertain terms. Indignation of the country's eminent leaders against the Macaulayan system of education came to be so pronounced that there arose an all-round demand for a system of national education rooted in the soil, respectful to our national heritage and yet conscious simultaneously of modern needs. The immediate utterance of that awe-inspiring spirit of revolt was the establishment of the National Council of Education, Bengal.

It may be recalled here that the birth of the National Council of Education, Bengal in 1906 was followed in the same year — a little earlier or later — by the death of the Dawn Society, which was set up by Satis Chandra Mukherjee. On this issue, Professor Haridas Mukherjee, now a Fellow of the Council and Professor Uma Mukherjee (since deceased), both close associates of the Council, write:

> By giving birth to the National Council of Education in 1906, the Dawn Society committed a glorious harakiri.[4]

In this connection, we may take a line from John Keats' *Hyperion* and put it, slightly modified:

> With fierce converse the Dawn Society died into life.

[**Note:** Perhaps a detailed elaboration on the history of the National Council of Education, Bengal is not considered necessary any further here except that many of you might be interested to know something about the origin of the Extension

---

4. Haridas Mukherjee and Uma Mukherjee, *The Origins of the National Education Movement*, National Council of Education, Bengal, 2nd revised edition, 2000, pp. 41-42.

Lecture Unit which we at the Council received as heritage from our revered predecessors in the first decade of the last century. The genesis of the Extension Lecture Unit of the Council to provide liberal education to its students goes back to 1906 when eminent persons like Mohini Mohon Chatterjee, Rabindranath Tagore, Gooroodas Banerji, Hirendranath Datta, among others, spoke on a wide range of subjects of diverse interest. In 1919, an Extension Lecture Committee was formed with Ramendra Sundar Trivedi as the President and Pramath Nath Mukherjee as the Secretary. During the period from 1919 to the third decade of the twentieth century, extension lectures on various subjects by august personages at the Council were a regular feature. In fact, this Extension Lecture Unit functioned regularly during the period 1929-43. Professor Kaliprasanna Dasgupta was in charge of it till his demise in November 1942. The Extension Lecture Unit, which thus blossomed into prominence, wilted before the fifties of the last century. Since 1992, however, the Council has again been organizing extension lectures popularly known as *Rabisandhya* lectures every Sunday under the able stewardship of two learned scholars viz. Professor Arun Kumar Gupta (since deceased) and Professor Rama Prasad De, who happens to be the Honorary Director of this Extension Lecture Unit. Of the 48 lectures organized every year, 46 are endowment lectures. Out of more than 600 lectures delivered by many eminent speakers during the past one decade, well over a hundred have already been published. The name *Rabisandhya* (i.e. Sunday evening) was given by Professor Rama Prasad De to the Extension Lecture Unit.]

Aurobindo Becomes First Principal of Bengal National College

After the Swadeshi movement swung into action, Aurobindo Ghosh was first seen in Calcutta in March 1906 and he was at that time in the service of the Maharaja of Baroda, drawing a handsome salary of Rs. 750/- per month. At a particular juncture of history in order to study the political maelstrom of Bengal at first hand, Aurobindo Ghosh came from Baroda to Bengal. When the National Council of Education, Bengal was constituted, the Memorandum of Association, which was submitted for registration on 23 May 1906, contained eight signatories of whom the fifth signatory was Aurobindo Ghosh. Of the thirteen members of the Executive Committee to run the Council, Aurobindo Ghosh was one.

Although it was Subodh Chandra Mallik, who invited him to be the Principal of the proposed Bengal National College, as indicated in Pramada Ranjan Roy's Bengali biography of Sri Aurobindo, the fact remains that the name of Aurobindo Ghosh was uppermost in the mind of Satis Chandra who lost no time in proposing the name of Aurobindo Ghosh to join as Principal, Bengal National College. This is because in the eyes of Satis Chandra, too, there was no other competent person than Aurobindo for the Principal's post. Aurobindo Ghosh's superb education, intelligence, scholarship, wisdom, patriotism and selflessness were considered beyond comparison.

Aurobindo agreed to participate in the great activities of the Bengal National College and after necessary talks with Satis Chandra, he returned to Baroda. He came back to Calcutta again in 1906 on long leave without pay and plunged himself wholeheartedly into the country's political movement. At the same time, there is no gainsaying the fact that both the name and fame of the Bengal National College enormously increased because of Sri Aurobindo's association with that Institute.

It would be of relevance to indicate here that both Jadavpur University, a university of excellence, in its golden jubilee year and the National Council of Education, Bengal in its centenary year, have been contemplating to reassess Sri

Aurobindo's contribution to the area of education and its applicability to the Indian context today. As we know, it is through the commendable efforts of some living scholars like Dr Kireet Joshi of the ICPR, Sri Samar Basu of the World Union of Sri Aurobindo Ashram, Pondicherry and other Sri Aurobindo scholars of repute that Sri Aurobindo movement is gaining ground not only in the country but abroad as well. It is a matter of satisfaction to note that hundreds of organizations in the country are up and doing to strengthen Sri Aurobindo movement through symposia, conferences, seminars, etc. which should not be mistaken as palavers for the shuffling of shibboleths.

Aurobindo's View on National Education

Needless to say, one of the principal components of Sri Aurobindo movement consists in the dissemination of Sri Aurobindo's concept of national education and integral education. In fact, Sri Aurobindo has spoken at great length on: (i) true education, (ii) national education, (iii) integral education, (iv) principles of true teaching, (v) how to study, and (vi) examinations. Let us have just a peep into the areas of his concept of education inasmuch as the National Council of Education, Bengal minus a consideration of Sri Aurobindo's concept of education looks like a ship without a rudder.

Any definition of true education counts on one's definition of knowledge. As Swami Vivekananda said,

> The goal of mankind is knowledge. That is the one ideal placed before us by Eastern Philosophy.[5]

As for the nature and kind of knowledge, Swamiji referred to *secular* and *spiritual*,[6] with spiritual knowledge figuring

---

5. Swami Vivekananda, *The Complete Works of Swami Vivekananda*, vol. I, p. 27.
6. Ibid., p. 28.

distinctly as the higher goal of the two. In Sri Aurobindo's philosophy is seen a synthesis of this twofold knowledge, as set forth in the *Muṇḍaka Upaniṣad* (1.1.4): (i.e. "Twofold is the knowledge that must be known of which the knowers of the *Brahman* tell, the higher and the lower knowledge.")

The central aim of education, as Sri Aurobindo observes:

> . . . is the building of the powers of the human mind and spirit. It is formation or, as I would prefer to view it, the evoking of knowledge and will, and of the power to use knowledge, character, culture — that at least if no more.[7]

To Sri Aurobindo it is not so much the nomenclature of "national education" as "a true and living education" that matters. As he says:

> There are three things which have to be taken into account in a true and living education: the man, the individual in his commonness and in his uniqueness; the nation or people; and universal humanity. It follows that that alone will be a true and living education which helps to bring out to full advantage, makes ready for the full purpose and scope of human life all that is in the individual man, and which at the same time helps him to enter into his right relation with the life, mind and soul of humanity of which he himself is a unit and his people or nation a living, a separate, and yet inseparable members.[8]

From this assessment of "a true and living education" by Sri Aurobindo, we can follow that Sri Aurobindo could have stopped by referring to true education of the individual. But he did not do that. He spoke of true education of the nation. Sri Aurobindo could have stopped by speaking of true

---

7. *Sri Aurobindo and The Mother On Education,* 1955, Pondicherry: Sri Aurobindo Ashram, pp. 9-10.
8. Sri Aurobindo, *The Hour of God* (cent. ed. vol. 17), pp. 198-99.

education of the nation. But he did not do that also. He spoke of true education of universal humanity. But why is this three-tier combination of parts for "a true and living education?" As Sri Aurobindo says,

> For within the universal mind and soul of humanity is the mind and soul of the individual with its infinite variation, its commonness and its uniqueness, and between them there stands an intermediate power, the mind of a nation, the soul of a people. And of all these three, education must take account if it is to be, not a machine-made fabric, but a true building or a living evocation of the powers of the mind and spirit of the human being.[9]

Thus, so far as these three things for "a true and living education" are concerned, the first and foremost consideration, which weighs with us, boils down to one indispensable point viz. man. This is because, as Sri Aurobindo says,

> India has seen always in man the individual a soul, a portion of the Divinity enwrapped in mind and body, a conscious manifestation in nature of the universal self and spirit.[10]

Coming to "national education," as conceived by Sri Aurobindo, we see that, towards the early part of 1907, Aurobindo Ghosh wrote in the *Bande Mataram* on national education as follows:

> National Education cannot be defined briefly in one or two sentences, but we may describe it tentatively as the education, which, starting with the past and making full use of the present, builds up a great nation. Whoever wishes to cut off the nation from its past, is no friend of our national growth.

9. Sri Aurobindo, *A Preface On National Education,* as contained in the book, *Sri Aurobindo and the Mother On Education.*
10. op. cit., pp. 199-200.

> Whoever fails to take advantage of the present is losing us the battle of life. . . . We must acquire for her the best knowledge that Europe can give her and assimilate it to her own peculiar type of national temperament.

Sri Aurobindo's ideas on "national education" are traceable to two principal dissertations on the subject, of which one captioned *A Preface on National Education* was published in two parts in the last two issues of the *Arya,* November-December 1920 and January 1921[11] and the other entitled *A System of National Education* was published in an authorized edition in 1924.[12]

Although the idea of "national education" is not preposterous, Sri Aurobindo was explicit enough when, in referring to the word "national," as prefixed to "education," he observed,

> There may be much virtue in an epithet but to tag on the word "national" to a school or college or even a Council or Board of Education . . . and think we have solved the problem does not really change anything.[13]

In the nineteenth century, Tolstoy wrote:

> The strength of the Government lies in the people's ignorance and Government knows this and will therefore always oppose true enlightenment. It is time we realize this fact. And it is most undesirable to let the Government, while it is spreading darkness, pretend to be busy with enlightenment of the people.[14]

---

11. op. cit., pp. 9-10.
12. Sri Aurobindo, *A System of National Education,* (some preliminary ideas) — ibid.
13. op. cit., p. 16.
14. Quotation occurring in an article entitled *Confronting Leviathan* by Asok Mitra, ICS in the journal *Frontier* (p. 5); month and year of publication not available.

Education in a Dismal Condition

Now, what in India has resulted from "people's ignorance" of which Tolstoy has spoken? Here in India we notice, much to our consternation, that colossal illiteracy of the masses, staggering unemployment, political skulduggery, massive scams involving crores and crores of rupees, notorious black-marketing, chicken-hearted bureaucracy and bureaucratic chicanery, militant trade unionism, intellectual hypocrisy in educational institutions, recalcitrant attitude on the part of sons and daughters towards parents, disrespect to teachers, horrible insubordination at offices, awful non-accountability to superiors, organized vandalism, criminal intimidation of the innocent people by the ruffians, never-ending terrorist and secessionist activities, odious espionage, gruesome murders, merciless torture on women, ruthless exploitation of child labour, alarming poverty, etc. have raised a monstrous Frankenstein staring grimly at the country. What are all these due to? The only answer is: absence of proper value-oriented education without which such a dismal picture cannot be got rid of and without which the idea of economic independence would remain a myth.

Despite all top-level parleys about a drastic reorientation of the present system of education, which still persists as an imperial relic of the British education in India, nothing tangible has so far been done to remedy the sorry state of affairs obtaining in the field of education. This indicates an evil augury when education gets stuck up with a utility-cum-production-oriented system alone to the total exclusion of values directed towards development of an integral personality through an "integral education."

Present System of Education

As a legacy of the British education in India, the present system of education refers to a three-tier faculty, viz. (i) faculty of arts or humanities, (ii) faculty of science & engineering, (iii) faculty of commerce. This triple division still aims at churning out white-collar workers, low-rung bureaucrats, lawyers, technicians, engineers, doctors, cost accountants and chartered accountants. Is that all? Moreover, the number of people in such occupations can be counted on fingers as against a population figure of well over 100 crores in our country. The spread of education is poor, perfunctory and has not succeeded in the least in liquidating illiteracy of the vast multitudes of our people who, without getting any chance to learn even the three R's, are deprived of the blessings of literacy. As a result of lack of education, what we find is criminalization of politics and corruption in every stratum of society.

Perusal of prescribed text-books by the students is extremely desultory. They cram answers to questions on these books with the help of myriads of key-books available in the market. The present system of education is thus more or less an imposition in the sense that the syllabus is so structured that the students are over-encumbered with a plethora of text-books and reference books. As Swami Vivekananda observed: "Education is not simply stuffing the mind with information that runs riot."

The students are forced to learn things by rote. They forget immediately after the examination what they read immediately before the examination. It is the case with most students, if not all. It is the defective system of education that accounts for lakhs of failures in the examination every year. Newspapers are flooded with reports of a large number of plucked students committing suicide. Then, again, many of the unsuccessful students are joining corrupt politicians and venal leaders as their active supporters. What is the result? "Mastanocracy" throughout the country — all masquerading as patriotic fervour and prejudicing our approach to the burning question of education.

An impression has gained ground in colleges and universities that the test of learning lies in the acquisition of the number of degrees, and for that matter, in flaunting a PhD or D.Lit after one's name. Research work has qualitatively suffered. After all, what is a doctoral thesis in most cases nowadays? It is a hefty document turgid with numerous lengthy quotations without throwing light on any new or original discovery through research. Of course, there are honourable exceptions.

Misconception on National Education

At this critical juncture, to quote Sri Aurobindo,

> . . . there is and can be no meaning at all or none worth troubling about in the idea of a national education and that the very notion is the undesirable and unprofitable intrusion of a false and narrow patriotism into a field in which patriotism apart from the need of a training in good citizenship has legitimate place.[15]

Sri Aurobindo adumbrated that there could be no point in making a fetish about any particular form of education for purposes of training to good citizenship, as palpable from his observations:

> . . . for that one purpose no special kind or form of education is needed, since the training to good citizenship must be in all essentials the same whether in the East, England or Germany or Japan or India. Mankind and its needs are the same everywhere and truth and knowledge are one and have no country; education too must be a thing universal and without nationality or borders.[16]

15. op cit., pp. 7-8.
16. Ibid., p. 8.

It is rather unfortunate that a misconception seems still to persist over what we call "national education." It appears to imply a resuscitation of the hoary past, which is an impossibility. As Sri Aurobindo says, "we do not belong to the past dawns but to the noons of the future."[17] Sri Aurobindo's ideas on national education include something very important when he wrote,

> After all, we live in the twentieth century and cannot revive the India of Chandragupta or Akbar; we must keep abreast with the march of truth and knowledge, fit ourselves for existence under actual circumstances, and our education must be therefore up-to-date in form and substance and modern in life and spirit.[18]

There is, therefore, no point in getting bogged down to any obstinately hidebound attitude and in dilly-dallying with, in the words of Sri Aurobindo,

> . . . the idea of national education which would make of it a means of an obscurantist retrogression to the past forms that were once a living frame of our culture but are now dead or dying things . . .[19]

In tinkering with the idea of capitalizing upon things retrospectively for construction prospectively in the context of our socio-economic constraints galore, let us not lose sight of the zeitgeist, i.e. the spirit of the age. As Sri Aurobindo says,

> The living spirit of the demand no more requires a return to astronomy and mathematics of Bhaskara or the forms of the system of Nalanda than the living spirit of Swadeshi a return from railway and motor traction to the ancient chariot and the bullock cart.[20]

---

17. Sri Aurobindo — *Essays on the Gita.*
18. op. cit., p. 8.
19. Ibid., p. 9.
20. Ibid., p. 9.

Integral Education and Aurobindo

As for "integral education," we see that, according to Sri Aurobindo school of thought, "Education to be complete must have five principal aspects relating to the five activities of the human being: the physical, the vital, the mental, the psychic and the spiritual."[21] Keeping these five components of "integral education" in view, we may divide Sri Aurobindo's scheme of "integral education" in two broad phases, viz. (i) the horizontal phase of education, and (ii) the vertical phase of education, which relate to two major fields of Consciousness.

I am reminded here of the Mother's message to the Education Commission, Govt. of India, with her blessings in 1965, which I quote below:

> India has or rather had the knowledge of the Spirit, but she neglected matter and suffered for it.
>
> The west has the knowledge of matter but rejected the Spirit and suffered badly for it.
>
> An integral education which could, with some variations, be adapted to all the nations of the world, must bring back the legitimate authority of the Spirit over matter fully developed and utilized.
>
> Blessings — The Mother[22]

Obviously, here we find an "integral education" being recommended for adoption inasmuch as an "integral education" is essentially a growth of consciousness, more conscious so as to be integrated with the inner personality (the Psychic Being and the Spirit). That makes the integral personality.

---

21. *The Mother On Education* (ed. 1960).
22. Obtained from Indra Sen of Sri Aurobindo Ashram, Pondicherry long ago.

Components of Integral Education

In the horizontal phase of "integral education," we are concerned with (i) physical education, (ii) vital education, (iii) mental education, and (iv) psychic education.

PHYSICAL EDUCATION

The first component of "integral education" on the horizontal plane is "physical education." As the Mother of Pondicherry says,

> The education of the body has three principal aspects: (1) Control and discipline of functions, (2) A total, methodical and harmonious development of all the parts and movements of the body, and (3) Rectification of defects and deformities, if there be any.[23]

In fact, proper cultivation of the physique ensures suppleness and beauty of the body besides adding to strength, valour, agility and alacrity. To quote Sri Aurobindo,

> I put a value on the body first as an instrument, *dharmasādhana*, or more fully as a centre of manifested personality in action, a basis of spiritual life and activity upon the earth but also because for me the body as well as the mind and life is a part of the Divine whole, a form of the Spirit and therefore not to be disregarded or despised as something incurably gross and incapable of spiritual realization or of spiritual use . . .. In my view the body as well as the mind and life has to be spiritualized or, one may say, divinized so as to be a fit instrument and receptacle for the realization of the Divine.[24]

The aim of "physical education" is thus to ensure proper formation of a healthy body and keeping up fitness of all

---

23. op. cit.
24. Sri Aurobindo, *On Himself SABCL,* vol. 26, p. 208.

bodily functions and systems and to remain open to the higher ranges of consciousness.

VITAL EDUCATION

The second ingredient of "integral education" is "vital education." Let us first understand what the vital being is. As the Mother of Pondicherry says,

> The vital being in us is the seat of dynamic energy and desperate depression, of passions and revolt. It can set in motion everything, build up and realize. It can also destroy and mar everything. It seems to be, in the human being, the most difficult part to train.[25]

At a time when sincerity is at a discount and patience is a thing of the past, training the vital seems almost preposterous, for, as the Mother further says,

> It is a long labour requiring great patience, and it demands a perfect sincerity, for without sincerity one will deceive oneself from the very first step, and all endeavour for progress will go in vain.[26]

Emotions or feelings, which are generally blind, constitute the "vital part" of the individual. If we are swayed by emotions and act according to the dictates of our emotional self by relegating reason to the background, our life is exposed to the risk of being divorced from integrality essential for development of an integral personality. Not that we are necessarily to extirpate our sensuous self from our "being" but that we ought to master the art of how to subordinate our sensuous self to our rational self.

The "vital part" in us mostly remains defiled and unrefined because of the absence of a sharp power of observation of the

---

25. op. cit.
26. Ibid.

functions of the vital, as distinct from other parts and also because of the absence of a ratiocinative capacity to judge impartially. It is only by developing our aesthetic faculties that we can so refine the "vital part" as to be able to ensure a transformation of character. Now, what is character? Character is the sum-total of one's habits. A man of good character means a man having good habits while a man of bad character means a man having bad habits.

Today crisis of character poses everywhere a problem of alarming proportions. As the Mother says,

> One must gain a full knowledge of one's character and then acquire control over one's movements so that one may achieve perfect mastery and transformation of all the elements that have to be transformed.[27]

Proper vital education automatically ensures moral education, the aim of which is character building. Utilization of the sense organs plays a vital role in the formation of character. That is why the Mother observes:

> The sense organs may be so cultivated as to attain a precision and power in their functioning far greater than what is normally expected of them.[28]

Thus, while touching upon the "vital being," we have by the way entered into "vital education" about which the Mother says:

> The education of the vital has two principal aspects . . .. The first is to develop and utilize the sense organs, the second is to become conscious and gradually master one's character and in the end to achieve its transformation . . .[29]

---

27. Ibid.
28. Ibid.
29. Ibid.

Let me quote Sri Aurobindo in this context,

> The Prāṇa (the vital) is everywhere in us supporting not only the action of our body, but of our sense-mind, our emotional-mind, our thought-mind; and bringing its own law or Dharma into all these, it confuses, it limits, it throws into discord their right action and creates that impurity of misplacement and that tangled confusion which is the whole evil of our psychological existence. In that confusion our law seems to reign, the law of desire.[30]

The aim of "vital education" is to ensure a harmonious working of the ordinary impulses of life relating to the demands of the flesh such as food, sleep, rest, work, bodily desires, social relations, etc., and to remain open to the higher ranges of Consciousness.

MENTAL EDUCATION

The third constituent of "integral education" is "mental education" about which the Mother points out that a true education of the mind, that which will prepare man for a higher life, has five principal phases. The five phases, in brief, are:

1. Development of the power of concentration, the capacity of attention.
2. Development of the capacities of expansion, widening, complexity and richness.
3. Organization of ideas around a central idea or a higher ideal or a supremely luminous idea that will serve as a guide in life.
4. Thought control, rejection of undesirable thoughts so that one may, in the end, think only what one wants and when one wants.

30. Sri Aurobindo, *Synthesis of Yoga.*

5. Development of mental silence, perfect calm and a more and more total receptivity to inspirations coming from the higher regions of the being.[31]

The aim of mental education is to ensure development of the capacity to handle ideas and words accurately in a comprehensive way with the integral truth of life and to remain open to inspiration from the Higher Sources.

PSYCHIC EDUCATION

So far as the "psychic education," the fourth element of "integral education," is concerned, the Mother says,

> The three lines of education — physical, vital and mental — deal with that which may be defined as the means of building up the personality, raising the individual out of the amorphous subconscious mass, making it a well-defined self-conscious entity. With "psychic education," we come to the problem of the true motive of life, the reason of our existence upon earth, the very discovery to which life must lead and the result of that discovery, the consecration of the individual to his eternal principle.[32]

The Psychic Being constitutes a Conscious Entity of the Revealing Divine Force in the process of evolution and is ensconced behind the trio, viz. the physical, the vital and the mental. Sri Aurobindo calls the "Psychic Being" *the spark of the Divine.*[33] Generally, the physical, the vital and the mental parts of our being remain so confused and jumbled up that it is almost next to impossible to separate the functions of the one from the other. This disorder is due to the fact that the individual generally remains stuck to the physical, the vital and the mental so much so that he finds no clue to this spark

---

31. op. cit.
32. Ibid.
33. Sri Aurobindo, *SABCL*, vol. 22, p. 293.

of the Divine, which remains veiled in him. That is why Sri Aurobindo says,

> . . . the most important thing for you is to develop the psychic fire in the hearts and the aspiration for the "Psychic Being" to come forward as the leader of the sādhana . . .[34]

The very nature of the physical, the vital and the mental is to run in opposite direction to the psychic. But the trio must need be conscious of the psychic entity and be identified with it. As stated, the aim of the physical, the vital and the mental is to keep open to the higher ranges of Consciousness. But the aim is not complete unless the physical, the vital and the mental maintain openness to the deeper guidance and control of the "Psychic Being" whose aim it is *to form an individual being . . . around the divine centre.*[35]

Thus, about the horizontal phase of education, it is considered a *sine qua non* that we should remain careful of two things, viz. (i) to ensure development of the physical, the vital and the mental, and (ii) to ensure development of the psychic. In fact, with the attainment of perfection in all these parts of education, the horizontal phase serves as a platform on which is raised the vertical phase for the "spiritual education" for us to grow upwards, i.e. to heighten our consciousness to a New Consciousness and be united with the Higher Divine Range.

Coming to the vertical phase of education, one has to remember that it is only when the psychic is awakened that the "spiritual education" starts. The Mother asks, "Why is it necessary to make a distinction between the psychic education . . . and the spiritual education . . .?"[36] The answer to the question comes from the Mother,

---

34. Ibid.
35. *Collected Works of The Mother*, vol. 4, p. 149.
36. *The Mother, On Education* (ed. 1960).

> It is necessary because the two are usually mixed up under the generic name "Yogic discipline" although the goal they aim at is very different in each case; for one it is a higher realization upon earth, for the other, an escape from all earthly manifestations even away from the whole universe, a return to the unmanifest.[37]

Sri Aurobindo school of thought teaches us that living a psychic life needs selfishness being banished while living a spiritual life needs being selfless.

One significant thing in regard to the vertical phase of education it that it brings about "spiritual ascent" and awakens a new consciousness. But this is not all. Earthly consciousness does not change into divine consciousness unless supramental light descends on earthly consciousness. That is why Sri Aurobindo attaches immense importance to a new education called "the supramental education" which, as the Mother says,

> . . . will, by its all-powerful action, work not only upon the consciousness of individual beings but upon the very substance of which they are built and upon the environment in which they live.[38]

Let us not labour under the erroneous impression that we have to get the education of the physical first, then the vital, then the mental and then the psychic and then the spiritual. All that we are required to do is to try to master the art and the technique associated with the horizontal and the vertical phases simultaneously. Otherwise, education, the soul of culture, will be barren, and the art of culture will be but a sham celebration of the disorders of the soul.

Ways and Means Committee of 1921, Bengal

It may be recalled here that the Ways and Means Committee set up in 1921 by the National Council of Education, Bengal

37. Ibid.
38. Ibid.

recommended means being adopted for the development of physique and character. This, therefore, is in consonance with the horizontal phase of education, as highlighted in Sri Aurobindo school of thought. Similarly, "to provide for denominational religious education" was one of the objects of the National Council of Education, as contained in its Memorandum of Association. Out of the endowment instituted by Brajendra Kishore Roy Chowdhury, religious education for the Hindu boys in the Bengal Technical Institute was arranged while a Standing Sub-Committee was set up in 1928 to oversee dissemination of religious education. A lecturer was engaged in 1919 to impart religious education to the students of the BTI. Baldeodas Jugalkishore donated Rs. 1,000/-, which was invested to fetch the value of a prize for proficiency in the *Bhagavad-Gītā.* The Council's founding fathers wanted to ensure that education ought to become the unfolding of inner faculties a man is endowed with and that education ought also to produce an edifying influence upon the student community. Tolerance of and respect for all religions was the keynote of religious teaching as the objective was to bring home to the students the core content of religious education, viz. spirituality. But what is spirituality minus Man, World and the Divine? In the philosophy of Sri Aurobindo, Man and the World constitute the dynamic aspect of the Reality while the Divine, on the other hand, constitutes the transcendental aspect of the Reality.

A question now arises: why was accent put on the physical education, character-building education, religious education, the study of the *Gītā* and even a teacher appointed to impart religious education to the BTI students pursuing technical and engineering studies? This was co-curricular and not extra-mural. The answer to the question is not far to seek. While it more or less conformed to the scheme of education evolved by Sri Aurobindo, this at the same time highlighted a very important aspect of education under the National Council of Education, Bengal.

Let not technical education lead to the building up of technopolis which, in turn, bids fair to build up necropolis. For, the National Council of Education believes, from technopolis to oecumenopolis to ekistics, such is the road to recovery.

Aurobindo As a Teacher

Sri Aurobindo has not yet been assessed as to how efficient and excellent he was as a class teacher. Paucity of time will not permit me to deal elaborately with this point. Let us, however, see what Sri Aurobindo says about the principles of teaching. He says,

> The first principle of true teaching is that nothing can be taught. The teacher is not an instructor or task-master, he is a helper and a guide. His business is to suggest and not to impose. He does not actually train the pupils's mind; he only shows him how to perfect his instruments of knowledge and helps and encourages him in the process. He does not impart knowledge to him, he shows him how to acquire knowledge for himself.[39]

At the Bengal National College, Aurobindo was a thorough and perfect teacher. From 15 August 1906 to 2 August 1907, Aurobindo functioned as the Principal of Bengal National College. During his Principalship, he was also the editor of the *Bande Mataram.* Notwithstanding his active participation in greater political movement, and despite his inability to bestow proper attention on the problems of the College always, he used to take class daily for two hours. Towards the early part of 1907, Aurobindo wrote in the *Bande Mataram*:

---

39. Sri Aurobindo, *The Hour of God* (cent. ed. vol. 17), pp. 204-05.

> We are dissatisfied with the conditions under which education is imparted in this country, its calculated poverty and insufficiency, its anti-national character, its subordination to Government and the use made of that subordination for the discouragement of patriotism and the inculcation of loyalty.[40]

So long as Aurobindo served as Principal and Professor, he took his duty seriously and taught about ten hours a week, taking his classes generally between 2 and 4 p.m. History, both Indian and European, and English Poetry were the subjects mainly taught by him. He did not have much opportunity to teach Political Science, because there was no student of Political Science during the early years.[41]

So far as I can remember, either I read somewhere or perhaps somebody must have told me that at Baroda, when Aurobindo Ghosh was one day teaching Milton's *Samson Agonistes,* one of his students — perhaps, maybe K.M. Munshi, who was also a student of Sri Aurobindo at Baroda, stood up and said, "Sir, the interpretation you are giving on Hellenism and Hebraism does not tally with that given in the annotated editions we read." Obviously, what surprise can there be that the architect of the Supramental Yoga will explain in a completely novel manner poles apart from the key-books, which are generally regarded by many students as Charon's ferry to cross the Styx of examination. Sri Aurobindo's reply to the inquisitive student was: "Why do you read the trash?"

Many of you know that in 1921 Gopal Chandra Sinha, Zamindar of Bara Jagulia in the Nadia district, created an endowment at the National Council of Education, Bengal for

---

40. *Bande Mataram,* dated 17.4.1907: *The Doctrine of Passive Resistance: Its methods.*
41. Amitava Mukherjee, 1992, *Fifty Years of National Education,* Calcutta: National Council of Education, Bengal, p. 59.

the promotion of agricultural education under the Council. His grandson, Sri Subhas Chandra Sinha, now an octogenarian and personally known to me, told me sometime ago when I called on him at his residence that he was a student of the Mitra Institution, Bhowanipur, Calcutta. Acharya Satis Chandra Mukherjee, who was one of the founding fathers of the National Council of Education, Bengal, was once a teacher of South Suburban Main School, Bhowanipur. Sri Sinha recalled his school days of the late 30's and early 40's of the last century, stating that there was a teacher of English who was a student of Sri Aurobindo at the Bengal National College. Sri Sinha regretted that he could not recollect the name of this teacher of English. But what Sri Sinha remembered was that one day the said teacher of English well over sixty-five years ago narrated to the students how great Sri Aurobindo was as a class teacher. The gist of what I remember to have heard is like this.

One day, in course of a discussion on William Wordsworth's *Daffodils,* the said teacher told him that Aurobindo Ghose (later Sri Aurobindo) was once explaining that poem in the class at the Bengal National College. Aurobindo was so deeply engrossed in explaining *Daffodils* in an altogether novel way that he forgot that two hours had rolled by and that the next teacher was waiting at the threshold of the classroom.

After sometime, Aurobindo realized that the next teacher was waiting. He expressed regret. But the teacher did not mind at all and humbly requested Aurobindo to continue as the interpretation was extremely sublime and absolutely novel. Yes, novelty of meaningful presentation, not pedagogic pedantry, was the quintessence of Sri Aurobindo's method of teaching. A pantheist that William Wordsworth was, the poet found manifestation of the Divine all around. Whether it is the mighty mountains or the roaring oceans, the singing cuckoo or the smiling primrose, the shepherd Michael or the old Cumberland beggar, everywhere the poet found divine beauty. But the most significant point for consideration is that the golden *Daffodils* were to Wordsworth more than everyday flowers. Actually, the golden *Daffodils* represented not only the living manifestation of beauty and grace of the Divine but also something else.

What Aurobindo seeks to hint at is that those who have eyes to see will not fail to see that even everyday flowers are not without an exhaustive manifestation of the Divine. Maybe, these everyday flowers seem to be a manifestation of the Divine without the touch of His transcendence. No doubt, this bears out Wordsworth's pantheistic outlook. But Aurobindo moves a step forward to say that the golden *Daffodils* represent more than the immanence of the Divine, i.e. the golden *Daffodils* speak both of the immanence and transcendence of the Divine.

As we know, pantheism emphasizes manifestation of the Divine to the exclusion of His transcendence. This is a half-truth. On the other hand, deism emphasizes the transcendence of the Divine to the exclusion of His manifestation. It is also equally a half-truth. In the golden *Daffodils,* Aurobindo could visualize both the manifestation of the Divine and His transcendence, too. The Divine is in the world and also beyond it. Transcendence is going beyond human knowledge and into a spiritual area. In the ultimate analysis, transcendence is transhumanism, which is perhaps the only true philosophy of civilization. Only "trans" does not abjure but transfigures. This is the evidence of wisdom. Thus, in his interpretation of the golden *Daffodils*, Aurobindo added a new dimension of an integral and all-comprehensive vision. The golden *Daffodils* as well as other beings and objects of Nature represent multiplicity of projection of an integral One Reality. This classroom lecture of Aurobindo as a teacher throws ample light on his integral vision of education on the vertical plane.

Like Swami Vivekananda who said, *Education is the manifestation of perfection already in man,*[42] Sri Aurobindo, too, believed in perfection. After all, the perfected human world can hardly be created by men who are themselves imperfect.

During his short stay at the Council, the change that came about of the national life, the inspiration that was aroused in the minds of the students and the way the country was galvanized into action under Aurobindo's leadership at that time are simply amazing.

Unfortunately, the Council came to lose the services of Aurobindo owing to a succession of political happenings. The office of the *Bande Mataram* was searched by the police. In a missive dated 8 January 1907 to the editor of the said paper, government cautioned Aurobindo strongly for writing and publishing seditious articles which, as the government opined, were couched in a language tending to provoke violence and to disturb law and order. From July 1907, the ball of the press prosecutions was set rolling by the government. Aurobindo smelt a rat and could understand that troubles were brewing. Lest any development might injure the academic interests of the College, Aurobindo resigned his principalship on 2 August 1907. Then on 16 August 1907, Aurobindo came to learn that a warrant of arrest had been issued against him on two counts, firstly, for reproducing translations of articles in English from *Jugantar* and secondly, for publishing in *Bande Mataram* of 28 July 1907 a write-up under the caption "India for Indians". Aurobindo lost no time and surrendered before the Detective Police, when he was placed under arrest.

Rabindranath Tagore was moved. To extol Aurobindo Ghosh's extraordinary patriotic spirit, which led to his arrest,

42. *The Complete Works of Swami Vivekananda.*

Rabindranath melted into poetry, singing: *Arabinda Rabindrer Laho Namaskar.*

Later on, however, Aurobindo was released on bail. Finally, on 23 September 1907, Aurobindo was set free. His acquittal was duly celebrated by the students. On being freed from the charge of sedition in the *Bande Mataram* case, Aurobindo returned to the Bengal National College not as principal but as Hemchandra Basu Mallik, Professor of History and Political Science at the College and worked till December 1907.

Aurobindo Resigns from National Council

In a few days, he had to leave the precincts of the College owing to divergence of views between the extremists and the moderates in politics on the question of freedom struggle. The moderates felt alarmed at the political views and activities of Aurobindo Ghosh. Those at the helm of affairs at the Council could not approve of the call that Aurobindo Ghosh used to give to the students to inspire them, and the office-bearers of the Council *did not find Aurobindo's company quite congenial.*[43]

The moderates became all the more alarmed when, on 2 May 1908 Sri Aurobindo was arrested *in connection with the Muzaffarpur murders* (30th April, 1908) *and the filing of the Alipore Bomb case. . . .*[44] Owing to this political trouble, his dissociation from the Council came to be just a matter of course. On 7 May 1908, a resolution was adopted by the Executive Committee of the Council requesting Sri Aurobindo to resign his membership of the Council and the Executive Committee. On 23 May 1908, Aurobindo resigned his membership of the Council and of the Executive Committee and the resignation was accepted on 4 August 1908. All connections of Sri Aurobindo with the Council thus ended.

43. Ibid., p. 95.
44. Ibid., p. 94.

How did Aurobindo Ghose react to this development? In this connection, we may recall the observation of A.B. Purani, the noted biographer of Sri Aurobindo, who wrote that the authorities of the Bengal National College wanted the Council to be *a place of learning* but Sri Aurobindo wanted the Council to be *a centre of life.* A.B. Purani was more than correct because we have already heard Aurobindo Ghose observing:

> We must . . . take the divorce of the National Council from the national movement as part of a deliberate and permanent policy . . .. All that we can now expect of the Council is to be a centre of scientific and technical education; it can no longer be a workshop in which national spirit and energy are to be forged and shaped.[45]

Aurobindo's Valedictory Speech

Today after a century if we ask ourselves: what did the National Council of Education actually get from Aurobindo Ghose? He was here as a principal for less than a year and as a teacher for a very short time. So, what did we actually get from Aurobindo Ghose? The first bequest that we got from Aurobindo was his name — the name Aurobindo — which has become a source of perennial inspiration for us. The second heritage, which we have got from Aurobindo Ghose but to which we do not pay much attention, is the historic address which he delivered to the students of the National Council of Education, Bengal. We have already noted why and how Aurobindo had to resign his principalship of Bengal National College on 2 August 1907. On 22 August 1907, his inspired students gave him an excellent farewell. On 23 August 1907, Aurobindo gave a historic address to the students, a little excerpt of which is quoted below:

---

45. "The Apostasy of the National Council" in *Karmayogin*, vol. 1, no. 16, Oct. 9, 1909.

> There are times in a nation's history when Providence places before it one work, one aim, to which everything else, however high and noble in itself, has to be sacrificed. Such a time has now arrived for our motherland when nothing is dearer than her service, when everything else is to be directed to that end. If you will study, study for her sake; train yourselves body and mind and soul for her services. You will earn your living that you may live for her sake. You will go abroad to foreign lands that you may bring back knowledge with which you may offer service to her. Work that she may prosper. Suffer that she may rejoice. All is contained in that one advice.[46]

From this valedictory address to the students, the conclusion that becomes irresistible is that, to Sri Aurobindo our country represents our Mother for whom whatever sacrifice is called for has to be made irrespective of any cost that it might involve. So profound was his love for the country! What is the picture today? Many of our political leaders whose names have been tarnished as corrupt with slurs of scams appear to value party above country. Education seems to be in uncaring hands, in the hands of those whose priorities lie elsewhere. Even in educational institutions, in the Universities, personal bickering, clash of ego, clash of personal interest, intolerance, envy and all negative qualities resulting from rude and crude politics rule the roost. In this connection, we may assert with all the force that we command that the message of Aurobindo Ghose, as contained in the said valedictory address, has now assumed limitless importance because it is incumbent upon the student community today for saving the country from all corroding evils.

---

46. Quoted from Sri Aurobindo's *Farewell Address* to the students of the National Council of Education, Bengal occurring in the booklet *Two Memorable Speeches*, published by the National Council of Education, Bengal.

Aurobindo Turns Saint in Pondicherry

On 2 April 1910, Sri Aurobindo left Bengal forever for Pondicherry where Aurobindo Ghosh, the principal of Bengal National College and the then top-ranking leader of our motherland and the prophet of nationalism turned into saint Sri Aurobindo, the maker and exponent of a new Vedanta. His connection with Bengal politics did not last beyond four years from 1906 to 1910. During this period of four years, he stayed behind the bars for one year from May 1908 to May 1909.

Sri Aurobindo's action and his original political thoughts, particularly his concept of a divine life and integral yoga are being assessed and reassessed in various ways. The process is continuous. But no tangible research appears to have been hitherto done on his contribution to education and culture and the field of poetry. I regard Sri Aurobindo not only as a great yogi but also as a great poet. It would accordingly be appropriate for both the National Council of Education, Bengal and Jadavpur University, of which the parent body is the National Council of Education, Bengal to concentrate their research today on the relevance of Sri Aurobindo which, as I feel, is to be ferreted out not only in his hermeneutics or interpretation of manifestation of supramental on earth but also in the concept of his national education and integral education and their applicability to the system of education prevailing in the country today.

In an article entitled "A Word in Time" published in the 3 May 1908 issue of the *Bande Mataram*, Sri Aurobindo wrote,

> The Council is not merely an educational body nor is the College merely an educational institution; they are trustees to the people of a great instrument of national regeneration and should work always in that spirit.

Beside this description of the National Council of Education, Bengal by Sri Aurobindo, my immediate feeling was that, with men like Sri Aurobindo, Satis Chandra Mukhopadhyay, Rabindranath Tagore and other luminaries at the helm of affairs, the National Council of Education would function as the watershed of our country with a wide catchment area and its waters would irrigate the country into giving us rich harvests of human resources. I have reasons to believe that, despite the mark of anomie not only in the political sphere but also in the intellectual and academic spheres almost all around, an institution like the National Council of Education, Bengal as the parent-body of Jadavpur University, can never fall into desuetude.

Aurobindo Ghosh, the principal and professor of the Bengal National College established by the National Council of Education, Bengal, to whom Rabindranath paid compliments by describing him as *Swadesh Atmar Vanimurti* (= personifed voice of the soul of the Motherland), who wanted to initiate the students into the *mantra* of the Motherland, to organize them at the altar of the Motherland — that Sri Aurobindo we remember with our heads down in all reverence. His farewell address to the students at the Bengal National College has set us thinking at the National Council of Education, Bengal so as to be able to understand the implications of his dream, a dream that constitutes the wealth of both the National Council of Education, Bengal and Jadavpur University today.

In the golden jubliee year of Jadavpur University and the centenary of the National Council of Education, Bengal, we may hope that, in line with the tradition and heritage handed down to us by the galaxy of luminaries of the late nineteenth and early twentieth century, the present authorities of the National Council of Education, Bengal and of Jadavpur

University will be pleased to do whatever is within the range of their possibility to ensure that education is spared the ignominy of being in uncaring hands. I am reminded of Dr A.P.J. Abdul Kalam, former President of India, who in a message sent to the National Council of Education, Bengal on the occasion of its Centenary Celebration on 11 March 2005 stated, *inter alia,* that one of the missions of the Council should be to inspire noble qualities in students and produce good human beings for the overall benefit of society.

Let me conclude by quoting verse 114 of Chapter II of *Manu-Smṛti*[47]:

> Sacred Learning approached a brāhmaṇa and
> Said to him: I am thy treasure, preserve me,
> deliver me not to a scorner; so (preserved)
> I shall become supremely strong.

---

47. Quoted from Sacred Book of the East translated by various oriental scholars and edited by F. Max Müller (vol. xxv) — Oxford at the Clarendon Press (1886).

8

History as Applied Metaphysics

Indrani Sanyal

SRI AUROBINDO and his illustrious contemporaries are held in high esteem for their epoch-making activities and for creating a history — rightly speaking, they heralded a new age, initiated a renaissance — in all spheres of life. They are revered for their contribution to politics, ethics, culture, society, literature and other domains of life. No texts on modern Indian history can afford to ignore their contribution to the cause of national history. However, here no attempt is being made to evaluate and assess the role of Sri Aurobindo and his contemporaries in the context of Indian history. My concern here is not with any "historical" events as such but to make it conceptually clear what constitutes historicity of history not only in this context particularly, but in all similar such contexts.

How should we understand the nature of historical facts? A philosopher of history as distinguished from a historian has a different way of understanding and interpreting history. One very illuminating way of drawing a distinction between a philosopher of history and a historian may be borrowed from Arthur C. Danto[1] who says a philosopher of history explains the "whole of history" and a historian explains the

1. Arthur C. Danto, *Analytical Philosophy of History*, p. 1.

"whole of past." A careful perusal of the above observation would not delude one in believing that the objective of philosopher of history is redundant or insignificant. In this article, I would like to focus on the appraisal and elaboration of the main observations of Pramath Nath Mukhopadhyaya,[2] also known as Swami Pratyagatmananda Saraswati with views of other well known philosophers of history, both Western and Indian. Sri Aurobindo himself was a great scholar of history and the present discussion would enable me to look at the philosophy of history as espoused by Sri Aurobindo in an unorthodox way.

Relations Between Purāṇas, Other Texts and History

In the preface to the first edition of the book *Itihas O Abhivyakti,* Pramath Nath himself begins by asking questions, as to what is history? What is the relation between the Purāṇa and other studies that go by the name of history in our country with true (*yathārtha*) history? What is the relation between that which is regarded as history in the West and true history

---

2. Pramath Nath Mukhopadhyaya (1880–1971) was among the first group along with Aurobindo Ghosh, Satish Chandra Mukherjee of Dawn Society, Benoy Kumar Sarkar, Radhakumud Mukherjee and other eminent educationists to join the National Council of Education, Bengal which was founded to reorient education in the direction suitable for the requirements of our people. He began his career as Professor in Philosophy and Physics in Ripon College, now known as Surendra Nath College. Pramath Nath Mukhopadhyaya had no preceptor, he had himself initiated into *saṅnyāsa* or recluse and was known as Pratyagatmananda Saraswati. He was very much interested in Western science and Indian spirituality. He has written some very important books, but most of these are not available nowadays. In this article, I would like to consider Pramath Nath as a philosopher of history and would try to explicate and analyse his idea of history as developed in his book, *Itihasa O Abhivyakti,* written in Bengali with a subtitle in English as *Philosophy of History With Special Reference to the Culture-Life of India,* National Council of Education, Bengal, 1929.

which is the object of his search? *Itihasa O Abhivyakti* is not to be considered as another text on history rather it is to be viewed as an attempt to find out proper significance of history. To establish his viewpoint he has given ample quotations both from Western texts and Indian texts.

Paradigms in the light of which history is to be viewed are varied and many. It was believed by some that the task of a historian is to give descriptions of deeds, events that occurred before their eyes and to give description of states of society that prevailed during that time. Royal historians, for example, were reporters of events that took place in the kingdom of their patronizing kings. Opinions differ very much as to whether history is to be taken as the study of the individual, an eminent personality who makes the history. Aristotle is one of those who says history is an account of what individual human beings have done or suffered. The idea of making history by an individual has not been acceptable to all. Rather it has given rise to lots of discussions and debates about the role of an individual in history. Indeed, there are historians who are inclined in favour of the view that activities of some individual are the main determiner of history and almost the only spring of any historical development. This view has been rejected on the ground of being too one-sided. The Biblical view of history that rests on a single event — the advent of Jesus Christ is often rejected on the ground of its being dogmatic.

Views on History and Study of Civilization

Is history the study of the civilization of the whole species? Immanuel Kant (1724–1804) in "Idea of a Universal History with a Cosmopolitan Purpose,"[3] observes that actions of men when considered individually add up to nothing significant.

3. *Idea for a Universal History from a Cosmopolitan Point of View* (1784). Translation by Lewis White Beck.

He suggests it is possible that Nature or providence is fulfilling some plan through these actions of which agents are not aware. The development of such capacities, according to Kant, belongs to the history of species as a whole. Karl Lamprecht,[4] the author of the History of the German people, whom Sri Aurobindo also admiringly quotes,[5] is among the representatives of the latter view. The stand of Lamprecht annoyed many critics and they thought that the German historians are incapable of assessing the role of the individual in determining the course of history. Lamprecht calls his view universal and thus may have prepared the course of Universal History. Marx's conception of history based on class struggle also draws attention to the importance of the role of social factors in history and not to that of an individual. Herbert Spencer writes,

> You must admit that the genesis of the great man depends on the long series of complex influences which has produced the race in which he appears, and the social state into which that race has slowly grown . . . before he can remake his society, his society must make him.[6]

Herbert Spencer makes it very clear that the manifestation of history that he is trying to elaborate and explain is not history as bound by a particular geographical region, or as placed under the authoritarian rule of a kingdom or as determined by any particular period of time. Pramath Nath quotes a passage from Acton's *Lectures on Modern History* (1911). Acton says,

---

4. *Deutsche Geschichte, Moderne Geschichtswissenschaft,* Freiburg i/B, H. Heyfelder, 1905.
5. Sri Aurobindo's *The Human Cycle,* p. 2.
6. English Philosoper, 1820–1903. The significant philosophical ideas of spencer are to be found in the *First Principles* (1862) and *Principles of Ethics* (1879–1893).

> By Universal history I understand that which is distinct from the combined history of all countries, which is not a rope of sand, but is continuous development, and is not burden on the memory, but an illumination of the soul.[7]

This idea of Universal History,[8] we shall see subsequently, is the key concept in the philosophy of history as developed by Pramath Nath or Sri Aurobindo. Sri Aurobindo in his *The Ideal of Human Unity* shows his disapproval for the ordinarily understood notion of history. About that type of history he remarks,

> History teaches us nothing, it is a confused torrent of events and personalities or kaleidoscope of changing institutions. . . . We do not seize the real sense of life in the channels of Time. . . . What we seize are current or recurrent phenomena, facile generalizations, partial ideas.[9]

History as Description and as Explanation

Sri Aurobindo in his *The Human Cycle*[10] refers also to the views of Lamprecht who maintains that human society progresses through certain distinct psychological stages which he calls respectively symbolic, typal, and conventional, both individualist and subjective. Sri Aurobindo observes one of the very important distinctions admitted in philosophy of history is between history as description and as an explanation. Pramath Nath also does not subscribe to the view that history is just a description and this is evident from his agreement with those who going beyond description try to account for or explain and interpret why did an event happen as it did.

---

7. This reference is from *Itihāsa O Abhivyakti*, p. 89.
8. Acton's *Lectures on Modern History*, 1911.
9. *The Ideal of Human Unity*, p. 261.
10. *The Human Cycle*, p. 2.

He makes an interesting distinction between *tathyer bojha,*[11] i.e. burden of information and *tattver alo*[12], i.e. light of truth.

The burden of information that passes for history may hamper the proper task of history. Pramath Nath does not say that the collection of data or facts which is done by the method of repeated observations (*bhuyodarśan*) which is also a part of scientific method, is not important. As history purports to deal with facts, there has been a strong urge to regard history as a natural science like physics, chemistry and others. In the Western philosophy the trend of empiricism was directed towards explaining historical discourses in purely mechanistic terms as domains of causal or functional correlations of human actions and natural processes. The fact is, the role of science in the growth and development of human civilization can never be ignored.

No responsible thinker whether Western or Indian can deny it either. But at the same time to overrate the success story of modern physical science and to be spell-bound by its achievements are not encourageable. This present age is so much overwhelmed by this materialistic expansion of science and its method that it does not care about things or realms over which science cannot reign. Pramath Nath observes that man of this age is only concerned with the this-wordly sentient and the present. This way of looking through the eyes of science has influenced our vision about history. Mostly discussions about the history of states, history of trade and commerce, history of literature and science are trendy in present time. From this observation, it is quite transparent that the present age has accorded more importance to the political-economic tradition of the Western civilization. What can be discovered

---

11. *Itihasa O Abhivyakti,* pp. 15-16.
12. Ibid.

by science and what can be brought by science to our knowledge are endless, but there are questions, searches regarding which science still leaves us wondering. However, with regard to any civilization, developed or destroyed, large or small, the question may be asked, "What is it all for?" It is not mere description of how did one live but also issues and questions relating to the meaning of life are worth considering.

Modern Science and Physical Discoveries

Pramath Nath in his endeavour to rekindle a new paradigm for history also echoes thoughts of Sri Aurobindo as stated in *The Human Cycle,* wherein he says as follows:

> Modern Science obsessed with the greatness of its physical discoveries and the idea of the sole existence of matter, has long attempted to base upon physical data even its study of Soul and Mind and those workings of nature in man and animal in which a knowledge of psychology is important as any of the physical sciences. It is not surprising therefore that in history and sociology attention should have been concentrated on the external data, laws, institutions, rites, customs, economic factors and developments, while the deeper psychological elements so important in the activities of a mental, emotional ideative being like man have been very much neglected."[13]

The new paradigm for history that Pramath Nath was trying to put before us bears similarities with Sri Aurobindo's views in this matter. Pramath Nath maintains what is generally called history concerns itself with the outer or external aspect — it is like dealing with the outer covering or bark of a living tree. If we cannot penetrate through the outer covering of the tree we cannot have any idea about the essence of the tree, its veins through which life flows; unless we track its pulses, we

13. P. 1

cannot reach the root of the tree. It is clear that he does not encourage looking at history from its outer shell, in terms of sickening details of intrigues, dates, facts. This crude outer shell may often make us overlook ever restless and eager expression of life that thrives within it. Pramath Nath makes it clear that it is man, an organic whole, that tries to fulfil itself through those events. According to him *rasa* or savour of history constitutes the inner essence of history and from this *rasa* all desires are born and all impetuses arise.

The proper subject matter of history is the study of man who is capable of knowledge and desire. History establishes a relation of an individual with another individual, of an institution with another institution, of the present with the past and also of the present with the future. It is very important that Pramath Nath does not consider history as only concerned with the past, but also relates to the future. The historical subject is not comparable with the subject of scientific enquiry. Facts of history are not natural events to be measured by dates and time of the present. It can be guessed that some ideas or thoughts enjoy more acceptance, credibility in one age or another. These *bhāva* or thoughts, *dhāraṇā* or ideas and beliefs are to be considered as the life or soul of history. Just by giving catalogues of all events no one can compose history. So-called historical events are so complex that we may not be able to trace all the details even if we proceed very carefully.

Method of Study of Natural Science and History

As a philosopher of history, he tries to find out what should be the method of study in this domain? In this connection he quotes a passage from Bernard Bosanquet's *Social and International Ideals* in favour of his claim that the method of natural science is not the method of history. Bosanquet writes,[14]

---

14. p. 40 (1917).

> In History I do not much doubt that co-operative narrative, directed so far as may be to the main connection of events which seem to have determined evolution, will play a greater and greater part, accompanied by the manual and corpus. But we will not, I think, admit a mere pulverization of great writings into a diamond dust of fact — or rather, we will observe that great works and actual spirits of *de facto* peoples as leading achievements of humanity, whatever the anthropologist — and we will listen attentively — may tell us about the realities of the race. And we shall not forget, I hope, that history, after all, like all other intellectual construction, must depend on the quality of the historian's mind.

Pramath Nath's attitude towards history is very much anti-positivistic as is evident from his rejection of the claim that the method of science and the method of history cannot be the same method. The adoption of the method that has led us to fruitful consequences in the realm of material science will be of no help in the realm of history, for it is not the aim of history to collate facts but to interpret facts. Strata or layers of earth's crust or chemical action and reactions of compounds can be described without reference to consciousness or life. It seems these phenomena are absolutely determined by the laws of motion. They do not have any spontaneity, they move like one billiard ball moving another. In support of his claim, Pramath Nath quotes a few lines from Cardinal Newman's writing which runs as follows: "Physical science never travels beyond the examination of cause and effect . . . The physicist will never ask himself by what influence, external to the universe, the universe is sustained."[15] But the data of history are never of this sort. He cites a quotation from Bosanquet to substantiate his viewpoint:

15. Cardinal Newman, "Christianity and Physical Science," p. 33.

> He (professional historian) is soon superseded; for touching but a few points in a vast fabric of life, he soon has to yield to deeper and more complex researches . . ..[16]

According to Pramath Nath events are external shell of history. Varied emotions of the soul, sorrows and desires are the birthplace of events that occur. Science, especially physical science, is pre-occupied with measurement, but historical facts are not measurable or calculable.

Historical Events Influenced by Associated Conditions

In the case of history, events are influenced by the totality of associating conditions but it can never be claimed that by all those conditions any historical event is absolutely determined. Man's desire, frustrations, emotions are behind all those events also. A seed of a tree definitely depends upon environmental factors for its growth but Pramath Nath points out that the seed must have some urge within itself for its growth and development. Apart from its own internal nature, the seed does not borrow this impetus for growth and development from something else. All historical events are like this, they are said to be organic in nature. Just by enumerating or analysing external factors it is not possible to explain these historical events. Behind all these external factors, some hidden force, or vital impulses wake up and become restless. In the language of the *Tantra*, it is said to be *ucchanavasthā,*[17] or swelled condition of *bīja* (seed) or *bindu,* when it is ready to create. Historical events are always viewed as expressions of life and product of life. Pramath Nath thinks that behind all historical events something is trying to express itself. In his opinion that is the soul of history and outer events are like the *śarīra*, i.e. body of history. Thus it can be said that in the

---

16. An address delivered to the London School of Sociology and Social Economics, 1911.
17. *Itihasa O Abhivyakti,* Chapter 5.

eyes of Pramath Nath history of the world is none other than the history of progress of *ātmā* or consciousness and it is our objective to study this progress. Philosophers of history may be classified into three broad groups according to the type of pattern they decipher in past events: they may view history either as linear, or cyclical repeating itself in subsequent periods of time or as chaotic with no definite order or plan. From the writings of Pramath Nath a linear approach to history is quite evident. Among the notable philosophers of history like Hegel and others also a linear approach to history is observable. Hegel believed that history proceeds in a line, hence linear. For those who hold linear theory, history is a process that unfolds towards a final goal. Hegel's belief in progress was also shared by Marx and both of them see progress of history as the outcome of a dialectic in which factors working in opposite directions are reconciled. Marx viewed the struggle of thesis, antithesis and the resultant synthesis as always taking place in materialistic economy.

Philosophers Differ Over the Exact Idea of Progress

It is to be seen that the very concept of progress is a controversial word and often different philosophers of history differ over the exact connotation of progress. It has been remarked that the concept of progress is the product of the ideas derived from the period of Enlightenment. Kant also believed in a kind of progress in history. According to him the hidden plan of history may be to provide conditions in which men move from barbarism to culture. Pramath Nath in his *Itihasa O Abhivyakti* quotes from Guizot's History of Civilization, vol. I, wherein Guizot says,

> For my own part, I am convinced that there is in reality, a general destiny of humanity, a transmission of the aggregate

> of civilizations; and consequently, a universal history of civilization to be written.[18]

Sri Aurobindo in his *The Human Cycle*, refers to the views of Lamprecht, the German historian who believes that human society progresses through certain distinct psychological stages which are called as symbolic, typal and conventional, individualist and subjective. Sri Aurobindo observes that Lamprecht's views suggest that a civilization passes through certain psychological stages. Sri Aurobindo does not think that dissecting any civilization into watertight compartments is feasible. However, the phrases employed by Lamprecht to describe psychological stages of the growth of civilization appear to be quite suggestive. To this scheme of Lamprecht, Sri Aurobindo includes the necessity of spiritual transformation which is absent in the former scheme of classification.[19] The subjective stage, the last one of a social cycle may find its fruition in a spiritualized society. Sri Aurobindo would like to incorporate a spiritualistic element in history.

In *The Ideal of Human Unity*,[20] Sri Aurobindo looks upon history as the progressive revelation and manifestation of the absolute spirit in and through time. In Sri Aurobindo's views man's destiny is to attain a divine life on the earth. This admission or realization that history is not mere narration of materialistic elements is important in grasping the views of Pramath Nath as well. Pramath Nath as a speculative philosopher of history tries to find a pattern behind all historical events and considers it an objective of a historian to discover that hidden pattern lying behind the given one. In his view history cannot wholly rely on observations and

---

18. Vol I, pp. 4-5. This reference is obtained from *Itihāsa O Abhivyākti, p.* 14.
19. Chapters XXI-XXIV, *The Human Cycle.*
20. Sri Aurobindo Ashram Trust, Pondicherry, 1971.

experiments, and he concludes it will be wrong to suppose that history is an inductive science. He states categorically that we need to apply deductive method in history. Hence we need some fundamental principles to function as premisses.

Who is a True Historian?

Who in the opinion of Pramath Nath is a true historian? To state Pramath Nath's view,

> One who is expert in the worship of Vaiśvānara is a true historian."[21]

According to the Upaniṣads, the individual cannot be conceived apart from the universe. According to the *Chāndogya Upaniṣad* the individual should realize his unity with Vaiśvānara, the universal-self. As Vaiśvānara, the individual realizes his unity not with all human beings but with all the living beings and with the whole universe. This is the gist of Vaiśvānaravidyā. In this connection, Mukhopadhyay is very much influenced by the Upaniṣadic thoughts and he derived his conception of the Vaiśvānara, which may be translated as the Universal Consciousness from the *Chāndogya Upaniṣad*.

In the *Chāndogya Upaniṣad*, the Vaiśvānara is a metaphysical concept; it is understood as the ultimate, which is essentially consciousness, spirit of *Ātman* inherent in all beings. In the *Chāndogya Upaniṣad* we find the anecdote of different sages, who, having not yet realized the ultimate, regard space as *Ātman*, or sun as *ātman*, or wind as *Ātman*, or water as *Ātman*, or sky as *Ātman*. These piecemeal approaches to *Ātman* are not able to comprehend the *Ātman* in its complete perfection.

Mukhopadhyay would like to project a historian or the *itihāsavid* as one who tries to achieve unification with the universal consciousness. His view of history is thus very much

---

21. *Itihasa O Abhivyakti*, p. 103.

coloured by his metaphysical belief and thus history for him is actually progress through the paths of *puruṣārthas*, pursuits of human life — *dharma, artha, kāma* and to the final *puruṣārtha, mokṣa*. Sri Aurobindo also develops his view of history from a metaphysical perspective of a divine life on earth. Sri Aurobindo looks upon man as a spirit encased in matter; the individual is looked upon as conscious power of the Eternal, and the goal of the individual is the realization of his unity with the totality of the *Brahman*. History records the movement of man as such towards accomplishing the completeness of this Eternal Consciousness.

Bibliography

Aurobindo, *The Human Cycle, The Ideal of Humanity, War and Self-determination*, Pondicherry: Sri Aurobindo Ashram, 1971.

Danto, Arthur C., *Analytical Philosophy of History*, Cambridge: Cambridge University Press, 1968.

Dray, William H., ed., *Philosophical Analysis and History*, New York and London: Harper and Row, 1966.

Kant, Immanuel, *The Idea for a Universal History from a Cosmopolitan Point of View*, Translation by White Beck, The Bobbs-Merrill Co., 1963.

Mukhopadhyay, Pramath Nath, *Itihasa O Abhiyakti*, (Philosophy of History with special Reference to the Culture-Life of Ancient India), National Council of Education, Bengal: Jadavpur University, 1991.

Reddy, Madhusudan, *Meta-History — The Unfoldment and Fulfilment of Human Destiny*, Aurodarshan Trust, 1984.

9

Some Renaissance Aspects of Vivekananda's Thoughts

Tirthanath Bandyopadhyay

THE idea I want to float is that Vivekananda, in an important sense, can be deemed to be a renaissance man. Renaissance, as we know, basically designates the revival of art and literature under the influence of classical models in the fourteenth-sixteenth centuries. It is believed that this revival would enhance the human condition as a whole. So understood, this revival may be regarded as a humanistic one. By the same token, a man may be deemed to be a renaissance thinker if his thoughts involve something which would foster some worthwhile betterment of the human condition through certain socio-cultural reformations.

Now I think there are some such thoughts scattered in Vivekananda's writings. I shall choose three of such thoughts. One, his emphasis on the universality dimension of morality. Second, his view on caste system. And third, his notion of *dharma*. I shall deal with them in the following and try to show that these are of great importance to all humanity and will help us to constitute a higher plane of existence for humanity.

Universality of Morality

The universality of morality amounts to the claim that moral views are meant to be universally valid, that is, they are to be applicable to all normal human adults. The significance of this contention lies in its demand that no one is morally entitled to go against moral requirements on grounds of one's own personal benefit, and in this way this article arrests the possibility of exploitation of man by man.

Now, Vivekananda affirms the universality of morality by his conviction that the same "universal soul" is equally present in each human being, so that each of us is one with the universal soul and hence one with each other. Obviously, this realization should lead man to have the same sort of regard for others as the one he has for himself, which ultimately means that we all are equal. This recognition in turn should breed in us the thought that each one is to be treated in the same manner as oneself. This we may call the principle of human oneness, and it is one of the cardinal principles of Vivekananda's overall thoughts. What this principle boils down to is that nothing could be truly harmful or good to me without, all things equal, being so to others, and vice versa. This being so, to harm any other person is to harm oneself. Vivekananda expresses this point when he says that "in injuring his neighbour, the individual actually injures himself." (Swami Vivekananda, "Vedanta as a Factor in Civilization" in *The Complete Works of Swami Vivekananda,* (henceforth *CWSV*), Advaita Ashrama, Calcutta, vol. I, 1984, p. 385). He further asserts: "As manifested beings, we appear to be separate; but our reality is one, ... From this monistic principle we get at the basis of ethics, and I venture to say that we cannot get any ethics from anywhere else." ("Practical Vedanta III" in *CWSV*, vol. I, p. 334). This clearly suggests that no ethics can afford to limit its scope to a part of humanity. And it immediately follows that none is, under normal circumstances, entitled to claim a moral stand which is valid exclusively for oneself. No maxim is a moral maxim unless it is universally applicable. This position would clearly prevent one from maltreating others and thus would surely tend to promote betterment of mankind as a whole.

Feeling of Brotherhood

Vivekanada wants to authenticate the doctrine of our basic oneness with each other by affirming a very intimate relationship of us with each other — which he calls the relationship of **brotherhood**. And Vivekananda regards this relationship not as a moral ideal but as a **fact:** We **are** brothers of each other. It is only by being guided by the sense of universal brotherhood in our daily interpersonal activities that we can ensure an **enduring** human fellowship. In order to secure fellowship, it is crucial that one would not appeal to human brotherhood on one level but practise egoism on another level. Brotherhood is bound up with co-operation and it is not to be found in escape from commitments to others, but in one's essential relations with others.

A cautionary observation is in order here. In treating **brotherhood** as the manifestation of our **oneness,** we must not take any of them in its literal sense, for in that case the position would involve absurdity. No man can literally be identical with his brother. So I should want to give an intellectually tolerable interpretation of Vivekananda's view. It might be agreed that the doctrine of our oneness, as per Vivekananda's arguments, amounts to the truth that the universal soul is not only present in each one of us but, more importantly, constitutes the essence of each of us. This may be interpreted as the position that, although as individual **jivas** we are different, we all have evolved out of the same Soul. Thus viewed, we all owe our individual being to the same

Soul and in that way we all are on the same level as human individuals. We all are brothers. In fact, one might argue on behalf of Vivekananda that in order to reckon that we are **equal**, it is not necessary to treat ourselves as literally identical with one another. The recognition that we all belong to the same Soul and hence are persons in the same identical sense would seem to be effective enough to spawn in us that feeling of intimacy or closeness to each other which we are expected to have for our brothers. So once we seriously recognize ourselves as **brothers**, we would readily become inclined to treat each other on equal terms. Thus, this recognition would tend to create and sustain in each of us a psychological climate conducive to the obtainment of human equality — so essential to the emergence of a befitting human community. For one thing, the realization that we all are brothers would promote in each of us an effective tendency to care for others. For, as Vivekananda observes, ". . . can man degrade his brother and himself escape degradation? (*Swami Vivekananda*: *Caste, Culture and Societies*, henceforth *CCS*, Advaita Ashrama, 1970, p. 40). So, given the realization of mutual brotherhood, we can scarcely remain callous to one another. On the contrary, this realization would prompt us to become more readily and reliably **available** to each other, in that, in terms of this fraternal mentality or attitude, we all would come to have an "inner readiness" to help others in their need ungrudgingly.

All this embodies the point that the universality of morality, ultimately, exhorts us not simply to live **among** others but — more importantly — to live **with** others. And it needs little effort to realize that not the former but the latter mode of living is essential to the emergence of a truly **humane** community.

Caste System

Vivekananda's view on caste system draws largely on his conception of **dharma**. **Dharma**, as Vivekananda conceives of it, does not lie simply in learning our moral duties but in our performing those on appropriate occasions as well. Now Vivekananda distinguishes between two kinds of **dharma**: (i) **Jāti-dharma**, i.e. the **dharma** "enjoined according to the different castes"; and (ii) **Svadharma**, i.e. "one's own *dharma*, or set of duties prescribed for man according to his capacity and position." (Cf. "The East and the West" in *CWSV*, vol. V, p. 455). It is to be observed that Vivekananda does not take ***jāti-dharma*** to mean or entail the view that the **so-called** higher castes are entitled to appropriate to themselves all privileges. In fact, Vivekananda does not accept the view that people own their castes just through their birth — castes are not hereditary. Vivekananda finds no rational grounds in support of the hereditary caste system; on the contrary, he believes it to be a severe hindrance to human progress. The hereditary caste system seems to derive its rationale from the presumption that qualities yield to birth in **all** the succeeding generations. This presumption Vivekananda finds wrong. In his opinion, "qualities yield to birth in two or three generations." (*CCS*, p. 14). And hence he holds: ". . . The son of a brāhmaṇa is not necessarily always a brāhmaṇa; though there is every possibility of his being one, he may not become so." ("Conversations and Dialogues" in *CWSV*, vol. V, pp. 376-77.) For, it is highly unlikely that an ancestor who had merit would, of necessity, bequeath it to his descendants. The latter need to acquire it for themselves. Since talents are not hereditary, and since birth is not a **deed** of the one who is born, no one can make, on grounds of birth alone, any special claim to his excellence. If so, there should be no **hereditary** inequity or favouritism.

Divide Caste Not by Birth But by Qualities

Vivekananda's view as regards caste would not incur any such injustice. For, he does not believe that man is at birth programmed to live in certain ways, only requiring to reveal certain talents which he just inherits. Vivekananda rather deems it proper to classify people into different castes, not on the basis of their birth, but on the basis of their individual qualities, that is the qualities which one owns as a **particular person** and not as a member of a specific caste or class. Individuals do differ in their capacities and talents in various ways, but no one receives any capacity or talent just from one's birth. The reason is simple: No caste has any exclusive territory of qualities. So membership in a caste is not had by birth, and a person can change his caste by birth by developing and sustaining in himself the appropriate qualities. Vivekananda has no condemnation for caste system based on people's individual abilities and occupations. So conceived, Vivekananda's notion of caste system would accommodate diversity of capacity and occupation but no **privilege**. By **privilege** he means the "enjoyment of advantage over another" (*CCS*, p. 46). And he observes: "The difficulty is not that one body of men are naturally more intelligent than another, but whether this body of men, because they have the advantage of intelligence, should take away even physical enjoyment from those who do not possess that advantage. The fight is to destroy that privilege." ("Privilege" in *CWSV*, vol. I, p. 435). Vivekananda is thus not against variety of castes but against any privileged caste. He thus comes out with the view that ". . . whenever privilege is broken down, more and more light and progress come to race." ("Vedanta and Privilege" in *CWSV*, vol. I, p. 423).

Untouchability is A Social Evil

Put differently, Vivekananda does not endorse the view that men are **racially** classed as superior and inferior. One does not have to be an astrologer to foresee that any rigid or static caste system would almost inevitably lead to the rise of permanently privileged classes. Indeed, it is this conviction that leads Vivekananda to repudiate the practice of privilege-allocation on the basis of heredity. This custom readily gives birth to many notorious social evils, such as untouchability. Vivekananda considers untouchability to be "an orthodox superstition which has interfered with national efficiency all along the line." ("Reawakening of Hinduism on a National Basis," Interviews, in *CWSV*, vol. V, p. 226).

This suggests that Vivekananda acknowledges no basic **discrimination** between man and man, so that no one would be morally or humanly be justified in handling others in the way in which he would not, in his senses, allow himself to be handled by others. Needless to say, this kind of social or interpersonal climate would pave the way for what may be termed a "humanly just society." For, in such a community no one would be considered **innately** superior or inferior to anyone else, which, therefore, would permit everybody to develop their individual qualities. So understood, Vivekananda may be said to show a pathway to human society of a free or open kind.

Three Qualities of a Man

Let me explain the view in more detail. Vivekananda believes that the three **guṇas** or qualities — **sattva**, **rajas** and **tamas** — are inherent in different degrees in each man and form in their combinations the basis of the distinction of the different classes of people, namely, **brāhmaṇas**, **kṣatriyas**, **vaiśyas** and **śūdras**. (Cf. "Conversations and Dialogues", X, in *CWSV*, vol. V, p. 337). But, and this is crucial, a person does not, of necessity, simply inherit the combinatorial whole of the said qualities that he owns. Consequently, the boundaries between different castes are not static. By relativizing in this way the caste-boundaries, Vivekananda strikes at the very root of any rationalization in defence of the view that people gain their rights and privileges through their birth or fate. This point is echoed in his following remark: "The idea that one man is born superior to another has no meaning . . ." ("Vedanta and Privilege" in *CWSV*, vol. I, p. 423). In a word, no one is privileged. No one is "born to serve" and no one is "born to lead." Castes thus, as Vivekananda understands, become **human** rather than **social** categories, and hence flexible rather than rigid groupings.

Vivekananda's contention that no one is born with hereditary prerogative, thus entails that the predominance of one or the other of the aforesaid three **guṇas** is due not to the chance of a person being born within a specific caste but is flexible. Vivekananda thus holds: "The same power is in every man, one manifesting more, the other less. The same potentiality is in everyone." ("Vedanta and Privilege" in *CWSV*, vol. I, p. 423). So, at times, one or the other of the three **guṇas** predominates in man in varying degrees and is manifested accordingly. Consequently, man in different pursuits acquires membership of different classes. When he is engaged in serving others for pay, he acquires **śūdrahood**; when he is busy in transacting some piece of business for profit, he acquires **vaiśyahood**; when he fights against wrong doing, he acquires **kṣatriyahood**; and when he contemplates or is in **dhyāna**, he acquires **brāhmaṇahood**. This is why Vivekananda concludes: ". . . it is quite possible for one to be changed from one caste to another" ("Conversations and Dialogues", X, in *CWSV*, vol. V, p. 377).

Prevalence of Rigid Social Network

Vivekananda's view on caste system thus may well undergo changes and hence may be viewed as a polemic against the sterile and stereotyped conception of "caste society" in which mobility of individuals among different social classes is excluded and the socio-economic status of an individual is fully determined by his origin. The free association of individuals on the basis of common values or interests is often thwarted by allegiance determined by birth in a particular caste. In such a rigid social network, people only swim with the social current instead of providing new directions in public life. To be sure, such a social set-up would tend to artificially restrict the natural unfolding of the qualities inherent in the individual. As this sort of caste system would put a barrier to the best service the individual could have rendered to the society, it would in effect put a barrier to human progress. But since in the caste system, as conceived by Vivekananda, there prevails the opportunity of moving from one social class to another so that there should be no definitive association between caste and occupation, there can be no job or status fixed a priori for any person. A **brāhmaṇa** (by birth) may be a good office worker, even a hand labourer, as readily as a priest. This is why I have remarked that Vivekananda's conception of caste system makes room for a society of an open kind.

As Vivekananda states: "All the members of a society ought to have the same opportunity for obtaining wealth, education or knowledge." (*CCS*, p. 79). So, in Vivekananda's view, all are equal as persons — no matter whatever occupation one is efficient in. Clearly, this kind of attitude towards work would leave no space for inherent antagonism between works or professions. By the same token, it would make it possible for more and more individuals to reach for their full potential in any discipline that is apt for them. More so, because this kind of outlook would pave the way for the increasing emergence of new occupations — manual as well as non-manual. As a consequence, people would be able to render their best service to the society, and society as a whole can only benefit. Furthermore, this would tend to make us free from the narrow disciplinary parochialism that bedevils our interpersonal life, especially when there exists a disparity in respect of economic standing.

Dignity of Work

This requires that individuals be serious enough in carrying out their jobs. So Vivekananda cautions that no one of any profession is to be esteemed valuable unless he tries hard and sincerely enough to do his job efficiently. As he puts the point: ". . . a man should not be judged by the nature of his duties, but by the manner in which he does them. His manner of doing them and his power to do them are indeed the test of a man. A shoemaker who can turn out a strong, nice pair of shoes in the shortest possible time is a better man, according to his profession and work, than a professor who talks nonsense everyday of his life." (On Karma-Yoga in *CWSV*, vol. V, pp. 239-40).

As is well known, Vivekananda vouches for the dignity of work as such. A sincere and efficient man of any profession is a man of value. Any such worker contributes to the good of the society. So conceived, occupations can hardly become the bases of inequalities and conflicts associated with differences of occupation. Someone may argue against this argument by pointing out that it is just not true that every kind of profession is good for the society. So the idea that professions are made good by the sincerity and efficiency with which they are executed becomes suspect. This being so, Vivekananda would need to indicate some grounds for deciding which profession is good for the society and which is not. But then I must confess that, to my knowledge, Vivekananda has not tackled this issue in any of his writings — not at least quite explicitly.

Nevertheless, subject to revision, I believe that he would agree to the view that a profession would scarcely be deemed good or valuable if it causes, in some way or other, harm to the people at large. To put the point the other way around, only that sort of profession is valuable which, in some important way, brings good to the broad social interest — especially to the poor class. And if anyone executes such a profession sincerely and efficiently, without ever making any effort to shirk what his work requires him to do, then he should be deemed a man of value.

Vivekananda's Notion of Dharma

In this section, I shall discuss Vivekananda's notion of **dharma**, thereby trying to show how it fosters human wellbeing. Vivekananda does not endorse an anaemic kind of **dharma** that consists in passively abiding by the stereotyped codes of conduct spoken of in the traditional caste system. **Dharma** is not indoctrination. **Dharma** must not remain apathetic to social agonies, and hence it should be what would constitute the paths to the expunction of the prevailing social wrongdoings, yielding thereby the betterment of people as a whole. In short, **dharma**, to worth its name, must express and confirm itself in the service of humanity. Vivekananda puts this point thus: "You may invent an image through which to worship God, but a better image already exists, the living man. You may build a temple in which to worship God, and that may be good, but a better one, a much higher one, already exists, the human body."("Practical Vedanta II" in *CWSV*, vol. II, p. 313).

Vivekananda, in this context, makes a very important observation. He exhorts us not to serve people condescendingly. While helping the poor, if someone flaunts his wealth, he misses the very point of charity, in that the befitting objective of charity is not to manufacture in the mind of the poor a sense of inferiority or hopelessness. In the help of this kind, what the helped one needs is money, and not another person; here money becomes the bond between them, a bond which takes on a life of its own and does not so much unite them as separate them. As a consequence, they fail to enter into a **human** relationship, fail to be **brothers** of each other. In light of all this, the true objective of helping the poor should be to help them to stand on their feet; as we shall shortly see, Vivekananda endorses this view.

True Help Means Helping Oneself

Vivekananda tells us not to serve people in the hope of gaining honour and admiration for ourselves. He puts this point thus: "One looks for name and fame and covers his efforts to obtain them with the enamel of charity and good works. He is working for himself under the pretext of working for others. Every so-called charity is an encouragement of the very evil it claims to operate against." ("The Practice of Religion" in *CWSV*, vol. VI, p. 101). As Vivekananda sees, to truly help others amounts to rendering help or service to oneself. For, in and through doing good to the world, one invariably undergoes oneself "moral excellence" (Cf. Karma-Yoga in *CWSV*, vol. I, p. 75); doing good to others, thus, gives one the opportunity to better oneself, all "good acts tend to make us pure and perfect." (Karma-Yoga in *CWSV*, vol. I, p. 76). Needless to say, the realization of this point would, in all likelihood, prompt one to help and serve others more readily than one would otherwise be inclined to.

For uplifting and bettering the condition of the downtrodden, Vivekananda thinks it essential to educate them in the proper manner, so that they could come to realize that they too have a right to welfare and thus come to develop the required determination to fight for themselves. Hence Vivekananda opines: "The only service to be done for our lower classes is to give them education, **to develop their lost individuality**." ("Our Duty to the Masses", in *CWSV*, vol. IV, 1978, p. 362). To enable the downtrodden to struggle for themselves, it is important to inculcate in their mind the sense that there is no essential difference between them and other people, that all **are** brothers and hence are kins of each other. This realization would help the downtrodden to come out of their sense of inferiority and indignity, so that the emancipation of them into **human beings** would eventually take place. As a result, they would become self-confident and self-reliant, and in the process would be able to meet their needs — along with developing within themselves the important mentality that their pain and misery must be regarded as warnings which it would be dangerous to disregard.

True Dharma Aims at Removing Ills

Be that as it may, in Vivekananda's opinion, **dharma** requires us to render service to the poor in concrete and specific terms, **and** to make them realize that they deserve this service. **Dharma** or duty, then, must aim at eliminating **real** miseries of **particular** individuals, and never by being guided by the condescending attitude.

Vivekananda's understanding of *dharma* is then imbued with a very important element — the element of this-worldiness, in that **dharma** must aim at enhancing the conditions of human beings in general, and of the poor class in particular, **in this world**. Vivekananda pronounces: "Who cares whether there is a heaven or a hell; who cares if there is a soul or not; who cares if there is an unchangeable or not? Here is the world, and it is full of miseries. Go out into it . . ., and struggle to lessen it or die in the attempt . . . this is the first lesson to be learnt, whether you are a theist or an atheist, whether you are an agnostic or a Vedantist, a Christian or a Mohammedan." ("Practical Vedanta" in *CWSV*, vol. II, p. 353).

Vivekananda's notion of **dharma** is thus humanistic in the most realistic or mundane sense.

Conclusion

I would like to conclude this essay with the following remark, which I think I am entitled to make upon the preceding observations. Vivekananda holds, as we have seen, three views: (i) There is a potential universality to moral claims in that moral views are intended to be universally valid; and hence no one is entitled, by invoking some moral maxim allegedly valid for oneself alone, to obtain any gain at the expense of others. Obviously, this would make it impossible for anyone to use a moral maxim simply as an instrument for oppressing others; (ii) castes are not inborn but have to be earned by individuals themselves, so that no one is allowed, by birth alone, to enjoy caste-related benefits over others; and (iii) **dharma** is a practical pursuit in that it is to be substantiated in terms of the sincere endeavour to render service in concrete terms to actual individuals.

Now I incline to think, as I have tried to argue, that these three views, if acted upon, that is, if they become a vital part of people's lives, would help us a lot to equate humanism by resolving or at least lessening the antagonism between man and man and in this way to develop and sustain a humanly better world in which there may be enough for everybody's need but never enough for somebody's greed. To be sure, in such a world, there would be people whose rights and concerns would not be constrained by race, caste, creed or gender, but would be safeguarded on humanitarian considerations. Given all this, Vivekananda may well be deemed to be a renaissance man — or so it seems to me. I want to say something more. Inasmuch as the goal of forming a humanly better world can hardly be ignored or denied at any developmental stage of man or society, Vivekananda's aforesaid thoughts would seem apposite to any human society, and in these terms, Vivekananda may also be deemed to be a man of any era. So we may end up with the claim that Vivekananda may be reckoned to be an eternal and hence always a contemporary renaissance man.

Abbreviations

CWSV — *The Complete Works of Swami Vivekananda.*

CCS — Swami Vivekananda, *Caste, Culture and Societies.*

10

The Western Imperialistic Challenge

Aurobindo, Tilak and Gokhale

Aparna Banerjee

THE great men whose views I have discussed in this paper belong to a vast spectrum of thinkers who have influenced the nationalist movement in India. Since I have presented my views with reference mainly to Sri Aurobindo, Tilak and Gokhale, this is bound to delimit the scope of even some of the basic concerned issues. I have explored the differences between these three great nationalists in terms of their reaction to the West, which was rooted in their encounter with it. It was not possible for any of them to discard the Western perspective completely and look at it from a prior unexplored position. The anglicized underpinnings in their political thought are more than evident. But unlike Tilak and Gokhale, Sri Aurobindo seems to have been more successful in overcoming it in a way that could be both Indian and yet could legitimately accommodate different ways of being without threatening them. The solution that he found ultimately lay in his theory of spiritual evolution.

Meaning of "Western Imperialistic Challenge"

The phrase "Western Imperialistic Challenge" has more than one layer of meaning. It is not only about political domination but also about cultural domination. The Indian nationalists had been fighting against the British rule after being "awakened" by European thought about nation, notion of liberty and equality. A sense of lack and urgency of finding Indian identity led to a division between the liberal nationalists like Gokhale on the one hand and the national revolutionaries like Sri Aurobindo and Tilak on the other.

While, the spirit of nationalism animated both the liberal nationalists and the national revolutionaries, they held fundamentally different views about the nation. But, it is interesting to note that a sense of deficiency worked in both the reformist and the revolutionary imagination. The reformists of the nineteenth century wanted to prepare the country out of its ignorance and false consciousness. The revolutionary often saw in this the threat of a loss of self-identity and wanted to go back to the past to revive the glory of the nation.

The "Pull" of Westernization

The reformist dilemma is more than evident in the nineteenth century. Bengali writer Bankim Chandra Chattopadhyay, who, in spite of his wholehearted commitment to the spirit of Hinduism, exposed many inequalities institutionalized within the Hindu society and did not hesitate to point out how inequality and servitude permeate through the whole society, while Europe and America were in a far better condition. Yet at the same time he could not accept the European and American brands of equality in toto. This is particularly evident in his discussion of gender equality. Gokhale and his mentor Ranade had been in the same predicament, who in their personal lives had to go through the pain of this double pull repeatedly.[1]

---

1. Gokhale had a very early marriage at the age of fourteen. See T.V. Parvate, 1959, *Gopal Krishna Gokhale*, Ahmedabad : Navajivan Publishing House, p. 471. Ranade married within a month of the →

We can illustrate this pull of Westernization and the quest for self-identity and self-respect with the help of an example. The case of raising up the age of marriage of girls had opened up a lot of controversy. Gokhale, and even Ranade, who was deeply religious, wanted the change. But Tilak protested vigorously against State intervention in matters of social and religious practices.

In fact, after the Age of Consent Bill was enacted, Tilak suggested the formation of *Dharma Rakshani Sabha* (Society for the Perservation of Religion). He said that the purpose of organizing such a society was protecting our society, our institutions and our civilization from being crushed under the heels of — here he uses the phrase — "the so-called" nineteenth century civilization.

British Education Policy Criticized

Gopal Krishna Gokhale was no less critical of the British Government in spite of favouring various social reforms. In the fifth National Congress he said, education, meaning Western education, had merely put a tongue in the mouths of the formerly dumb people and the people of the educated class were the spokespersons of the country. He added that it was unwarranted on the part of the British administrators who lived secluded and luxurious lives, to claim that they knew more about the wants and wishes of the masses of India than the educated Indians who were in daily contact with their countrymen.[2] In the Indian National Congress at Calcutta he spoke for reducing the Salt Tax because it pressed heavily on the Indian masses. He also pointed out the heavy burden

→ death of his first wife, a girl of twelve, at the age of thirty-two. See A. Sharma, 2002, *Modern Hindu Thought: The Essential Texts*, New Delhi: Oxford University Press p. 156.

2. *Sarvajanik Sabha*, Quarterly Journal, January 1980, p. 8.

of Income Tax on the poorer people of the country. His patriotism and concern for the country is thus unquestionable.

However, his mode of appeal is sometimes conciliatory, appealing to the sense of justice of the Government of India. For example, at the second Bombay provincial conference, he had moved the resolution against the reduction of Government expenditure on education. But while doing so he expressed his great faith in Western learning as a liberating force in India, and his trust in the British nation that it was her noblest instinct to deliberately prefer to instruct the people of India in Western learning.[3]

Boycott of British Goods

It may be noted that Gokhale was not a coward. After the partition of Bengal, when as a protest the boycott of British goods had started, he was sent by the Congress to England to campaign, along with Lajpat Rai. Since the boycott and the Swadeshi movement had spread a feeling of anger among the British people, especially in Manchester, he was warned by his well-wishers not to go there. But Gokhale was not perturbed. Addressing the people there, he said that he realized how much the people there suffered on account of the boycott. But he asked them to imagine how much more the Indian people have suffered in their own country being at the mercy of the British officials who are sent there to govern them.

Yet in spite of his boldness and patriotism, he had deep faith in British ideals of liberalism, equality and fraternity. His dream was to build a reformed modern India on the basis of such ideals. At the same time, he was aware that the anti-foreign feeling in the country could load the scales heavily on

3. Proceedings of the Second Bombay Provincial Conference, May 1889.

Tilak's side.[4] This is why after Tilak's release from jail in 1914 the two sides in spite of their genuine attempt could not reconcile. The feelings of lack or deficiency did not have a convergence which was one of the reasons that made the Indian nationalist movement complex in character.

Tilak Professed Vedic Theory

The task of the revolutionary leaders was not easy either. They needed to unify the people with a common nationalist feeling. Bal Gangadhar Tilak sought to do this by reminding them of their past glory. He undertook the project of writing Vedic history. In spite of his revolutionary spirit, he too, no doubt suffered from a sense of urgency to deal with the problem of re-establishing the Indian identity at a time when circumstances made India come closely under the Western civilizational impact. He had to prove to the Europeans as well as to his countrymen, many of whom were already exposed to the influence of Europe, the antiquity of the present Indian history within the Western model by providing evidences that could be acceptable as historical evidences as distinct from myths, to the "Westernized" readers. He worked out the thesis of the antiquity of the Vedas to a period not later than 4000 BCE by means of astronomical data recorded in the hymns. He wrote a masterly book, *The Orion,* in 1833 on the subject. In his second book, *The Arctic Home in the Vedas,* Tilak went further to determine the antiquity of the Vedas with the help of geology. His argument was that the primitive Aryan home was in the Arctic region. He professed to prove that the level of civilization attained by the Aryans before 8000 BCE was higher than that of the culture of the Stone Age or even that of the age of metals. Tilak argued that the Hindu

---

4. He had expressed this view in a letter to Annie Besant, dated 26th January, 1915.

theological claim that the Vedas were eternal without a beginning could thus be proved on scientific and historical grounds.

Commenting on Tilak's thesis of Vedic history, Wolpert wrote: "In a land where antiquity was generally equated with superiority, few contributions to the inflation of the national ego were of greater significance than Tilak's attempt to prove that his Aryan forebear had not merely been among the first people to attain a high level of civilization, but actually planted the seed of civilized existence in the world."[5]

The tendency of the Europeans to see the whole enterprise as an attempt to cover up a lack is discernible in these comments. The British had already represented the Indian past through a periodization of the ancient, medieval and the modern. The medieval was called "despotic" and the modern "the rule of law." The imperial ideology was to label the native as not mature enough (which actually means Europeanized enough) for political freedom. But precisely because borrowed European concept of freedom or liberty was not enough to inspire the educated Indians, some Hindus looked for their own identity in Vedanta philosophy. The emphasis was on *Karma-Yoga* — action as a detached duty, rather than on spiritual liberation. Active self-realization through service for the society was propagated as the true message of Vedanta philosophy. Vivekananda was the advocate of this new thought.

Unification Through Popular Religions

Now, although such philosophical reflections had roused nationalist feelings in the educated Indians, Tilak realized that the masses could be inspired for self-governance and brought

5. A. S. Wolpert, 1962, *Tilak and Gokhale: Revolution and Reforms in the Making of Modern India*, Berkeley: University of California Press. pp. 64-65.

together on the basis of popular religion. Just as in Bengal, the hymn of the Bengali national revolutionaries was "Bande Mataram," in Maharashtra, Tilak organized festivals in honour of the popular God Ganapati. Similarly, the great Maratha hero Shivaji's fight against the Mughal Emperor Aurangzeb was taken to be analogous to the fight against British foreign rule. His strategy was to unify the Indian society through the feeling of *Hindutva*.

It should not be hastily concluded that Tilak wanted to exclude the Muslim people from the nationalist movement. In fact, while addressing the congregation of Shivaji Festival in Bengal he is on record to have said that a great hero like Shivaji could have been Mohammedan.[6] Similarly, towards the end of 1916, in the Joint Session of the Indian National Congress and the Muslim League at Lucknow, Tilak had moved a resolution to the effect that if the British were prepared to leave the country and wanted to hand over the reigns of the country into the hands of the Muslims, the Hindus should not have any objection. Tilak had realized that the nationalist unity could be strengthened or reinstated by recalling an antecedent culture or history. But evidently such a strategy can also be malignant causing a sense of exclusion in the minorities. This is particularly true of a country like India with its variety of languages, customs and religions. This seems to be the main limitation of his programme of the nationalist movement.

Aurobindo's Affinity With Bal, Pal

Sri Aurobindo had started his political career as a nationalist revolutionary and sided with Tilak. His agitation against the partition of Bengal was carried out in his writings in the English weekly called *Bande Mataram.* He had affinity of thought with

6. *Mahārāṭhā*, 24th June, 1906.

such political leaders as Lokmanya Bal Gangadhar Tilak and Bipin Chandra Pal, belonging to the extremist division of the Congress, who aimed at freeing India through revolutionary acts. In an article written in 1907, he refers to the *Gītā* to show that Hinduism has not made the impossible demand that the masses of mankind should rise to a level of saintliness and tolerance towards the oppressors. Thus he says, "Politics is the field of the kṣatriya and the morality of the kṣatriya ought to govern our political actions. To impose on politics the Brāhmanical duty of saintly sufferance, is to preach *varnasaṅkara*."[7]

The main flaw in the programme of social renovation of the liberal reformists in his view was that what they were aiming at was to change the machinery of the Indian society. He saw it clearly that through social reforms like adult marriage, intermarriage or interdining between castes alone, India could not be put on her path of progress towards political independence.

Moreover, even before he went through a spiritual transformation after being jailed in 1909, he had written something in *Bande Mataram* that shows his already developing awareness of the problem of unification. He wrote "the winning of freedom is an easy task; the keeping of it is less easy. The first needs only one tremendous effort in which all the energies of the country must be concentrated; the second requires a united, organized and settled strength."[8] He emphasized upon a basic distinction between uniformity and unity.

---

7. Sri Aurobindo, 1999, "The Morality of Boycott" in M. Paranjape (ed.), *The Penguin Sri Aurobindo Reader*, New Delhi: Penguin Books, p. 10.
8. *Bande Mataram*, March 21, 1908.

Maintain Self-identity : Aurobindo

Although, humanity is ultimately one, different peoples from different cultures are variants of this common humanity. No doubt, our ultimate aim should be to reach that supreme oneness. But the way is not one of destroying variation. For this reason, uniformity is not real unity. Rather, it is a unity that is attained at the cost of death of human vigour and energy of variation. Hence abolishing our own distinctive identity would be a regression.

Many reformists have proposed the idea of retaining our strong qualities while purging off the weak ones. From the Western culture, we should, in their opinion, take the qualities that need to be emulated. But, this was an oversimplification which Sri Aurobindo saw clearly. "If we take over a Western ideal, we take it over from a living form which strikes us; we imitate that form, are subjugated by its spirit and natural tendencies, and the good and bad intertwined in the living growth come in upon us together and take united possession."[9]

On the other hand, although our attempts at imitating the West have (fortunately) failed, we cannot blame our countrymen completely for having tried to imitate. When India, due to historical reason, came across the Western culture, it had already lost its old vigour. Hence, coming across a very active and pragmatically successful civilization, the very instinct of life makes it natural to be impelled to imitate. In fact, Sri Aurobindo points this out to be a constant phenomenon in the history of civilization.[10] But the main point once again is that a healthy growth can be possible only when instead of mechanical imitation there is successful assimilation of the positive aspects. That has already happened repeatedly in

9. Sri Aurobindo, "Indian Culture and External Influence" in M. Paranjape, p. 44.
10. Ibid., p. 45.

Indian history. But then any specific reformist programme like widow remarriage or raising the age of marriage cannot be an effective idea to borrow from the West, unless we can find corresponding to it something in our own conception of life. Our aim, however, cannot be to go back to the past; for that is neither desirable nor possible. In fact with the passage of time, different cultures have come closer to each other in the sense of being thrown together. Thus while on the one hand we need "the fidelity to our own spirit," on the other hand, a strong and masterful dealing with external influences "is also necessary."[11] The main aim remains one of the successful assimilation which is a very difficult task.

In fact, Sri Aurobindo found the solution only after his spiritual transformation. He realized that collective identities at the national level could be oppressive just as they could help empowerment. They could give birth to new hegemonies that are disastrous to the maintenance of a freer and more enabling society. On the other hand, the question remains as to how much diversity clashes with the mainstream. It is usual to think that reason can take a positive role in solving such problems. But, Sri Aurobindo disagreed on this point. Man in his view is primarily spiritual just as society is. The true self of the individual is to be sought neither in his body, nor in his ego, nor again in his rational power. Our realization that we cannot live only for ourselves but in solidarity and mutual interdependence with others need not be based solely on pragmatic considerations. In fact, the solidarity cannot break only if it is based on the spiritual realization of essential human unity. This is the ultimate project for man in all societies and India can play the role of a guide in this matter.

---

11. Ibid., p. 51.

Conclusion

Finally, regarding Indian national consciousness, Sri Aurobindo, like Tilak, was convinced that it was not imported from the West. He believed that the national consciousness was already present in the soul of the nation and that it could not be roused by external pressure alone. In fact, he pointed out, how nationalism in a non-spiritual form was already present in India in the Rajputs, the Sikhs and the Marāṭhās. Thus he denied that India had any such basic deficiency in national consciousness that she had to import from the West. If British imperialism could overpower India, it was not because the original ideas of this country were false. It was because India had turned away from these original ideas into conventionalism. Hence, the form of incompleteness that Sri Aurobindo finds in the emergence of the Indian nation does not lie in any inadequacy or deficiency of Indian history specifically. He could even appreciate the West for its positive features. Thus he says, ". . . it is to its passion for the discovery of the actual truth of things and for the governing of human life by whatever law of the truth it has found that the West owes its centuries of strength, vigour, light, progress, irresistible expansion."[12]

But when the aim is to achieve human unity, Sri Aurobindo was convinced that it is ultimately the East which can solve the problem without suppressing the diversities — both at the individual and at the aggregative levels. We should realize that nation is essentially spiritual in character, but first we have to understand that the basic unity underlying a nation is not domination but mutual respect for freedom and equality. This spiritual enlightenment alone can generate the sense of a

12. Sri Aurobindo, 1971, *The Human Cycle* included in *Social and Political Thought*, Pondicherry: Sri Aurobindo Birth Centenary Library, vol. 15, Chapter II, p. 11.

deep fraternity and unity of mankind. Whatever reform India needs is only rediscovery. It is the rediscovery of human spiritual unity that it once knew only symbolically. Such a unity is neither in conflict with the growth of individual nature nor does it base itself on exclusion. This brings into centrestage the deep bond between individual diversity, national growth and finally the unity and growth of humanity.

We find that Sri Aurobindo had overcome the twin pressures and pulls of Europeanization and national identity through a notion of nationalism that was Indian in nature and yet universal in its appeal to mankind in general.

11

Significance of Tagore's Poetry in the Indian Renaissance

Sri Aurobindonian Perspective

Supriyo Bhattacharya

More strange than true, I never may believe
These antique fables, nor these fairy toys.
Lovers and madmen have such seething brains,
Such shaping fantasies, that apprehend
More than cool reason ever comprehends.
The lunatic, the lover, and the poet
Are of imagination all-compact.

— *A Midsummer Night's Dream*,
5.1.1-27; William Shakespeare

IN the din and bustle of a hackneyed existence, one gets a reassuring sign of hope as one reads these memorable lines on the imaginative power of "the lunatic, the lover, and the poet." We may leave aside for the moment the lunatic and the lover. As for the poet, we may pick up Rabindranath Tagore who proved to be, as Krishna Dutta and Andrew Robinson (now famous biographers on Tagore) put it, "the most dazzling instance" of the benefits of "cultural collision" — that is, the Bengal renaissance on the one hand and the "high noon" of the British Empire on the other.[1] In his little gem of a book,

1. *Rabindranath Tagore : An Anthology*, 1997, ed. by Krishna Datta and Andrew Robinson, London: Picador.

The Renaissance in India (1920), Sri Aurobindo places Tagore in the third step of the process which led up to the Indian renaissance. The first step was the "reception of the European contact, a radical reconsideration of the many of the prominent elements and some revolutionary denial of the very principles of the old culture."[2] The second step was, according to Sri Aurobindo, a "reaction of the Indian spirit upon the European influence, sometimes with a total denial of what it offered and a stressing both of the essential and the strict letter of the national past, which yet masked a movement of assimilation."[3] The third step was a process of "new creation" in which "the spiritual power of the Indian mind remains supreme."[4] In this stage, the Indian mind "recovers its truths, accepts whatever it finds sound or true, useful or inevitable of the modern idea and form,"[5] but it does not merely accept, it so "transmutes and Indianises it, so absorbs and so transforms it entirely into itself that its foreign character disappears and it becomes another harmonious element in the characteristic working of the ancient goodness, the Shakti of India mastering and possessing of the modern influence, no longer possessed or overcome by it."[6]

The works of the great Bengali novelist Bankim Chandra Chatterjee and the poet Rabindranath Tagore, the two minds of "the most distinctive and original genius"[7] in literature represented, according to Sri Aurobindo, the stages of this third step.[8]

---

2. *The Renaissance in India, Sri Aurobindo*, 1920, Pondicherry: Sri Aurobindo Ashram (1st edn., 6th impression 1996).
3. Ibid.
4. Ibid.
5. Ibid.
6. Ibid.
7. Ibid.
8. Ibid.

Sri Aurobindo here speaks primarily of the poetry of Tagore, when he singles out Tagore as a creative writer in the time of Indian renaissance — not the whole range of Tagore's poetry, but Sri Aurobindo bases his analysis upon what the poet wrote up to 1920 or thereabouts. The question is: how does this poetry which is recognized by Sri Aurobindo as a "profounder voice," "a voice of the dawn,"[9] reflect the characteristics of what Sri Aurobindo calls the third step of the process that led up to the renaissance?

Sri Aurobindo does not make any analysis of Tagore's poetry, (up to the period we have already mentioned) in *The Renaissance In India* to answer this question. But he makes a superb analysis (though brief) of one of Tagore's poems in the English journal *Karmayogin* edited by him in an article somewhere in between 1909 and 1910. And he takes up a fuller analysis of the significance of Tagore's poetry in the pages of the *Arya* from 1917 to 1920 and this was later collected and published in a book entitled *The Future Poetry*.

The Influence of Renaissance

Take the article of *Karmayogin* first. Lately, there has been much talk about the question whether the "Indian renaissance" actually happened or not. Some feel that no such thing happened, while others believe that even if something of the kind happened, it was truly not Indian; it was restricted to a particular class and not something touching and influencing the life and culture of the masses. As to the first question whether the renaissance truly happened, the answer can best be found in Tagore's creative work itself. Sri Aurobindo's analysis of only one poem points to the creative ferment that went into developing a process of reawakening — the finding of one's ture self once again and expressing its experiences in

9. Ibid.

newer modes or forms accommodating new complexities of the age and hitherto undiscovered subtleties of soul-experience. The awakening was on two fronts: on the one hand Tagore did capitalize — as any genuine poet does — on the traditions of his own country (and that included the Upaniṣads, the Buddhist legends, the Sanskrit literature, the Vaiṣṇava poetry, the songs of Bauls, etc.); and then he gave an expression of his soul-experience in a language of his own, taking the elements of his traditions as a fertilizing agent on the humus of his inner consciousness. The other front on which the awakening took place was the sphere in which Tagore absorbed the useful hints and suggestions coming from his reading of Western literature. Here, as we shall see, the absorption was not so much in the form of borrowing certain ideas or substance, as in the form of imbibing certain idea-forces and naturalizing certain poetic techniques of some of the greatest poets of the West and making variations of those techniques in a way all his own.

But to come back to Sri Aurobindo's article of *Karmayogin.* This article refers to the brief poem *Duhkhabhisar* of Tagore published in the Bengali monthly *Suprobhāt* (in the issue, Śrāvaṇa 1316 *BS*), edited by Kumari Kumudini Mitra, daughter of the great Krishna Kumar Mitra, editor of *Sanjibanee.* "It is one of those poems," writes Sri Aurobindo, "in which the peculiar inimitable quality of *our greatest lyric poet* comes out with supreme force, beauty and sweetness."[10] Next come the most significant sentences: "one of the most remarkable peculiarities of Rabindranath's genius is the happiness and originality with which he has absorbed the whole spirit of Vaiṣṇava poetry and turned it into something essentially the same and yet new and modern. He has given the old sweet

10. *The Harmony of Virtue,* 1972, Sri Aurobindo Birth Centenary Library, vol. 3; Pondicherry, Sri Aurobindo Ashram.

spirit of emotional and passionate religion an expression of more delicate and complex richness voiceful of subtler and more penetratingly spiritual shades of feeling than the deep-hearted but simple early age of Bengal could know. The old Vaiṣṇava *bhāva* — there is no English word for it — was easily seizable, broad and strong. The *bhāva* of these poems is not translatable in any other language than that the poet had used."[11] The first few lines of the poem can be freely rendered into English (in Bengali, the first line begins with "*kothāy ālo, kothāy ore ālo*") thus:

> *Where is the light, oh where is the light!*
> *Do kindle it by the fire of separation.*
> *The lamp is there, it does not*
> *burn into flame; was it thus ordained?*
> *Better than this is Death.*
> *Oh kindle the lamp by the fire of separation.*

The few sentences of Sri Aurobindo (quoted above) seize the heart of the matter: how Tagore absorbs the essence of tradition and on the strength of that how he wakes up to himself and finds his own voice, thereby widening and deepening the tradition and the frontiers of our consciousness.

Impact of Western Literature

Next, does Tagore's poetry have anything to do with the impact of Western literature? Was it "influenced" by the poetry of the West or was the literature of the West more in the nature of a stimulus, a kind of persuading wind that opened the doors of the many possibilities of self-experience and ways and avenues of self-expression? The latter hypothesis seems nearer to the truth. Let us first note that when the poet was only 17 years old he published a few literary essays in *Bharati* in 1878, which show his familiarity with the work of the poets

11. *The Harmony of Virtue.*

of Europe. In a piece written by him in *Contemporary Indian Philosophy*, edited by S. Radhakrishnan in 1937, the poet remarks: "I myself have tried to get at the wealth of beauty in the literature of the European languages, long before I gained a full right to their hospitality" (quoted by R.K. Dasgupta in his *East-West Literary Relations*, 1995, published by Papyrus). His essays published in *Bharati* (namely "Saxon Jati O Anglo-Saxon Sahitya," "Beatrice, Dante O Tanhar Kavya," "Petrarch O Laura," "Goethe O Tanhar Pranayinigan") bear eloquent witness to his knowledge of and interest in European poetry. Add to this his visit to England where he studied English literature for four months with Professor Henry Morley at the University of London. Even in 1881 when he was 20 years old he could say in an essay published in *Bharati*: "In English literature a great epic is being written which we may call the spirit of man; it is the work of many poets writing through the ages" (Translated by R.K. Dasgupta).[12] In another beautiful essay "Sonar Kāthi" in 1915 and later included in *Paricay* (1916) he captured with a fine simile the impact of English literature on our literature: English literature is like the Prince crossing the seven seas to reach the sleeping princess of our literature and waking her up by the touch of his golden wand. Tagore, however, hastens to add that the literature then produced bore the stamp of our national genius. R.K. Dasgupta points out that the same idea is stated once again in his foreword to *The Bengali Book English Verse* (1918) edited by T.O.D. Dunn where Tagore says: "Bengal's response through literature to the call of the West is something unique in the history of the modern East. . . . The breath of inspiration coming from the West has kindled the original spark in us into a flame that lay smothered in the ashes of dead habits and rigidity of traditional forms."[13]

12. East-West Literary Relations, 1995, by R.K. Dasgupta; Kolkata, Papyrus.
13. Ibid.

How it happened in the case of Tagore can best be illustrated from his own poetry and from a study of the techniques that he gradually developed on his own and by his closeness to some Western poets — Shelly, Yeats, Goethe, Keats and Whitman especially. In a brilliant essay "Western Influence on the poetry of Tagore", Tarak Nath Sen, the late legendary scholar and teacher of English literature, presents some cogent arguments to drive the point home.[14] The main conclusion that Sen arrives at after a series of detailed arguments is this: "Traces of Western influence in the poetry of Tagore in the shape of specific echoes and borrowings are not many. For Tagore did not set himself to imitate in deliberate fashion. He was not the kind of poet who seeks to make up for the lack of native genius or talent by a sedulous imitation of foreign models (all too common a feature of modern literature). Western influence in his case acted rather as a stimulant and opener of mental horizons, enlarging for him the area of available spiritual companionship, giving him a heightened awareness of the possibilities of poetry — the realization that there are more chambers than one in the mansion of the Muses."[15] As illustration for explaining what he means in the last sentence, he says: "Keats' most fruitful gift to Tagore seems to me to have been not so much a certain style or manner or poetic slant, or specific patterns of attitude or subject-matter, as a particular form of verse. That was the run-on and enjambed rhymed couplet, where the rhymes are so swamped by the modulated overflow of sense and rhyme from line to line that the couplets read almost like blank verse . . . in Bengali verse the end-stopped and self-contained rhymes couplet had been the staple metre for centuries. It was Tagore who naturalized in Bengali the run-on and enjambed rhymed

14. *A Literary Miscellany*, 1972, by Tarak Nath Sen; Kolkata: Rupa and Co.

15. Ibid.

couplet, and in doing so he must have taken his cue from Keats."[16] (In poetry in some lines the sense is enclosed within the single line, which is then called "end-stopped." If the sense flows over into two, or several lines, they are then called "run-on"). Why this run-on and enjambed couplet appealed to Tagore is explained by Sen: "The sinuous movement of the run-on and enjambed heroic couplet appealed more to the romantic taste than the rectilinear movement of the neo-classical variety, being more in accord with the romantic principle as enunciated by the landscape gardener William Kent: "Nature abhors a straight line" . . . Keats thus gave him (i.e. Tagore) an instrument that served him splendidly for nearly the entire length of his poetic career."[17] Sen cites quite a few examples from Tagore's poems to illustrate his point. Poems from *Manasi* (particularly *Meghdut, Ahalyar Prati, Viday, Ses Upahar, Naivedya, Ses Saptak,*) are examples of this type of couplet which saves the poetry from hybridization with song.[18]

The other technique from another Western poet was in the realm of "prose-poetry" and free verse and this too Tagore turned to splendid account. Sen remarks, "If there was any Western poet who gave him his cue for "prose-poetry" and free verse, it was rather Walf Whitman than any other. . . . It should be noted . . . that Tagore's "prose-poetry" and free verse are just another facet of the same magnificent mastery of rhythm that he shows in his metrical verse."[19] Sen cites, for example, Tagore's magnificent poem on the earth in *Patraput*.

Tagore's Contribution Through Poetry

All this is of secondary importance when we come to the real achievement of Tagore as proof of his positive contribution to

16. Ibid.
17. Ibid.
18. Ibid.
19. Ibid.

the Indian renaissance through his poetry (and other works) that is pointed out by Sri Aurobindo in his masterly analysis of poetry (and in course of that, the poetry of Tagore) in the pages of *The Future Poetry* whose first unrevised form appeared in a series of brilliant essays in the journal *Arya*, during 1917-20. Sri Aurobindo first takes a close look at the turn of poetry in the age which we have left behind, particularly the middle nineteenth century in England and America. In that poetry there was a "pre-occupation with reflective thought and therefore with truth," but it was not "at its core and in its essence a poetic thought and truth and its expression, however artistically dressed with image or turn?"[20] This was, as Sri Aurobindo rightly says, "inevitable in a reign of dominant intellectuality."[21] But he points out that an excess of reason and intellectuality is not congenial to "moved vision and the uplifting breath of life"[22] that gives birth to that fire and boundless ether called poetry. "A poetry which is all thought and no life," says Sri Aurobindo, "or a thought which does not constantly keep in touch with and refresh itself from the fountains of life . . . suffers always by lack of fire and body, wants perfection of grasp and does not take full hold on the inner being to seize and uplift as well as sweeten and illumine, as poetry should do and all great poetic writing does."[23] When the poet's medium is the "outward life" of things or the "surface inward life" of the passions and emotions, the poet is moving in a "strong and fresh natural element and in an undivided wholeness of the inner and outer man"[24] and his work has all the vitality of a thing "fully felt and lived." But

20. *The Future Poetry* (Ch. XXVII), 1972, by Sri Aurobindo; Pondicherry: Sri Aurobindo Ashram.

21. Ibid.

22. Ibid.

23. Ibid.

24. Ibid.

Sri Aurobindo points out, when intellectual thought has begun its "reign in the mind of a more cultured race," the difficulty of the poet also begins and increases, as that reign becomes "more sovereign and imperative." The reason is, according to Sri Aurobindo, that intellectual thought makes a sort of "scission" in our being with the result that on the one hand, the vital urge is carrying on life and on the other, the "deliberate detached reason" tries to observe it and to take an "intelligent view" and extract from it all its "thought values."[25] The poet too, as a child of the age, is moved to follow this turn (Sri Aurobindo cites the example of Browning). But, Sri Aurobindo goes on to warn that this can only be done without any harm to the "vital power of the poetic spirit" and the "all-seizing effect of its word" when a balance is maintained between thought and life, "the life passing into self-observing thought and the thought returning on the life to shape it in its own vital image."[26] A just balance between thought and living word was, for example, found by the Greeks and also in the classical literature of India. But such a balance is easily lost and then we get more of "studies of life than of creation," thought about the meaning of character and emotion and event and elaborate description rather than the "living presence of these things."[27] Passion, direct feeling, ardent emotion, sincerity of sensuous joy are "chilled by the observing eye of the reason," and give place to a "play of sentiment."[28]

It is curious that in 1921 the great Nobel Laureate Poet T.S. Eliot was expressing the same concern for the crisis that English poetry was then facing. Sri Aurobindo was writing "The Future Poetry" during 1917-20 and he did not see Eliot's

25. Ibid.
26. Ibid.
27. Ibid.
28. Ibid.

essay *"The Metaphysical Poets"* (1921) in which Eliot presented his diagnosis of the problem. But the analysis presented by two different minds in two different parts of the world ran on more or less similar lines. Eliot goes as far back as the seventeenth century and makes this trenchant remark[29] : "In the seventeenth century a dissociation of sensibility set in, from which we have never recovered." To illustrate his point, Eliot picks up Tennyson and Browning who, according to him, "are poets, and they think"; but they do not "feel their thought as immediately as the odour of a rose."[30] In contrast, in Chapman, Eliot points out, there is a "direct sensuous apprehension of thought or a recreation of thought into feeling."[31] And this is also true of Donne, the great metaphysical poet.

Eliot's analysis brings out Sri Aurobindo's point more forcefully. "A thought to Donne," explains Eliot, "was an experience; it modified his sensibility. When a poet's mind is perfectly equipped for its work, it is constantly amalgamating disparate experience; the ordinary man's experience is chaotic, irregular, fragmentary. The latter falls in love, or reads Spinoza and these two experiences have nothing to do with each other, or with the noise of the typewriter or the smell of cooking; in the mind of the poet these experiences are always forming new wholes."[32] Almost echoing the words of Sri Aurobindo, Eliot concludes: "The sentimental age began early in the eighteenth century and continued. The poets revolted against the ratiocinative, the descriptive; they thought and felt by fits, unbalanced; they reflected. In one or two passages of

---

29. "The Metaphysical Poets", 1921, in *Selected Essays*, T.S. Eliot; London: Faber and Faber Limited, 1980.
30. Ibid.
31. Ibid.
32. Ibid.

Shelly's Triumph of Life, in the second Hyperion (of Keats) there are traces of a struggle toward unification of sensibility. But Keats and Shelly died, and Tennyson and Browning ruminated."[33]

Eliot does not pursue his analysis further, nor does he offer any solution to the problem. But Sri Aurobindo goes further. First, he notes that there is an attempt to get back to the "natural fullness of the vital and physical life."[34] But the endeavour fails in sincerity and success because, Sri Aurobindo explains, "Life, action, vital power are great indispensable things, but to get back to them by thinking less is a way not open to us in this age of time, even if it were desirable remedy of our disease of over-intellectuality and a mechanized existence."[35] Eliot too admits that, "it appears likely that poets in our civilization, as it exists at present, must be difficult. Our civilization comprehends great variety and complexity."[36]

What, then, is the way out? "The way out," says Sri Aurobindo with great insight, "lies not in cessation of thinking and turn to a strenuous description of life, nor even in a more vitally forceful thinking, but in another kind of thought mind."[37] We gain this higher reach of the thought mind when we get above "the limited crude physical mind," "the vital power and its forceful thought and self-vision," and "the intellect and its pondering and measuring reason" and tread instead "the illumined realm of an intuitive and spiritual thinking, an intuitive feeling, sense and vision."[38] But, Sri Aurobindo adds the caveat: "This is not the vital intuition

---

33. Ibid.
34. *The Future Poetry*, (Ch. XXVII), 1972, by Sri Aurobindo; Pondicherry: Sri Aurobindo Ashram.
35. Ibid.
36. "The Metaphysical Poets."
37. *The Future Poetry*, Ch. XXVII.
38. Ibid.

which is sometimes confused with a much broader, loftier, vaster and more seeing power, but the high original power itself, a supra-intellectual and spiritual intuition."[39]

This is the solution that the new age, of which Tagore and a few Western poets are forerunners, demands. "The all-informing spirit," concludes Sri Aurobindo, "when found in its fullness, heals the session between thought and life, the need of a just balance between them disappears, instead there begins a new, luminous and joyful fusion and oneness."[40]

The reason why the "supra-intellectual and spiritual intuition" is the key to the problem is also pointed out by Sri Aurobindo with rare clarity. He would have us remember a profound truth of the spirit: "The spirit gives us not only a greater light of truth and vision, but the breath of a greater living; for the spirit is not only the self of our consciousness and knowledge, but the great self of life. To find ourself and the self of things is not to go through a rarefied ether of thought into *nirvāṇa*, but to discover the whole greatest integral power of our complete existence."[41]

Sri Aurobindo mentions the work of a few poets of the West and from India, that of Tagore, in whom the double seeking of the twofold power, "the truth and reality of the eternal self and spirit in man and things and the insistence on life," finds increasing expression. It is the "highest note" of Walf Whitman; it is constantly repeated from the "earth side" in Meredith; comes down from the "spiritual side" in all A.E.'s work; moves between "Earth and the life of the worlds behind" in Yeats' "subtle rhythmic voices of vision and beauty"; echoes with, "large fullness" in Carpenter.[42] But,

39. Ibid.
40. Ibid.
41. Ibid.
42. Ibid.

coming to Tagore, Sri Aurobindo generously admits that Tagore gives us "more of this discovery and fusion for which the mind of our age is in quest than any other creative writer of the time."[43] His work (i.e. Tagore's), declares Sri Aurobindo, "is a constant music of the overpassing of the borders, a chant-filled realm in which the subtle sounds and lights of the truth of the spirit give new meaning to the finer subtleties of life.[44]

Conclusion

Tagore's work, or for that matter, that of the other poets mentioned here, has not indeed done all that has to be done; nor have they given, as Sri Aurobindo reminds us, the "complete poetic synthesis and fusion."[45] But, in the Indian renaissance, Tagore's poetry has been to create what Sri Aurobindo calls a "new and deeper manner of seeing life".[46] To use the beautiful words of Sri Aurobindo, Tagore's poetry built "bridges of visioned light and rhythm" between "the infinite and eternal and the mind and soul and life of man"[47] with the result that "at the subtlest elevation of all that has yet been reached, stands or rather wings and floats in a high intermediate region the poetry of Tagore, not in the complete spiritual light, but amid an air shot with its seekings and glimpses, a sight and cadence found in a psycho-spiritual heaven of subtle and delicate soul experience transmuting the earth tones by the touch of its radiance."[48]

The adventure of poetry did not stop with Tagore, as he himself never stopped progressing. The exploration into the

43. Ibid.
44. Ibid.
45. Ibid.
46. Ibid.
47. Ibid.
48. *The Future Poetry*, Ch. XXXII, by Sri Aurobindo.

different realms of higher intuition was continued and Sri Aurobindo himself embarked upon a new journey on a road less travelled by. Sri Aurobindo gave the world an illuminating exposition of the various grades of spiritual intuition starting from what he called the "Higher Mind," "Illumined Mind," "Intuitive Mind," to "Overmind" and beyond that, to "Supermind" in the pages of the magnum opus *The Life Divine*. The poetry coming from these levels is what he called the "Overhead Poetry." A brilliant example of what poetry is like when it comes from the higher overhead plane is the epic *Savitri* written by Sri Aurobindo himself. Sri Aurobindo also gave examples of a few passages from Homer, Milton, Shakespeare, Wordsworth, Virgil and a few other poets (See his *The Future Poetry*). But a wonderful manifestation of the initial promise of a spiritual intuition was adumbrated in the Indian renaissance by the best of the poetry of Tagore as well as the ceaseless marvel of his songs and other creations.

12

The Revolutionary Movement
Tagore and Aurobindo

Manjula Bose

THE struggle for India's independence gradually started gaining in strength from the early years of the twentieth century. The struggle proceeded along two channels. One was that of peaceful, non-violent protest and agitation as pursued by the Indian National Congress. The other was the path followed by the groups alternatively known as Revolutionaries, the Extremists or the Hardliners. The latter believed in armed struggle and did not hesitate to use violence. Armed struggle was not open warfare as yet. Generally the *modus operandi* was that of isolated attacks on and killing of British officials or their Indian henchmen here and there by one or few revolutionaries. The idea was to create terror among the British rulers as also to take revenge against particular officials who had become hateful for their oppressive policies or the cruel treatment meted out to the freedom fighters.

The activities of the revolutionaries consisted of making arrangements for building up the physique of young men, imparting them training in the use of arms, and schemes for collecting arms, mostly illegally. Their programme also included collection of money through any means, including robbery and intimidation. Except the physique-building programme everything else was conducted in a clandestine fashion up to the plan of attack on the intended victim. Irrespective of whether they were successful or not in fulfilling their target, they were mostly apprehended or died on the spot fighting. Those who were caught generally faced the death penalty or deportation.

The activities of the revolutionaries gained momentum through the first two decades of the twentieth century. It may be said that such activities reached a climax with the Chittagong Armoury Raid case. After this since the thirties the revolutionary movement was on the wane.

Extremism is a Crime — Tagore

Rabindranath was not generally involved directly in any political activity, either of the non-violent Congress variety or of the revolutionary variety. As he wrote in a letter to C.F. Andrews, "Politics are so wholly against my nature, and yet, belonging to an unfortunate country, born to an abnormal situation we find it so difficult to avoid their outbursts" (May 6, 1921). Keenly aware of the political trends and developments of his time, he went by his own judgements and ideas about the wellbeing of the country.

Rabindranath's attitude towards the revolutionary movement can be summed up as follows. At the personal level he had great respect for the revolutionaries because of their patriotism, courage and self-sacrifice. But he had difference with them both on the ideological plane and on the methods adopted. He held that violent means taught men to deviate from their humanity by enjoining hatred and killing of others. There was no sanctity of the human life to the hardliner. He would throw moral principles to the winds for achieving immediate goals. Even if one achieves the goal, the sense of right and wrong is destroyed forever — which is a great loss. He says, " . . . what we recognize as extremism is neither decent, nor legal, nor open; that is, extremism means giving up hope of achieving one's objective through the straight path and treading a devious, distorted path. That is why I have told my own people quite forcefully that this path is entirely wrong; that is why I have the right to say emphatically that extremism is a crime according to the Government's rules also.[1] In the same essay he says that when a result is obtained through unfair means the unfairness itself extracts a heavy price.

The mental condition of Atindra, a revolutionary character portrayed by Tagore in *Char Adhyay* may be recalled in this connection. He laments for the criminal acts in which he has taken part as his revolutionary duty. These included plundering and killing an old lonely widow. Rabindranath questions in agony, "The lamp of patriotism is kindled, but what scenes does this light reveal — those of thefts, dacoities and secret murders? When God has made His appearance, shall we then worship Him with the offering of sin?"[2] The deterioration of moral standards is also revealed through Atindra who is critical of falsehood, meanness, mutual distrust, conspiracies to capture power and the habit of spying on each other that he witnessed among his revolutionary comrades.

Tagore Objected to Revolutionary Ideas

Another reason for Tagore's objection to the revolutionary ideology was the complete regimentation of thought. Once a man joins a revolutionary group he is bound by an oath of allegiance. The slightest deviation from the path laid out by the group has disastrous consequences. The tragedy of Atindra

---

1. *Chhoto O Baro, in Kālāntar* (1975), Visva Bharati, p. 101.
2. Ibid., p. 103.

arises from a conflict between loyalty to the group and the call of conscience.

Not only did Tagore find the methods and ideology of the extremists morally untenable, practically also they were not expedient. When the minds of men of the whole country were not ready for revolution, scattered and sporadic acts of violence were bound to fail, the consequent sacrifices by a few individuals were fruitless too.[3]

Tagore Shows Respect, Sympathy Also

Yet his great respect for the revolutionaries is evident in many ways. He says " . . . that they offered themselves as sacrifices in the fire of doom has rendered them worthy of adoration not only in our country, but in all countries."[4] While condemning criminal acts like theft, robbery and murder he says "One cannot forget that we not only saw the thief and dacoit in light of patriotism we also saw the hero."[5] The revolutionaries discarded all personal interests and were ready to sacrifice their whole life to the service of the motherland. They had no prospect of government service or honour from royalty. Such men would be assets to any country. But in India they were thwarted and crushed by the ruling power and bureaucracy.

Tagore's sympathy towards the revolutionaries was manifest in many forms. He reacted strongly against the severe persecution of the passengers of the ship Komagatamaru in 1914. They were being persecuted for their revolutionary tendencies. Rabindranath was so much perturbed by their fate that in 1916 he declined an invitation of the Government of

---

3. *Call of Truth* (Satyer Ahban) *in Kālāntar,* p. 198.
4. *Call of Truth,* p. 198.
5. *Chhoto O Baro,* p. 105.

Canada to visit their country because he felt that the distress of the passengers of Komagatamaru could be traced to the refusal of the Canadian Government to let them disembark at Vancouver. A number of ex-revolutionaries were given employment in Santiniketan. In 1930 in a statement to a reporter of the *Manchester Guardian* he said that harsh and arbitrary punishment of revolutionaries by a harsh and irresponsible government was driving the people to despondency, frustration, insanity, even suicide. He raises these issues in his poem *"Prasna"*.

Tagore Showers Praises on Aurobindo

While he was respectful towards the revolutionaries in general, his reverence was particularly manifest in the case of Aurobindo. The ovation that he offered to Aurobindo or the eulogies that he showered on Aurobindo were really without parallel though there were basic differences between the two. One common ground between them was the intensity of their patriotism. The early blossoming of this patriotism in Aurobindo is difficult to explain inasmuch as he was uprooted from his native soil at the age of seven and kept with an English family with strict instructions that he must be kept totally aloof from any contact with Indians. His revolutionary inclinations were evident very early. While in England he joined a secret society called the Lotus and Dagger. The society failed to take root. Nevertheless it promised to be a genuine revolutionary society. When he was in service of the State of Baroda he wrote a number of articles in the Marathi paper *Indu Prakash*. According to M.G. Ranade, if the series had continued, Aurobindo would definitely have been charged with sedition. As early as 1902, Aurobindo was working for the spread of revolutionary and nationalistic propaganda in Bengal although he was physically not present on the scene. He sent his emissary Jatin Banerji, a Bengali soldier in the Baroda Army for this purpose. Sister Nivedita was one of the few who knew of Aurobindo's directing brain being behind the nationalistic movement although he himself was not physically there. Thousands of young men were enlisted in the nationalist movement through his efforts.

Similarities and Dissimilarities Between Tagore and Aurobindo

Aurobindo was critical of the Congress and here his viewpoint converged with that of Rabindranath. One reason was that Congress did not adopt a clear-cut goal of national resurgence but was bothered with inconsequential trifles — demanding only a few paltry administrative reforms. One would remember Rabindranath's essay *"Mantri Abhisek"* (1896) in this connection. The issue then was how many members of the Viceroy's Executive Council would be Indians and how many of them would be elected and how many nominated. Secondly, Aurobindo protested against the Congress habit of appeasing the British with flattery to gain their goodwill. He thoroughly condemned the mendicant attitude. This is similar to Tagore's reaction to what he describes as **আবেদন আর নিবেদনের থালা বহি বহি নতশির.** Thirdly, he felt that the national movement was not a mass movement. It was confined to the middle class. Rabindranath was also critical of Congress politics because the voiceless masses were overlooked. In his essay "Call of Truth" (1921), he asserted that Gandhi was the first national leader who approached the masses.

But there was a basic difference. At no time did Aurobindo reject the use of force as and when necessary. Rabindranath was opposed to violence, at least of the underground, conspiratorial variety, attacking isolated individuals. He abhorred other crimes like theft and robbery too. Aurobindo believed that in the conditions then prevailing in India a successful armed revolt was not within the realm of possibility. So individual acts of assassination and violence directed against

British officials or their Indian henchmen were the only way out. Such violent methods might be branded as criminal and wicked. But this was the view of the oppressor and Aurobindo had no scruples about it. He believed that armed revolt was the swiftest and most thorough in its results. Tagore on the other hand felt that scattered use of violent methods by a few was bound to fail. His point was that in order to attain something one has to pay a full price. Otherwise the price offered is wasted and one does not get the desired commodity. "When the country was not ready an attempt at revolution meant deviation from the straight path and adopting a wrong one. The wrong path may be shorter in span, but by following it one does not reach the destination, rather one's feet are lacerated by thorns. The sacrifice of the revolutionaries was very great from their point of view, but it was too poor a price to be paid on behalf of the whole country."[6]

For both *swarāj* was not just throwing out the British and having an alternative form of government. It meant the fulfilment of national life. But they differed on the meaning of fulfilment of national life. Rabindranath felt that people should be endowed with courage and self-esteem. They should get rid of their self-deprecation and helplessness and try to achieve a life worth living through their own efforts. Both valued India's culture. But to Aurobindo it was imbued with a religious connotation. He was more akin to Bankim Chandra than Rabindranath. The *mantra* of "Bande Mataram" was the key to an understanding of Aurobindo's concept of a nation. India was Goddess incarnate, the mighty mother. Rabindranath was equally patriotic, he would look upon India as the mother, but not as the Goddess. Aurobindo, on his part, never had any sympathy with Rabindranath's programme

6. *Call of Truth*, p. 198.

of social and moral regeneration, his schemes of rural reconstruction or his principle of co-operation between nations.

They came into contact with each other over the National School of Education and both had reason to be equally disillusioned. Rabindranath held Aurobindo in the highest esteem, knowing fully well that he was encouraging violent activities, for Aurobindo never made a secret of his views. Aurobindo was a protagonist of Sanātan Hindu Dharma. Rabindranath was not; in fact he was not the protagonist of any particular religion. Aurobindo was an Extremist and the quarrels between the Extremists and Moderates had taken an unseemly turn in the Surat Congress fiasco in 1907. Aurobindo brought out the factional quarrels of Congressmen in the pages of *Bande Mataram.* Rabindranath, who earlier believed that *Bande Mataram* was an excellent paper now felt that *Bande Mataram* was no longer giving out the fearless calls for freedom.

In spite of all these, Rabindranath was unshaken in his estimate, one may even say reverence, of Aurobindo as shown by his poem, *Namaskār.* The poem's name is self-explanatory. After Aurobindo left politics and became Sri Aurobindo, the yogī, they met once in 1928. Rabindranath had a different realization this time. That is another story. But the refrain is the same. He still had this to say:

অরবিন্দ রবীন্দ্রের লহ নমস্কার।

(Aurobind accept the salutation of Rabindra)

Note: All quotations have been translated from original Bengali into English by the author.

13

Philosophy of Krishna Chandra Bhattacharyya

Tara Chatterjea

KRISHNA CHANDRA BHATTACHARYYA (1875–1949) was an exact contemporary of Sri Aurobindo. He has been hailed as the most original and creative thinker among the Indian academic philosophers of the last century. He was a profound thinker but he published little. The story goes that he scribbled his thoughts on pieces of paper and threw them away. His able son, late Professor Gopinath Bhattacharyya collected some of his articles and published them in two volumes as *Studies in Philosophy.* Besides this, very little work is available to us. I, personally, have come across only two other works. One of them is a short article captioned *Swaraj in Ideas* and the other one is written in Bengali called *Kantdarsaner Tatparya.* It is very difficult to have a proper understanding of his philosophy, because his writing is terse, pithy and he seldom gives examples to elucidate a point. He uses many familiar terms which mean and do not mean what we are accustomed to mean by them. Yet in his works we feel the presence of an acutely analytic mind and a deeply authentic thinker.

It is said that his thinking was highly influenced by Kantian philosophy and Advaita Vedānta. But the mark of his creative mind is present everywhere. His philosophy is not a commentary on those thinkers' works. There are clear-cut points of departure. Even his articles on traditional Indian philosophy are more of constructive interpretation than elucidation. He was interested in Indian idealism and has written extensively on Advaita Vedānta and Samkhya-Yoga. This led to his emphasis on two ways of apprehending experience — the subjective way and the objective way. He has been interested in the Jaina theory of *anekānta,* and the idea of many faces of reality ultimately ended in the concept of alternative Absolutes. He spoke of Absolute as truth, which he reaches by analysing thinking; similarly by analysing feeling he reaches Absolute as value; and by analysing willing he reaches Absolute as freedom. He attributes these ideas to Advaita, Hegel and Nihilistic Buddhist, respectively. But he reaches the conclusion through analysis of experience, and it is not just a summary of conclusions reached by other thinkers.

Thought Philosophy of Krishna Chandra

In his personal life Krishna Chandra was a devout, practicing, conservative Hindu, but he treated philosophy as purely an exercise in theoretical consciousness. He tells us what he means by philosophy in an article titled *The Concept of Philosophy,* which was published in 1936 and is a product of mature thinking. I have largely depended on that article for what I write here.

He says that "Theoretic consciousness at its minimum is the understanding of a speakable."[1] To speak is to formulate a belief and beliefs are understandable and communicable. These have also been called thoughts. Krishna Chandra himself says that only one form of thought is literal thought, and others being symbolistic thought, should not be called thought at all, but then he uses the term "thought" to present theoretic

1. Krishna Chandra Bhattacharya, "The Concept of Philosophy," in *Studies in Philosophy,* Volume II, edited by Gopinath Bhattacharyya, Progressive Publishers, Calcutta, 1958, Section 6, p. 101.

consciousness as such, and we have followed him. He speaks of four grades of thought. These are empirical thought; pure objective or contemplative thought; spiritual or subjective or enjoying thought; and transcendental thought. The role of speech is so important in theoretic consciousness, that Krishna Chandra says that "The so-called grades of thought are really grades of speaking."[2] But we shall see that he maintains a difference between thought and speech.

Empirical thought is thought of an object perceived or imagined as perceived or is perceivable. By empirical thought he is mainly talking about scientific thought. But there are contents which are objective, yet have no reference to perception, such as the logical forms. Thoughts which have these contents constitute the second grade of thought. These thoughts are also called contemplative thoughts. It is to be noted that contemplative thoughts are directed towards pure objects, i.e. a priori objects, and contemplation is not necessarily *dhyāna* or religious meditation. Usually, these two types of thoughts are expected to exhaust all our thinking. But Krishna Chandra progresses further. When the contemplative attitude is completely dropped, and a radically different subjective attitude is adopted, we have spiritual thought. The content is subjective, and the attitude is called enjoying attitude. Here enjoyment stands for simply subjective attitude, and the content is not necessarily bliss as the name may suggest. All these attitudes are transcended in transcendental thought, where the content is neither subjective nor objective. Because he defines the final grade in this way, there is a tendency to conclude that Krishna Chandra's philosophy ultimately ends in mysticism. To my mind such a view is incorrect. I shall come back to this later. It is to be noted that whereas in the first grade of thought, Krishna Chandra does not speak of

2. Ibid., Section 9, p. 102.

attitude, in all other three grades the change of attitude is emphasized. The contents of the four grades of thought are called fact, self-subsistence, reality and truth, respectively. Science deals with the first grade, and philosophy deals with the last three grades of thoughts.

Science, Philosophy and Relation of Thoughts

The difference between the first two stages constitutes the qualitative difference of science and philosophy. Philosophy is in no sense a continuation of science, nor is it a world view which emerges out of a summary of the conclusions reached by various sciences. Their contents are different and the attitudes are different, too. Science deals with empirical facts and treats objects as usable. Thoughts in this grade are directed towards objects which are perceivable; such objects even constitute the meaning of the words in this grade of thought. The relation of speech with object is contingent; it does not in any way affect or constitute the content of thought here. Speech is used here literally and the judgements which express the thoughts are proper judgements.

When the same world of object is approached philosophically, connection of language with content becomes necessary. In his unique style Krishna Chandra says that in science the content is *spoken of* so that there is a clear cut distinction between the linguistic expression and the corresponding object, whereas in philosophy they are merely *spoken.* Kalidas Bhattacharyya quotes two sentences from the article to explain this statement. First, "Pure thought is not thought of a content distinguishable from it," and second, "The content that is spoken is not intelligible except as spoken."[3] In science one is dealing with empirical particular

3. Kalidas Bhattacharyya, *The Fundamentals of K.C. Bhattacharyya's Philosophy*, Saraswat Library, Calcutta, p. 182.

facts and empirical concepts which are perfectly understandable without any appeal to speech; pure objects are a priori concepts and categories, which are understandable only through their spoken form.

Krishna Chandra holds that only in science the judgement form is real. In all three grades of philosophical thinking the judgement form is apparent. In ordinary judgement the predicate amplifies or explicates the subject; in philosophy the judgement arises by presupposing the predicate, and there is nothing there to add or explain. In this sense philosophy is self-evident elaboration of the self-evident. He also holds that in science one thinks literally, whereas in philosophy one thinks symbolistically. Then he explains how in the three grades the symbolic nature is different. But with speech, the situation is slightly different. In the first three grades speech is literal, and only in the fourth grade speech is used symbolistically. Here I see a subtle distinction between thought and speech.

Both science, comprised of empirical thought, and philosophy of object involve contemplation. Both of them have the same objective attitude. The judgement in empirical thought is of the form "A is related to B," which may be paraphrased as "A as related to B is." If the contingent empirical factor is removed and the empty "is" is left behind, it is called the content of contemplation. It has been called self-subsistence. To explain this Krishna Chandra brings in the concept of proposition. We can assert or deny or have different attitudes towards it, because we have ideas about pure objectivity. Contemplative thought is not an extension of empirical thought; in empirical thought the content is concrete contingent fact but in the other the content is the self-evident structure of the object. Krishna Chandra shows that pure objectivity is not any generalization from empirical facts, and we come to know the attitude as contemplation only in contrast of the enjoying attitude. Contemplative thought and empirical thought have this in common that they are both directed towards some object. Science deals with objects but any reference to subject is irrelevant and immaterial. When philosophy deals with objects, a reference to subject becomes necessary, and it is intelligible as object only, as what the subject is not, and as symbol of the subject. This means that only when we transcend the second stage and reach the third, in the consciousness "I am", one comes to know the contemplative attitude as distinct from the subjective attitude and the corresponding difference in content.

In a very condensed form much is being said here. Object is that which is *meant.* Meaning conveyed by the speaker is what the hearer would try to convey, if he used the same word. So it is something public. This is object. In the next grade the *I* is enjoyed, i.e. subjectively experienced. Here, we find that the word I has no meaning, the hearer of the word does not understand the same I, he understands by it "you." The word *I* has a uniquely singular reference, the hearer understands it, through the word, and not through its meaning. It is a symbol of I, it is speaking subjectivity. The self incarnates in the word *I,* and that is subject.

Spiritual or the Thought of Self

The third grade has been called spiritual thought and this spirit is nothing but the self. Such thought is expressible as "I am." Krishna Chandra holds that in this stage the "am" is used symbolically. Here the contemplative attitude is dropped, the content is not objective, but is expressed as objective, so this is apparent objectivity. I quote: "What the word 'am' means is not contemplated in the objective attitude, but is subjectively enjoyed and only spoken *as though* it were objectively contemplated."[4] It is to be remembered that *understanding* is a

4. *The Concept of Philosophy,* Section 11, p. 104.

necessary feature of his philosophy. Krishna Chandra's point is that *I* may be enjoyed, that is felt and appreciated in the subjective attitude, but for *enjoying understanding* it is symbolized by objectively contemplated meaning. We see that adequate concepts are not available and speech fails to express the exact experience, then for understanding, and communication it has to be expressed as *meant*. This is symbolization. The subject is at once felt as opposed to object, and is symbolized by it. I quote again: "The content is I or implies I and although it is spoken as though it were an object, it is understood as what object is not, as the speaking subjectivity."[5]

With our training in Advaita, we find Krishna Chandra's approach easy to follow, as he says that the objective and the subjective attitude are radically opposed to each other, and we expect them to be like light and darkness but we stumble to find that the content of the enjoying attitude is individuated consciousness. He holds that individuated self, with some more epithets, is caught in enjoyment. To quote him: "Something else is always enjoyed along with the subject and enjoyed in reference to it."[6] I have argued elsewhere that if enjoyment be radically opposed to objective attitude, how can it grasp individuated consciousness? He further says that we have the awareness "I (as individual subject) am not." This consciousness involves an awareness of over personal self. This is the springing board for reaching the Absolute. Because there is demand to know the Absolute, the self can be negated. It definitely marks the difference from the classical Advaita position. Sankara says that the self can never be negated, whereas Krishna Chandra says here that by saying the individual self is nought, we arrive at the concept of the limitless Absolute. This would also be accepted by Advaita, only the

5. Ibid., Section 32., p. 113.
6. Ibid., Section 34., p. 114.

denial is of ego, which is not the real self. Krishna Chandra holds that denial of self is possible because we have a belief in the Absolute, although the speech here is wholly symbolic. My point is that here we are talking about individuated consciousness, and such consciousness obviously involves objective limiting attributes, and can it be the content of enjoyment? And I quote a very interesting comment of Krishna Chandra: "Individual subject is understood to be real as subject and not as object though it may be individual through some sort of identification with object."[7] I have already said that Krishna Chandra makes use of the subjective and the objective way of looking at things. Here, we either have to say that his description of the subjective attitude is not acceptable, or we have to revise our ideas about subjective cognising.

Transcendental Thought and the Concept of the Absolute

In the last grade we reach the concept of the Absolute. It is at once the negation and continuation of the subject. It is beyond all subjectivity and objectivity. It is the content of transcendental consciousness, which can be expressed only symbolically. If this is the scenario, if the transcendental is beyond both the objective and the subjective attitude, if it cannot be spoken literally and has to be expressed only through symbols, then what is the need of accepting it at all? Krishna Chandra says that in the spiritual grade we feel the demand for this stage. He says that fact can be denied only because we have an idea of the self-subsistent, and the self-subsistent is denied only when the reality of the subjective emerges. But "We may also deny reality in the form "I (as individual subject) am not."[8] He claims that this is a new grade negation. After shredding off individuality, one reaches the ultimate stage of pure

7. Ibid., Section 13., p. 105.
8. Ibid., Section 13., p. 105.

subjectivity. But in the *Concept of Philosophy* he decides to speak in a different way. My question is that if self is deniable and object is also deniable, why should the self be called real? The position in *The Subject as Freedom* is easier to apprehend.

It is to be noted that he does not speak of different sections of philosophy, but he speaks of grades. This implies that each grade is better than the former one, and it naturally involves the idea of a goal. Is this goal the reaching of Absolute? Experience comes to us as a fused jumbled up whole, and the Absolute is present in it and he moves towards it by peeling off the layers. As he has spoken of the Absolute as unspeakable, so his philosophy has been described as mysticism. But I do not accept this comment. Transcendental Absolute is still a content of theoretic consciousness. Kant speaks of the things in themselves as unknown and unknowable but that does not turn his philosophy into mysticism. His Absolute is not a lion's den which devours up everything. He is searching for the Absolute which is beyond all categorization. In one stage of his philosophical life he held that experience comes to us as indefinite, and through gradual dissociation we reach the ultimate definite, where no more dissociation is possible. This ultimate one is the Absolute. The Absolute prevades our experience. In every level it is rendered more definite than the previous one, and "The indefinite completely definitized is what is called Absolute."[9]

The Alternative Absolutes

He speaks of alternative Absolutes, which are reached through analysis of thinking, feeling and willing. He is interested in consciousness with its three faces. An over-simplified version of approach through feeling is as follows. A child plays with a toy and has a feeling of joy; a grandma who watches the play has a sympathetic feeling for this feeling, a second order,

9. *The Fundamentals of K.C.Bhattacharyya's Philosophy*, p. 31.

reflective feeling; an artist can have a third order feeling for this sympathetic feeling — the supra reflective feeling. This feeling, which is completely free from all objective mooring is Absolute as value. This does not look like mysticism.

However, another critic thinks that he has spoken of philosophy as constituted of belief, which carry a demand for knowledge. He contrasted his position with that of Kant. Kant spoke of postulates as thoughts, which are not knowledge; Krishna Chandra says that this ultimate knowledge is that which does not involve any thought. What such knowledge means he does not explain. The critic says that to speak of knowledge which goes beyond thought is to land into mysticism. Evaluation of this comment would require a thorough examination of the concept of knowledge, which is beyond the scope of this paper. However, it is to be noted this demand is not to be mistaken as a demand for self-realization. The self-subsistent demands to be known in absorbed contemplation, the real *I* demands to be known in pure enjoyment. The speaking attitude is not discarded here. The transcendental, which is spoken only through symbolization, completely dispenses of with speech when it is known completely. But I have said that to call it unspeakable is not to land into mysticism.

14

Acharya Brojendranath Seal
His Aesthetic Ideas

Sudhir Kumar Nandi

ACHARYA BROJENDRANATH SEAL and Rabindranath Tagore were contemporaries and we know that Dr Seal had very close and intimate understanding of Tagore literature. His review of Tagore literature is worth reading.

Brojendranath offered constructive criticism of Tagore's literature which Rabindranath valued a great deal. The poet asked the philosopher to preside over the inaugural ceremony of Visvabharati as he considered Dr Seal to be eminently suited for the purpose. Rabindranath's tribute To Brojendranath Seal (A tribute, Acharya Brojendranath Seal Birth Centenary volume, Calcutta, 1969) in verse is worth quoting:

> Pilgrim, the highest peaks of knowledge, hard to climb you have scaled;
>
> There on imagination's canvas, in diverse tints and colours is painted the invitation of Eternal Beauty;
>
> The radiance white from there, of glory that is
>
> The goodness of Wisdom's caressing hand, plays round your noble brow.

Thus while felicitating Dr Seal, Tagore has in mind a double image of the philosopher — an image resplendent with the glory of a seeker after truth and another in quest of the Eternal Beauty. Thus Tagore admirably refers to Dr Seal both as a thinker and as a poet. In the pages to follow we will try to analyse Dr Seal's aesthetic ideas in the context of his "synoptic view of things" and ascertain his position as a poet of the Quest eternal. That would give us a complete picture of Dr Seal both as a creator and as a critic.

Seal's Concept of Art and Criticism of Life

Dr Seal thought, individual scheme of life, an individual outlook on the universal to be the norm of poetry. This was consistent with his concept of art as the criticism of life and his preference for the whole — the *bhūmā* of the Upaniṣadic texts. His idea of the whole was also inspired by the Aristotelian idea of the "beginning middle and end theory." His craze for the totality was amply "reflected in his postulation of an "individual scheme of life" when he wrote:

> No doubt, all emotions are proper plastic stuff for constructions in aesthetics as well as ethics but as building materials, experience, in all its forms, is intrinsically valuable — ideation, imagination, instinct, no less than emotion. But none of these enter into the norm. What does enter into the norm and text of poetry is not emotional exaltation, imaginative transfiguration or disinterested criticism but in and through them all the creation of a personality with an individual scheme of life, an individual outlook on the universe.

The critic and the poet in Dr Seal combined to give us a unique individuality, that is the content of all art-work.

Art was looked upon by Dr Seal as the friction and practical consummation of experience. So far as Dr Seal was concerned the differentia between art and craft was this *ānanda* and herein he agreed with the Tagores, i.e. Rabindranath and

Abanindranath. Dr Seal, while working out this differentia follows the traditional Indian thinking on *rasa*. He tells us that *rasa* or the aesthetic sentiment or the aesthetic enjoyment is the characteristic element of art. This sentiment as sentiment is the same in different arts and not marked off by distinctive psychological character. The aesthetic sentiment then, is the same in different arts but the latter are marked off from one another by the medium in which they worked. This distinguishing of the subjective and objective aspects of experience hardly bears phychologial examination. This distinction is not maintainable from the standpoint of modern psychology. Representations, symbols, conventions constitute such a medium in every such art. But in the plastic arts only objective aspects of experience are directly represented. Experience, however, on the subjective side may not be represented directly but only symbolically.*

ART OF ARCHITECTURE, SCULPTURE AND PAINTING

It is the objective medium through which the *rasa* is excited that distinguishes an art and constitutes in what it is and not the essence of the *rasa* itself which, as *rasa*, is psychologically the same in all the arts. The three plastic arts — architecture, sculpture, and painting — are distinguished from one another by the number of dimensions of the medium in which they work. Architecture works in all the three dimensions fully and freely so as to form an all-sided representation of any given situation. Sculpture works in three dimensions, but with a limited field and circumscribed space and time in each direction. Painting works in two dimensions and achieves its purpose with the help of perspective, when so desired.

---

* For a detailed study, please refer to *Studies in Modern Indian Aesthetics* by Dr S.K. Nandi, 1975, Simla: Indian Institute of Advanced Study, pp. 93-155.

ART OF MUSIC AND MATHEMATICAL RHYTHM

But radically different from these plastic arts is the art of music which marks no objective aspect of the imagination but excites the evolution directly and not symbolically. Here ideas and representations are only indirect aids and nothing more. The objective medium is constitued by *air waves* (vibrations, rhythms), and whether in the form of melody or of harmony, mathematical proportions furnish the objective basis. It is interesting to note here that there is another sphere of rhythm which is entirely without any implication of sound or air waves, viz. mathematical rhythm which the mathematicians perceive in the evolution of pure mathematics, a rhythm which, perhaps, is what may have been symbolized in the music of the spheres.

THE ART OF ARTS — POETRY

Coming now to the final art — the art of arts, poetry, it is distinguished by the fact that it excites the *rasa*s (or the aesthetic sentiment) directly by means of language, movement and visual imagination working either separately or jointly. Its advantage is that it can bring the other arts (plastic as well as vocal) to its aid so as to give rise to composite forms of art.

Finally in this context, Dr Seal tells us that it may be noted that various composite types of art now being experimented upon, in which plastic, vocal and visual experiences are sought to be fused or thrown together as in medley, e.g. Imagism, Scintillism, Cubism, Naturalism (with the ugly and the nude as motives of art) and so on, and there is no end to such experiments.

But these experiments in the Occident are yet radically marked off from the domain of Eastern art such as the Chinese, the Japanese, and the Hindu. Taking Hindu art for example, it is not fair to say that Hindu painting paints the soul. This no art can do, and this would not be art, if attempted, but the distinctive feature is that it does not copy a model objectively presented to the artist but seems to image forth in the mind's eye an objective conceived by *dhyāna* and subsequently embodied in some sense-medium.

Another characterisitc feature of Hindu art is that the artist seeks individual expression only within the limits furnished by the type or model conceived by the master artist (or by tradition) to whom (or to which) he attaches himself. In the same way, the Chinese and the Japanese masters display their individuality within the limits furnished by the types or traditions to which they attach themselves and the individual element in art works more felicitously by working within the limits of the central type.

Seal's View of Aesthetics and Art

In the study of Dr Seal's view of aesthetics, it is essential to note that there are three typical and radically divergent views of art (as noted by Dr Seal) in his magnum opus: *The Autobiography* (unpublished).

1. The aesthetic values or satisfactions are finite values viewing Reality as temporal experience which cannot testify to any ultimate and immutable ground.
2. The aesthetic values or satisfactions (*rasa*) are emergent, being manifestations in time of an ideal ground which is infinite or timeless (or eternal).
3. The aesthetic satisfactions (or *rasa*) testify to a unique reality which may be termed the momentary, a sort of exaltation in which the experience of a moment is transfigured so as to assume an infinite value. In this respect Dr Seal comes close to the traditional Indian concept of the identity of the aesthetic joy with the Absolute Reality, *rasa vai saḥ*, and thereby he discloses a close affinity with Rabindranath's ideas in point. The unique reality of the art-work is hard to define and as

such Rabindranath characterized its essence as *māyā*. We know that this idea of *māyā* does not suggest illusion but lacks in ultimacy. This point had already been explained earlier and that is why perhaps Dr Seal uses the expression unique reality. Reality is there but it is unique and hence indefinable. According to him, literature (its relation to life) is twofold: (1) as the representation (not presentation of life), and (2) as the unfoldment of the meaning of life (in other words, its interpretation). Besides, it may be incidentally noted that there are other types of literary art, viz. those that are subsumed under post impressionism. Criticism is often vitiated by its ignoring the fundamental differences in aim and method between the above types of literary art. It must be carefully noted that the mere presentation of life for its raw material, as distinguished from its representation or its interpretation of meaning, is not art.

Greek Concept of Art Dominates the World

Though art as the expression of life must be as broad as life itself, it is unfortunate that the world has been dominated by the Greek concept of art which though supreme in its own way and exquisitely finished in form and meaning, has notional and even insular limitations of its own. The Greek pantheon, which is so human and has two characteristic human prototypes in Hercules (the unconquerable redeemed in his strength) and Psyche (redemptive love), is undoubtedly, matchless in form and type, but it is defective and even rudimentary in its expression and symbolization of nature and super-nature. Contrast with this the Egyptian, the Babylonian, the Indian and other culture types. To describe these in merely general terms:

1. The vast, the massive, the terrible or the grotesque in early Egyptian Art, with its sphinxes, its half-beast deities, its triad (Osiris, Isis, Horus) and finally its prototype of the Sun god in Amenophis, the first Exemplar of man-in God and God-in-man;
2. The asymmetrical and non-natural (but powerful and mysterious) in Babylonian Art (early middle and late) down to the new developments codified by Hammurabbi; or
3. The typical Hindu *mūrtis*, symbolical forms which manifest themselves to the devotee in meditation (*dhyāna*), such as the dancing Śiva (*Naṭarāja*), the Indian Buddha (not the Greek) or Viṣṇu and his consort or the divine figure of Sarasvatī; these being revealed to the artist in *dhyāna* (meditation) and not drawn as in the West after an objective model, which from the oriental point of view, would at once degrade them to the level of artefacts.
4. The Negro type with its peculiar physiognomy and its symbolic music and dance, its drumming and its signalling by flashes of light for communication of news from one corner of Africa to the other.

There may be instances of a few characteristic specimens of the wealth of non-Greek human types, which only prejudice can ignore in any comprehensive classification of art-types and art-systems. But all that can be conceded to Greek sculpture is that it executes its own representative idea and image with a perfection which neither the Egyptian nor Babylonian could achieve in its own respective world of art. But Hindu paintings and Chinese architecture exhibit the same superb mastery as Greek sculpture. To the Greek aesthetic sense, all non-Greek types are uncouth and monstrous, if not ugly.

But it is idle to claim that there can be any finality in art. Robin, for example, creates new types of humanity including the commonplace and the ugly and makes these last as proud denizens of the world of art as the classic or neo-classic types.

Such were Dr Seal's early views of literature and literary art and he brought them into line with his general philosophical outlook which by that time was markedly Hegelian.

Seal Gave Left-handed Compliment to Music

Music, for Dr Seal, posed a problem as he found in music nothing but mathematical proportions. Music received a left-handed compliment from Dr Seal in his Autobiography. The plastic and pictorial arts brought to Dr Seal revelations of a new world but music offered him a stumbling block. The mathematical proportions came home to him; they were only an evolution of mathematical proportions and nothing more. So appreciation of music was not so much dependent on the innate sense of harmony of the appreciation as it was on his acquired sense of proportion. This was training-based, and without appropriate training the appreciation of music was not at all possible. We note here that artists like Abanindranath repeatedly spoke of training and discipline for a proper understanding of fine arts whereas Dr Seal considered this training to be essential for a proper appreciation of music. He specifically told us that an understanding of Hindu music was impossible without such training of the ear as would enable it to catch the *śruti*s, the twenty-two intervals in which the octave is divided in that music; and *śruti*s imply a finer and more discriminative appreciation of natural gradations than the twelve semi-tones of occidental music.

Dr Seal found, however, that the usual notion that the Hindus had no idea of harmony at all was not altogether correct. Polyphonic music as intermediate between melody and harmony was of course nothing new to them. But this was not all. They had the elements of harmony as Dr Seal had shown, in his noted book *Positive Sciences of the Ancient Hindus.* This harmony as evidenced in music and other forms of plastic art was a phenomenon not only of the aesthetic world but of the phenomenal world as well. Love was instrumental in the discovery of this harmony for without love this harmony was not discernible in the empirical world. This hypothesis of love has been regarded as a condition precedent for the proper understanding of the problem of communication in art. This concept of love has a wider meaning in the context of modern aesthetics and it helps empathy or Einfuehlung to operate for a proper appreciation of art. That beauty could communicate or express in and through love, even though it was transfigured appetite, is evident from contemporary reviews of ancient and modern art-historians. We may, to illustrate our point, refer to the chapter entitled "Sources of Data" in *Sexual Behaviour in Human Female* (ed. by Kinsey and others). We should specially direct our attention to the section on art-materials, wherein the author tells us how elements contributed to the development of the word's fine arts persistently. Love in the lower sense equally fed the fine arts of the world as it involved the ideal love of the Platonic type as it's a priori prius. Strictly speaking this higher and lower love concept was not maintainable. Love, whatever moral appendage we may ascribe to it, is and has been pursuing the vision of beauty, which Dr Seal discovers in Endymion.

It may be noted that during the period of his writing *New Essays in Criticism*, young Brojendranath in his study of the "New Romantic Movement in Literature" showed no lack of self-confidence in his criticism of Hegel. Dr Seal accounted for this repudiation of his master in his address to the post-graduate students of the Calcutta University: (*New Essays in Criticism*, Soin Brothers, Calcutta, 1903, p. 25):

> You see I have been a seeker after flawless, full-orbited perfection throughout and in every walk of my life and this my hankering after perfection, after a finished product everywhere and always, has baffled me in all my endeavours to accomplish anything worthy of mention. Whenever I have sat down to compose anything I have been haunted by the fear that I may have thereby committed myself to the keeping of some closed system of truth and this is precisely what I am constitutionally incapable of doing.

New Essays in Criticism contains interesting revelations of young Brojendranath's self-assurance in expounding his early master Hegel's "Theory of Art" and pointing out where he began to differ from his master. We shall give below two instances. In the opening page of his preface, Dr Seal writes:

> Hegel's view of historic development as unilinear series, a position to which his dialectic of the categories commits him, can no longer be maintained. The Egypto-Babylonian, the Graeco-Italian, the Indo-Sino-Japanese art series and culture histories, cannot be evolved one from another and are relatively independent in origin as well as in development. In tracing the historic world process, at whatever point we begin and whether we proceed up or down, the genealogical line breaks up more and more into a network of relationship so that the Hegelian conception of a punctual movement in a unilinear series is as obsolete from the standpoint of the philosophy of history and the historic method proper, as the Lamarckian view in the domain of biology.
>
> At the same time, the recognition of the diverse origins and independent developments of the separate culture histories is not inconsistent with the assertion of an immanent world movement in which they all participate, each in its own degree and extent and it is the business of Dialectic to trace the outlines of the cosmic movement to formulate its

> successive categories or regulative ideas and to work out their rational and systematic filiation, without pretending to anticipate history or seeking to close the vista of the future.

Progress of Biological, Historical Sciences and Art

Dr Seal tells us that the progress of the biological and historical sciences has made it necessary to formulate this more correct philosophical view of development. The diverse historic cultures, arts, religions, philosophies, codes and race-consciousnesses are not partial phases or aspects of humanity or of the absolute idea; they are the developing whole and express, more or less fully and accurately, the idea of universal humanity, reproducing like the Leibnitzian monad, the entire cosmic movement, each in miniature and each from its own individual place and position in the long scheme of things (p. iv). It was rightly pointed out by Dr N.V. Banerjee, "Acharya Brojendranath Seal, the versatile thinker and the passionate humanist" (*Acharya Brojendranath Seal Centenary Commemoration Volume*, pp. 122-28) that Dr Seal's philosophy was an interpretation of culture, comprising science, art, religion and morality. His philosophic outlook sought a synoptic view of things, its characteristic being comprehensiveness and anthropocentricity.

Where young Brojendranath expressed his deviation from Hegel's theory of linear progress in art, his use of metaphysical expressions like immanent world movement and reproducing like Leibnitz's Monads the entire cosmic movement brought him close to the historicists who said similar things in another way: that each epoch, each society is of equal value and the linear idea of progress is untenable. Later Spengler in his detailed study of historic cultures concluded that each culture, similar to living organism passes through a cycle of growth, maturity and decline uninfluenced by others.

The Real is Always a Whole : Seal

While studying Dr Seal's later writings on aesthetics one has to note his still wider divergence from Hegel. The dialectical process was conceived by Hegel as a movement from aspect to aspect, from moment to moment, until it was completed in the Absolute Idea or the Absolute whole. The Law of Evolution was similarly taken to simplify a differentiation of parts, of organs and functions, which go on developing each in its own line until they are reintegrated in a coherent whole. Both these conceptions, Dr Seal thought, required a radical correction. The real is always a whole; the abstraction of phases, aspects, moments is unhistorical; and organs and functions evolve, never idependently but always as participating in and dominated by the life of the organism as a whole. The earlier stages were as real and concrete as the later ones. His idea of coherent whole as the matrix of all contraries and contradictions has been shared by many a modern critic and their resemblance or approximation in similar thinking is not a peculiar phenomenon in the history of aesthetics. The historico-comparative method reveals such resemblances; they might look paradoxical at times. Engelberg for example, while discussing the aesthetics of Yeats speaks in the same vein as Dr Seal. His thesis runs on the same lines. In *The Vast Design: Patterns in W.B. Yeats's Aesthetics*, Engelberg has endeavoured to arrange them in intelligible patterns which obey the Yeatsian laws of the contraries, seeing Yeats's whole art as a long exercise in trying to eat his cake and keep it too, an attempt to achieve what might be defined in Auden's word, as a poetry which is the clear expression of mixed feelings. In his first chapter, on first principles, Engelberg shows how Yeats was attracted by opposite ideals and determined to preserve them both — the grandeur and vastness mainly associated with the epic as well as the passion and intensity mainly associated with the lyric,

Western Renaissance individualism and the cult of personality as well as Eastern serenity and vague immensities.

Thus, Dr Seal's idea of a synoptic view finds its echo in Engelberg and the latter puts up an unwitting support for Dr Seal. Quite consistent to his adherence to the idea of a synoptic whole, Dr Seal wrote that antithesis as a mere negation (as conceived by Hegel) was a logical fiction. The organic whole developed and passed from a relatively less stable to a relatively more stable equilibrium and the balance of powers, which maintained the whole life, corrected undue emphasis in the one direction by developing a counter emphasis in a complementary (not opposed) direction. Dr Seal readily agreed with Mc Taggart, a Hegelian, when Dr Mc Taggart considered that Hegel in the later categories, more or less discarded the antithesis as an abstract negation.

Seal's Aesthetics : Relation With Hegel

But it must be said that Dr Seal's aesthetics had its roots in Hegel and he himself made it amply clear while he discussed the role of critics since Hegel. Philosophical critics since Hegel, Dr Seal writes, have either been content with diversifying and amplifying the materials that are illustrative of Hegel's classification of art, or what is very rare, have followed tracks of their own, thus losing the advantage of building on a solid foundation already laid. Ulrici, Lotze, Michelet among philosophers, Barante and Sainte-Bauve and Quinet, Gervinus and Taine among the historians of literature, Otto Bauer and Schlosser among the writers on Staatswi ssenschaft and political history (all of whom Dr Seal referred to) dealt in the spirit of comprehensive thought with theories and type of art. Dr Seal thinks that Michelet's relation to Hegel was that of a disciple and commentator. He considers Lotze to be at his weakest in aesthetics.

According to Dr Seal, Ulrici was more "possible in his theory of art, than in his doctrine of religion but the best event of his theory of art and art-criticism was the stress he laid on the central or regulative idea in his analysis of the products of art and that was Hegel diluted down to Ulrici. Bauer and Sainte-Bauve Schlosser and Gervinus gave us either fragmentary theories and generalizations or admirable galleries of portraits unmatched for brilliance and historic verisimilitude. It was Dr Seal's considered opinion that young among post-Hegelians, Taine alone fashioned a new theory on aesthetics and contributed elements of permanent value which fairly supplemented and corrected the Hegelian doctrine.

However, it may be safely said that the historic classification of art begun by Lessing Winckelmann and systematized by Hegel had some abiding influence on the thoughts of Dr Seal, as is evident from his own words:

> In respect of historic genesis and comprehensive classification, in the department of aesthetics, Hegel must remain the ground-plan for all future superstructures.

Seal Critical of Three Constituents

Nonetheless Dr Seal was critical of the three constituent factors in art. Dr Seal writes, of every artistic product — **the idea, the symbol** or **matter** and **the representation** or **reflection** — it is important to bear in mind that it is the character of the last which alone determines the type of art. It follows that the idea and the symbolical material may vary and yet so long as the relation between the two or what is the same, the character of the representation of the former by the latter, does not change, the type of art will remain the same. On this view it is easy to understand how different arts, like poetry and painting, operating upon different materials, may belong to the same type, such as the classical or the romantic. Within the domain of literary art, the same observation holds good. The epic, dramatic, and lyrical varieties are broadly distinguished in matter as well as in form, but this distinction of representative material is incompatible with their belonging to the same type of art.

Again, Dr Seal points out, taking individual differences among poetic creations, the Hell of Dante with its realistic hard-featured outlines, differs in embodiment and configuration from the ideal shadows and supernatural horrors of Milton's bottomless abyss, but there is no difficulty in classing them together as products of romantic art. Similarly, the other element, the idea may vary widely without correspondent variations in the type of art. With these critical notes on Hegel, Dr Seal drew some conclusions which considerably modified and enlarged the Hegelian theory on fine arts. To quote Dr Seal:

> It is idle therefore to say, as Hegel says, that the romantic type (re: his oriental-classical-romantic classification) is final and that art, as a historic movement, culminates, after the romantic type in religion and philosophy. Taine's conception is true. Art, instead of passing over into and being consummated in philosophy, run in parallel lines with the latter and is destined to new developments, along with the movement of speculation and with changes in the social environment.

Moral and Aesthetic Considerations: Modern Parallels

It has been said that Dr Seal was the first significant literary critic of the last one hundred years. His synoptic view of criticism comprised the entire panorama of human existence including man's endeavours in diverse fields and directions. It entails the problem of deciding whether judgements on literature are also judgements passed on contemporary society, social values, social ideas and ideals.

Incidentally morals *vis-à-vis* art come up before our mind and this vexed problem of art-morality relation has been tackled by Dr Seal in his own inimitable way. The issue had been discussed threadbare when Dr Seal spoke of *moral teaching by aesthetic culture.*

In his reply to a government circular, Dr Seal discussed the need of "moral teaching by aesthetic culture" by which he meant the regulation of emotions and the inculcation of habits and modes of conduct prompted by such emotions. Morality, for Dr Seal, had a positive social basis dissociated from those beliefs regarding ultimate realities, which are definitely formulated in the articles of religious faith. Moral teaching to him, had two positive foundations:

1. Social wellbeing and the inculcation of habits and conduct which promote such wellbeing.
2. Culture of the emotions, what Dr Seal called aesthetic culture, based not on religious principles or motive but on instinctive reactions in typical situations and relations of life. This was according to Dr Seal our objective.

The capital error was to teach religious beliefs and doctrines first and to follow them up by moral rules and precepts — a course which promoted enslavement and by reaction engendered skepticism. The proper course, on the other hand, was exactly the reverse. Theory of utimate beliefs ought to have been left to a later stage in the development of reason when religious beliefs and metaphysical principles would properly engage our interest. Dr Seal points out that Sanskrit dramatists had a sense of propriety, and moral equilibrium, which is offended by the final triumph of vice over virtue or of an unmoral fate over the human demand for equity and justice. For such triumph would offend the moral sense which was more fundamental if not more powerful than aesthetic sentiment. The Greeks believed in Fate or Destiny which was stronger than even Zeus, and the Greek moral sense, which was so elastic, was contrasted with the Sanskrit dramatist's demand for justice and moral balance. Dr Seal noted in this connection that Johnson too among the moderns was rigorous in his demand for proper moral proportions and "poetic justice."

Milton ultimately accepted this concept of poetic justice in preference to "political justice." Here we may further point out that Dr Seal noted in the section on abnormal psychology in his Autobiography that Freud being confronted by criticism of his pet theory of sexual love being directed by the male child to his mother and by the female child to her father, fell back on the idea of love as such minus the sex taint as a principle of explanation of such infantile love. And Dr Seal spoke on this point in Freud with great enthusiasm as he had a moralistic basis as was found in many other modern thinkers such as Croce and Cassirer.

Uniqueness in Tagore's Poems, says Seal

Of course, in modern times we have seen storm raging round Ezra Pond on his being awarded the Bollingen Prize for his noted work, *The Pisan Cantos*. The issue involved therein was whether art was purely formal and as such amoral in character. From Dr Seal's point of veiw such a position was untenable as according to him, aesthetic world was concentric with other worlds of discourse. Dr Seal is not alone in his belief. His concept of sympotic view finds its echo in a modern critic, Yvor Winters, when he distinguishes five steps in the critical process:

1. to state the relevant, historical and biographical material,
2. to analyse the writer's relevant literary theories,

3. to make a rational criticism of the paraphrasable content,
4. to make a rational criticism of feeling, style, language, and technique, and
5. to make a final act of judgement.

All these might be considered to lie within Dr Seal's synoptic view of literature. Judged by the time and context of Dr Seal, he may be looked upon as extremely original in his formulation and application of this synoptic view and his genetic method.

Adjudged by the above criterion, i.e. viewed as a whole, Tagore's poetic achievement was characteristically complete. That is the view held by Dr Seal in spite of his earlier adverse criticism of Tagore. Dr Seal considers that Tagore's early poems are exercises in emotional exaltation. To this he soon adds the art of imaginative transfiguration (as in *Urvaśī*). In his maturer achievement he develops the criticism of life without sacrificing either exaltation or transfiguration. Finally in this, his consummate later art, he has summed up all these elements and achieved the supreme mastery — the creation of a personality with an individual scheme of life, an individual outlook on the Universe. Thus, Dr Seal aptly brings out the uniqueness of Tagore's creative activity and that could alone be properly understood if he had viewed Tagore from this viewpoint of the totality. Judged piecemeal, Tagore had many shortcomings and when his creations were considered as a whole, his towering genius becomes evident.

Seal was Averse to "Artificiality"

Dr Seal's notion of the full-orbited perfection implies this point of view concerning the totality of things and whenever anything was judged from a clouded partial point of view, it was destined to end in a futile intellectual exercise. Anything, circumscribed, limited, or provincialized might represent some "closed system" of truth and hence a distortion of truth which was not worthy of pursuit. We all know that he had been a seeker after flawless, full-orbited perfection and this vision of the perfect unity did not allow him to build up any closed system as it did not approximate this vision of perfection. Maybe, it was the inherent weakness of discursive reason or of language itself that it could not reflect the totality, the vision of the whole and we may note in passing that for this inaptitude, the analytical method was rejected by Dr Seal. His distaste for this "closed system" was shared by Romain Rolland, and his fashionable art-connoissuer Sylvian Kohn speaks ill of "closed chamber-music" or "Sofa music." Anything closed smacked of "artificiality" and that was exactly what Dr Seal was averse to. This ghost of perfection haunted him and he was never satisfied with what he wrote. Tagore's poetic works (as judged by Dr Seal) somewhere reached his ideal of completeness. We may suggest here that judged thus, Tagore was a greater artist than Dr Seal as Tagore could come closer to Dr Seal's idea of "compactness." Dr Seal could not approximate his own ideal. That was exactly what Dr Seal wrote by way of confession which was to the effect that he could never approximate his ideal of perfection and completeness.

Dr Seal is known to have characterized his philosophy as "synthetic philosophy" as he took a view which considered all probable aspects of the problem in question. But his methodology was marked by keen, penetrating analysis and as such Krishna Chandra Bhattacharyya rightly remarked that his (Dr Seal's) real interest was in the abstract analysis of logic and epistemology. This penetrating analysis is present in every thing Dr Seal thought and wrote. In a letter dated 29 May 1914, written to Tagore from Cambridge, Dr Seal told him frankly that *Gitanjali* as rendered into English, was not his best creation and a correct appraisal of Tagore's genius would not be possible if he were judged solely by his *Gitanjali* as rendered into English. The English-speaking people branded Tagore as "mystic" without knowing fully the peculiar character of Tagore's mysticism and Dr Seal vehemently disliked it.

Dr Seal, though a mystic, was of a rational type, and according to some, this rational approach to problems, intellectual understanding of phenomena, was not incompatible with mysticism. He did not hesitate to say that Yeats and Underhill did not very well appreciate Tagore when they considered him to be a mystic poet. Dr Seal thought that Tagore was the best even amongst the modern poets. He wanted that people all over the world should know that there was much better stuff in Tagore's other works, e.g. his dramas, novels, stories and poems than in *Gitanjali* as catered to the Western readers. This evaluation of *Gitanjali*, for not being a criticism of life, was not quite in keeping with Dr Seal's postulation of a synthetic outlook. We consider that *Gitanjali* offered some transcendental principles of explanation which not only explained the ultimacy of human life in the context of God-man relation but also thus explained human existence as a total, completed phenomenon.

Seal's Interpretation of Artwork

Art, as interpretation of life, or criticism of life gives a piecemeal view. It had certain innate weaknesses. If such a business of art is essential for art qua art, art must be vested with a purpose, not quite in keeping with the freedom of the artist. To interpret life means stressing of an arbitrary function of fine arts and it is made a matter of intellectual apprehension only; this goes against his synoptic view of art. Art as such cannot be considered intellectual; Kant's characterization of the aesthetic purpose as "purposiveness without a purpose" fully brings out its enigmatic and indefinable nature. So this characterization of Dr Seal cannot be accepted without reservation. And we think that Dr Seal also did not uphold this position when he visualized the future of art in his Autobiography. Dr Seal felt that the future lay with a composite form of art, free from the limitations of an individual art like sculpture, painting or music. But it would have free recourse at pleasure to several media, individually or collectively, such as colour, sound and motion and would appeal to all the senses at once and to the soul as well, all these being consummated in poetry which appeals to the imagination and generalizes the senses. So herein the role of art as criticism of life has been subservient to something which had a greater appeal to imagination.

Intellect and discursive reasoning have been relegated to an inferior position and as such art as the criticism of life was not given the highest premium. But Dr Seal's flare for analysis and critical evaluation did not leave him and he repeatedly told that one should be critical enough in appraising an art-work. Other considerations should be avoided. Dr Seal amply demonstrates this critical attitude when he reviewed Tagore's earlier works. He applied the genetic method in the field of aesthetics, from the philosophico-historical, the comparative and the psychological points of view. His understanding of the different phases of the evoluton of art is noteworthy.

THREE MAIN BASES OF ART DEVELOPMENT

Dr Seal noted three main bases of art development in the history of world-art and we may refer to his Autobiography in point for a detailed account of the different periods in art history:

1. **Hellenic** — It would be wrong to say that Greek art confined itself to the body or to the mind as expressed in the body. In fact, it expressed the soul as well, so

far as this could be done in and through the body but it considered as beyond art whatever could not be expressed or adumbrated in body, nerve and muscle or in pose and situation.

2. **Renaissance** — In contrast with this Michelangelo, Titian and Leonardo da Vinci depicted the soul magnifying or idealizing nature so far as nature could express the Christian concepts and experiences of the soul. Rembrandt also expressed this in his chirascuro.
3. **Hindu** — The Buddhist-Hindu idea of art was again different from this, drawing its inspiration not from a living model of flesh and blood but from *dhyāna* or ecstatic meditation which revealed the form and figure to the eye of the mind. Moreover what was sought to be represented was not the individual but the type expressed in and through the individual and this type was more and more realized in and through *dhyāna*.

This classification is certainly an improvement on what Hegel did in point. Dr Seal virtually offers a transcendental principle as the guiding principle of art classification insofar as the Hellenic and the Renaissance periods were concerned and sought to adumbrate this principle through *dhyāna* on Hindu art; his criticism of Hegel's classification of fine arts may be looked upon as "constructive" when judged in the light of this new model.

Neo-Romantic Art: Analysis

Let us have a peep into Dr Seal's way of looking at the neo-romantic art movement. In section II of the *New Essays in Criticism,* Dr Seal placed before us some canons of neo-romantic art in a convenient formula:

1. A sense of discordance between the inner and the outer, between spirit and nature, the ideal and the

real. The social environment is one of *Sturm und Drang*, of fret and fury, of ideal revolt or uprising of the human spirit. The movement takes its actual rise, however, not in an unhealthy ferment of dissolution, but in an inevitable process which transfigures the old order and lifts it up to the absolute by raising it into self-consciousness and subjectivity. Thus a current of transfiguration sets in, and its significance was of considerable magnitude.

2. The second element is that of subjective egoism, which arising in the passage from a mechanical subjectivity, sets up the gratification of the individual consciousness as the standard in questions of truth and falsehood, right and wrong, beauty and ugliness. No stage of mind or art, Dr Seal contends, can subsist in an atmosphere of mere negation; and accordingly we find that in the course of the development of the neo-romantic art and consciousness, the negative element — the deadly strife with doubt and despair, and the subjective egoism — tends to disappear, and critical and constructive elements come into play. At this stage there is a fusion of the two streams; the current of transfiguration of the old order mingles with the stream of positive reconstruction of the new. The confluence results in a mighty stir and commotion. An objective basis is sought for life, so as to lift it out of the plane of over-subjectivity and morbid self-consciousness.

In the reconstruction or new synthesis of life and consciousness thus attempted, novel ideas as to the place and position of man in the universe and his destiny, a new criticism of social life and relations and new ethical and religious ideals, possess the minds of men. The function of neo-romantic literary art, Dr Seal points out, is to embody these regulative ideas and ideals in correspondent types and symbols, to invest them with appropriate emotions and images to interweave them with the sympathies and affinities, the historic associations and the imaginative interests of the race and thus to make them essential conditions of the conservation and solidarity of the social regime. The critical and constructive elements of neo-romantic literary art have been systematically analysed and methodically registered by Dr Seal with the help of a convenient formula of criticism (as stated above) and it takes note of these three fundamental aspects:

(a) The ideal content of consciousness, the regulative idea of central conception, which is here an objective criticism of life;

(b) The mythopaeic process or embodiment of this idea in a Vorstellung — which may be termed "the mythology of literary art"; and

(c) The crowning transfiguration or the birth of a new emotion, as of a new tone or harmony, transfiguring the imaginative material.

His Quest Eternal: An Analysis

Herein Dr Seal combines mysticism with pure poetry. We have already noted in the preceding pages how mysticism and poetry fused and blended in Tagore's poetical works. Mysticism of a certain kind was an inseparable and indigenous feature of the intellectual school. In Tennyson this type of intellectuality blended in mysticism; again this blending gives a type of obscurity that is evident in such mystic poets as Tennyson and Browning. Dr Seal is no exception to this rule and he is obscure at places. This obscurity might have been a product of Seal's revolt against individualism which in turn may be looked upon as a product of his mental evolution and a byproduct of his postulation of a synoptic view of life. Individualism had been considered to be the sheet anchor of all art but curiously enough this idea of revolt against individualism was incorporated in his new concept of art as enunciated in his Autobiography. The successive steps, according to him in this revolt are:

1. The mass-consciousness or mass mind working in and through the aggregate of individual minds: This is not organized, nor expressed through any particular organ or vehicle but is recognized as the consensus working in and through the "proletariat."
2. The community consciousness or the community mind: The community is held together by bonds of a common tradition and practice, is a more organized expression of the consensus than the mass mind.
3. The age consciousness or age mind: This is a living force and develops from age to age.
4. The race consciousness or race mind: By race consciouness Dr Seal here means the human race in general and not any particular race or people. By race consciousness, accordingly, is meant the stage of human evolution which has been attained by men at the particular turn of human history.

Dr Seal herein noted that the world had entered on a new phase of art ideals and art-constructions. The ruling ideas of this new world of art are the mass consciousness, the community consciousness, the age consciousness, and the race consciousness as explained above. The hero and the heroine will no longer be "individuals" as such in their own right, but individuals as representing or typifying the ruling forces in the mass consciousness, the community consciousness, and the race consciousness.

Conclusion

Before we conclude this dissertation, we may refer to "Quest Eternal" trying at a descriptive formulation of its subject-matter and critical evaluation of its aesthetic qualities. The poem opens with the gorgeous picture of a mighty ocean heaving and falling under the canopy of a silent sky spreading to the end of vision. The hero, a Greek priest familiar with the Indian lore, relates the story of man commencing from the stage of his cultural infancy. He has travelled as far East as Taxila or Mathura in India and spent quite sometime in Bactria. In the course of his world-travels, he has made it a point to study the philosophy, God-lore and fine arts of the Hindus. He watches and observes how in the primitive man consciousness emerges out of dumb matter and blind sense. He is overwhelmed with a sense of wonder at the beauty of the universe, sees himself silhouetted everywhere in the skies among the stars. Similar experiences in the East and the West are revealed in their mythologies. The milieu that created this ancient ideal as conceived by Dr Seal was half-agnostic and half neo-Platonic. The humanism of Dr Seal's ancient hero finds expression in the following invocations.

Thee nothing human doth displease,
For thou has not disdained to wear the human face,
Thy Muses, Graces, Charities
Are human mysteries,
Thou tastest of the cup from which
Thou freely serv'st man's race.

15

Outlook Towards Women
Influence of Indian Renaissance

Madhumita Chattopadhyay

In the history of Indian culture, the last part of the nineteenth century and the first part of the twentieth century constituted the birth of a new era, which has often been described as the Renaissance in India. Under the long period of domination under the Muslim empire and subsequently by the British Government, the Indian mind had completely withdrawn herself into a shell; and so when change came in, she felt herself in a dilemma between her own culture which had been lying dormant on the one hand, and the challenging, stimulating influence of Western culture on the other. In face of such dilemma, India was not only to wake up with an awareness of its past but also had to face the new and unprecedented cultural crisis with her own vigour and courage revived from her past glory. Thus the renaissance for India was "an attempt of a reawakened national spirit to find a new impulse of self-expression which shall give the spiritual force for a great reshaping and rebuilding." The motive behind the Indian renaissance was not only "to break the moulds of the past, but also keep safe its gains and its spirits" without which the future of India will not be possible. In this respect Indian renaissance exhibited a great resemblance to the Celtic movement in Ireland rather than to the Renaissance in the

West in the fifteenth century. Sri Aurobindo described the Indian renaissance as:

> a new age of an old culture transformed, not an affiliation of a new-born civilization to one that is old and dead, but a true rebirth, a renascence.
>
> — *The Renaissance in India* — 2, p. 17

Though this Indian renaissance occurred under the influence of modern Western education, it cannot be described to be a mere "Asiatic modification of Western modernism" but as a new and original thing in the spirit of her own national life and culture. To quote Sri Aurobindo again,

> The national mind turned a new eye on its past culture, re-awoke to its sense and import, and also, at the same time, saw it in relation to modern knowledge and ideas. Out of this awakening vision and impulse, the Indian renaissance is arising, and that must determine its future tendency.
>
> — Ibid., p. 17

Self-Conscious Spirit Asserted in Later Renaissance

The first stage of renaissance was marked by the opening of the eyes of the country people with the dazzling brightness of the new landscape and everything of the West came to be admired and imitated by scoffing at what belonged to our own tradition. But in the later phase of the Indian renaissance, there was assertion of the self-conscious spirit of the identity and uniqueness of Indian culture. Swami Dayananda Saraswati, Swami Vivekananda, and Sri Aurobindo were exemplaries of this phase, each in his own distinct idiom and style — Swami Dayananda emphasizing the Vedic past, Swami Vivekananda and Sri Aurobindo beckoning to a future brighter than the dawns of the past. It was not to be a restoration only but a reconstruction and re-creation. The lesson of the Indian renaissance, however, is that no rebirth is possible without the recovery of the spirit of one's own national life and culture.

This spirit of Indian renaissance exerted its influence on every aspect of her life — literature, art, education, lifestyle, religion, etc. that led towards different kinds of socialistic reforms. In this write-up our objective is to discuss the influence of renaissance only in respect of the change in the outlook towards women. Out of great compassion for the women, many great thinkers in that period tried to save women from their miserable conditions and open up a new enlightened world before them. Mention may be made of the contributions of Raja Rammohan Roy, Derozio and his young followers, Pandit Ishwar Chandra Vidyasagar, Madanmohan Tarkalamkar, Sri Ramakrishnadev and his disciples, Sri Aurobindo and others. Though all of them worked hard for the elevation of the position of women in one aspect or another, in the scope of a single article it would not be possible to discuss the contributions of all. So we have confined our discussion to the contributions of two great thinkers of Bengal, namely Swami Vivekananda and Sri Aurobindo in this regard. We are considering their views together as both of them felt that the upliftment of women was not possible from outside. They were convinced that "no law can liberate women unless they liberate themselves" (The Mother). Hence their objective was not to change the position of women by formulating laws, but to highlight the glorious pictures of the women as found in our tradition, in the Vedas, in the Upaniṣads so that the reform can come in a natural process. They believed in the process of self-reformation. Swami Vivekananda strongly argued that:

> Women must be put in a position to solve their own problems in their own way. No one can or ought to do this for them. And our Indian women are as capable of doing it as any in the world.

Presence of Male Chauvinism

Not only in our own country but also in many countries of the world, male persons possess a sense of vanity in being male; as a result there arises in them a desire to oppress the female and dominate over them. On the other hand, the female persons being of the weaker sex and also having less physical strength in comparison to their male counterparts always suffer from an inferiority complex. But in spirit they cannot tolerate the dominance of the male persons. As such there arises a sense of revolt in them that in most cases remains unexpressed. In other words the social positions of the men and the women are in two completely opposite poles. This gulf between men and women continue from the beginningless past till the present. That is the picture of almost all countries of the world. The liability of such conflict one puts on the other — man accuses woman for the conflict while the woman accuses the man. But the truth is that the liability of this conflict lies on both and one cannot claim superiority over the other.

As ardent believers in the doctrine of monism upheld in the Advaita Vedānta, Swami Vivekananda and Sri Aurobindo both could not accept the inequality between men and women as prevailing in society. They were supporters of women's equality. But they felt that unless we remove the inferiority–superiority complex regarding sex from the minds of the people, we cannot get rid of the false idea of inequality of men and women.

> The question to be solved, the real question is then not only that of a better utilization of their outward activities, but above all that of inner spiritual growth. Without inner progress there is no possibility of outer growth.
>
> — *On Women*, p. 42

Swami Vivekananda accused his male disciples of dishonouring the women by binding them with hard rules —

> You always criticize the women, but say what you have done for their uplift? Writing down *Smṛtis* etc., and binding them by hard rules, the men have turned the women into mere manufacturing machines. — *CWSV*, vol. 7, p. 214

Sri Aurobindo in the same tone said:

> What men have mainly demanded of them — to be their servants, nurses, cooks, children-bearers and rears, ministers of their sex-desires, etc. That has been their occupation and aim in life and their natures have got adapted to their work. . . . And then man smiles a superior smile and says it was all due to woman's inferior nature, not to the burden laid on her. — *On Women*, p. 18

Both of them were pained at the disrespect shown to women. Woman for them is "the living embodiment of the Divine Mother." Swamiji vehemently said,

> The principal reason why your race has so much degenerated is that you have no respect for these living images of Śakti.

Manu says:

> Where women are respected, there the gods delight; and where they are not, there all works and efforts come to naught.

Vivekananda said:

> There is no hope of rise for that family or country where there is no estimation of women, where they live in sadness. For this reason, they have to be raised first.
> — *CWSV*, vol. 7, p. 215

Union of Puruṣa and Prakṛti Must for Creation

But our tradition has taught us that the play of world and life, i.e. creation is possible only in the union of *puruṣa* and *prakṛti.*

That is why we want to keep humanity within the household and society, to get established in the proper *dharma* of the household and society and to express therein the supreme consummation. Man alone is only a half, woman too alone is only a half. Man and woman coming together will achieve each one's fullness and lead the world also towards global perfection. Man and woman are like those twin birds referred to in the Upaniṣads — *dvā suparṇā sāyujā sakhāyā samānaṁ vr̥kṣam.* The Upaniṣads describe the relation between man and woman as two halves of one and the same thing, for example two halves of a single shell — *ardhabr̥galamiva.* When man approaches man or woman approaches woman, two integral things are added together which are complete in themselves. But, when man and woman are associated with each other we find a sort of compounded multiplication — it is not merely a mixture, but a novel alchemy as it were. Accordingly in Indian mythology the idol of Hari-Hara (a combination of Lord Viṣṇu and Lord Śiva) reveals not the whole truth, "but a greater truth, a deeper mystery is revealed in the idol of Hara-Gaurī or Rādhā-Kr̥ṣṇa." (*About Women,* p. 42)

In our scriptures woman is said to be an equal partner in following the *dharma* — *sahadharmiṇī,* she is as if the other wing of man. With her help man is capable of giving an expression to his own complete *dharma* of life and embrace his own greater self. Man is like empty space without woman. Woman fills his emptiness — *ayamākāśaḥ striyā pūryata eva.* If a man remains engrossed within his own shell, the human being becomes dwarf and shrinks himself. That is why the Upaniṣads have said that the *puruṣa* did not enjoy all alone, from then on nobody ever enjoys alone. *Puruṣa* wanted a companion, that's why he formed himself in such a way that he became the dual form of male and female — *sa vai naiva rame, tasmād ekākī na ramate, sa dvitīyam aicchat, sa haitavānāsa yathā strīpumāṁsau sampariṣvaktau."* In other words in the Upaniṣadic ideal male and female are not two competing forces, rather complementary ones, manifestation of one and the same fundamental principle.

Sri Aurobindo harps on this notion of woman as *sahadharmiṇī* of Hindu religion and explains in clear language what its implication is. In a letter to his wife Mrinalini he writes:

> The wife shares the *dharma* (law of conduct) of her husband. She must help him, counsel him, encourage him in whatever work he accepts as his *dharma*. She should regard him as her god, take joy in his joy, and feel sorrow in his unhappiness. It is for a man to choose his work; the woman's part is to give help and encouragement."
>
> — Letter to Mrinalini, August 30, 1905

Woman is Both Guru and Disciple

Woman is *sahadharmiṇī* not only because she is a companion in *sādhanā* but also because she is the symbol of execution and realization as well. In the philosophy of Sri Aurobindo woman is considered to be *guru* and disciple at the same time of the man. She is considered a *guru,* as she can look into man's soul and understand it, awaken the indwelling god by the force of a unique oneness, who unerringly feels all his moods, that is the will of the indwelling *puruṣa* and with an eye on it directs him accordingly. She is considered a disciple of man because she has poured her all for him, her fulfilment coincides with his fulfilment, she has made her soul to dance in harmony with the rhythm of his soul. Each phase of man's *sādhanā,* each phase of his *siddhi,* his realization, she makes her own automatically and effortlessly. Man's *sādhanā* and *siddhi* get doubled being more visible, more concrete, unfailing and vast, under the influence of the woman. To quote Sri Aurobindo:

> We say that the wife is the husband's *śakti,* his strength. This means that the husband's strength is redoubled when

> he sees his own image in his wife and hears an echo of his own high aspirations in her.
>
> — Letter to Mrinalini, August 30, 1905

The question inevitably arises in our mind, what special role does a woman play in the life of a man so that she is viewed as "the husband's *śakti*?" The answer has been well-given in Sri Aurobindo's explanation in line with the Sāṁkhya thought. Woman is the mirror in which man sees the reflection of his own self, his hidden and dormant powers of genius, when she comes and stands before him; immediately he becomes awake and energetic with the inspiration of fully manifesting and expanding himself. That is why woman is *śakti* — without a touch of this force of woman man cannot attain full awakening and integral self-realization. As such in the Sāṁkhya system *puruṣa*, though even conscious, cannot indulge in activities unless he comes in contact with the principle of *prakṛti*. Without the touch of a woman it is as if the *jīvātmā* cannot open his thousand petals in full bloom. Man's whole power gets manifested by the touch of the woman, and it is for this a man requires a woman in his attainment of fulfilment. This is not a demand of sexuality, but one of completeness.

The moment one views one's wife in this spirit, the whole attitude towards women will alter — one will not feel any sort of sexual urge for the women. The senses will not be senses any more, sex is no longer sex, but takes on a new birth, a new form. Since the wife is the equal partner of man's spiritual being, for the very same reason she is the equal partner too of his physical being — all separation, all contradiction between spiritual and physical, soul and body, God and the creature will disappear. And both get mingled into one in a marvellous alchemy.

Create a Man-Woman Equality Feeling

When there will arise the true sense of equality between man and woman the idea of marriage will also change. The system which admits of inequality between man and woman, believe that the only role a wife plays in a husband's life is that of giving birth to his children (*putrārthe kriyate bhāryyā*). Naturally in such a system the basic feeling that a man feels towards his wife is one of sexuality and the woman is considered as an object of sensual enjoyment. But the moment the sense of equality arises between man and woman, the moment one realizes that one and the same Supreme *Brahman* is immanent in both of them, then sensual enjoyment will no longer play any significant role in a man's life. At that time, sharing material interests, aesthetic enjoyments or even mutual tenderness and affection, will not be considered as enough for marriage, though each of them is necessary. So the true spirit of marriage consists in being one in aspiration and ascension, moving forward at the same pace on the same spiritual path, and that alone contains the secret of lasting union. (*On Women,* p. 25).

We find that Swami Vivekananda in the same spirit had made attempts to remove the stains of inequality from the mind of the Indians. He appealed to the Vedantic ideals for this purpose. According to the Vedanta philosophy, one and the same conscious Self is present in all beings. That conscious Self is the only reality. Man and woman are different manifestations of that Supreme Reality. In that respect, how can there be any discrimination between one and the other. It is only because people fail to realize the nature of the Supreme Self and out of ignorance think of the distinction between male and female. So the entire way of discrimination between male and female is a creation of the human mind, is due to our ignorance. So the only way to solve the problem is to remove this ignorance and cultivate proper understanding among the people. For this the two great thinkers adopted two different means — Sri Aurobindo insisted on the *method on Integral Yoga* while Swamiji insisted on giving *proper education to the women* so that they themselves can change the scenario.

Realisation of Absolute Spirit Through Integral Yoga

In his philosophy, Sri Aurobindo distinguished between different planes, the first of which is the physical plane. This physical plane, according to him is the stage of animality where one is concerned with his physical body only. But man is not composed of physical body only but possesses intelligent will which is the manifestation of the psychical being. This intelligent will makes man conscious of the divinity in him, and gradually makes man progress towards his higher being when he will no longer be guided by his intelligent spirit but by his own intuition. In the words of Sri Aurobindo,

> when the mind is perfectly silent, pure like a well-polished mirror, immobile as a pond on a breezeless day, then, from above, as the light of the stars in the motionless waters, the light of the supermind, of the Truth within, shines in the quieted mind and gives birth to intuition.
>
> — *On Women,* p. 90

When this intuition arises, we will have the realization of the Absolute in us and then the sense of equality of man and woman will be revealed. Then alone will arise the true significance of marriage. The whole philosophy of Sri Aurobindo is attempted towards the realization of this Absolute Spirit and for this he has proposed his theory of Integral Yoga.

Swami Vivekananda also emphasized on the Upaniṣadic idea of the equality of man and woman in his writings. He felt that this equality was there always in our tradition, it was nothing new. But due to a particular situation this equality was given up and people forgot that the inequality was situational, context-dependent, and hence made it a custom to degrade the women. "Circumstances have forced upon us, for many centuries the woman's need of protection. This and not her inferiority, is the true reading of our customs." (*CWSV*, vol. 7 p. 228). Swamiji referred to our scriptures, our epics to justify the position that reverence for women is the true spirit of our tradition.

> . . . the race that produced Sītā — even if it only dreamt of her — has a reverence for women that is unmatched on the earth. There is many a burden bound with legal tightness on the shoulders of Western women that is utterly unknown to us.
>
> — *On Women*, p. 231.

With this firm conviction in mind, Swamiji was very much confident that:

> women must be put in a position to solve their own problems in their own way. No one can or ought to do this for them. And our Indian women are capable of doing it as any in the world.

It is out of this belief that Swamiji felt that no amount of man's endeavour would bring good results for women. It would be a mistake on our part to ask man to employ men to work for the upliftment of the women.

Self Reformation is Best Way to Reform

The best way of reformation was self-reformation. So he clearly said that women did not require any help from men, they were themselves capable enough of solving their own problems. The only duty of men towards women was to give them proper liberty. Liberty was the only condition of growth. In this context, Swamiji says,

> women will work out their own destinies — much better, too, than men can ever do for them. All the mischief to women has come because men undertook to shape the destiny of women.

Thus it is observed that Swamiji had a unique idea of reformation. He was of the opinion that when man was pure, perfect and divine, how could he be reformed? By reformation, he simply meant growth — not from outside but from within. As he believed in inner growth, he always suggested people to follow the path of self-reformation. Self-reformation, according to him, is only possible from freedom. And so he again and again emphasized on giving liberty to those who are to be reformed.

Swami Vivekananda was not hesitant in criticizing the social reform of the widow-marriage by saying:

> Our modern reformers are very busy about widow remarriage. Of course, I am a sympathizer in every reform but the fate of a nation does not depend upon the number of husbands their widows get, but upon the condition of the masses.

He felt that a look at the history of our country will disclose the fact that the main cause for the degradation of Indian society was due to two factors — one, making the castes other than the upper ones ineligible for the study of the Vedas, and secondly depriving the women members also of the right to education. If proper education is rendered to them all, they will realize that there is no harm in educating a woman. The doctrine of the Vedānta teaches us that:

> in the highest reality of the *Parabrahman*, there is no distinction of sex. We notice this only in the relative plane. And the more the mind becomes introspective the more the idea of difference vanishes. Ultimately when the mind is wholly merged in the homogeneous and undifferentiated *Brahman*, such ideas as "this is a man" or "that is a woman" do not remain at all . . . Therefore do I say that though outwardly there may be difference between man and woman, in their real nature there is none. Hence, if a man

> can be a knower of *Brahman*, why cannot a woman attain to the same knowledge? — *CWSV*, vol. 7, p. 219

What Sri Aurobindo had described as the physical plane dominated by the animality in man, Swami Vivekananda described as "the relative plane" or the plane of the "I-Thou". This animality or relativity determines that "this is male," "that is female," etc. But as we transcend this stage and proceed towards the mental or the psychic, there is gradual manifestation of the divinity in us. With this manifestation of the divinity the false sense of discrimination among the sexes will disappear and there will arise the sense of spiritual equality. As Sri Aurobindo remarks,

> it is in the recognition of this fundamental spiritual equality that can be found the only serious and lasting solution for this problem of the relation of the sexes. It is in this light that it must be placed, it is at this height that must be sought the focus of action and new life, around which will be constructed the future temple of humanity.
>
> — *On Women*, p. 43.

Implementation of Female Education

The only hindrance in the path of self-reformation in the case of women rests in their lack of proper education. So Swamiji insisted on the implementation of female education in our country. He pleaded for women's education in India by reminding us of our glorious past. Women had always been treated by men in India as equal from the Vedic period. Our women were always advanced in the fields of education. He expressed his pride for Indian women in the following words — "Do you remember how Yājñavalkya was questioned at the court of king Janaka? His principal examiner was Vacaknavi, the maiden orator *Brahmavādinī* as the word of the day was."

"Like two shining arrows in the hand of the skilled archer," she said, "are my questions." Her sex was not even commented upon. Again could anything be more complete than the equality of boys and girls in our old forest universities? Hence for the progress of Indian society Swamiji's appeal was to spread education among all — "Educate, Educate, *nānyaḥ panthā vidyate 'yanāya* (there is no path other than this)."

Swamiji could not remain satisfied with the sort of female education that was being provided by some Christian missionaries and some Hindu social reformers, as most of them were governed by Western ideals. However, he did not underestimate the efforts of the pioneers of female education for that. He told his disciples, "When a new idea is preached in the country some fail to grasp it properly, and go wrong in that way. But what matters is to the well-being of the society at large. Well, those who are pioneers of the little bit of female education that now obtains in the country were undoubtedly very great-hearted." (*CWSV*, p. 220). In his conception, spirituality is the essence of Indian culture. Hence any education that is to be provided to people must contain that element of spirituality in it. Religion must play the central role to such education. The female education which has obtained up till then in India, lacked that character — religion had been assigned a secondary position, and hence the defect. So he planned to establish a new Mission (*maṭha*) for the women where he proposed to impart them proper education.

> There shall be a girls' school attached to this women's *maṭha*, in which religious scriptures, literature, Sanskrit, grammar, and even some amount of English should be taught. Other matters such as sewing, culinary art, rules of domestic work, and upbringing of children will also be taught while *japa*, worship, meditation, etc. shall form an indispensable part of the teaching."
>
> — *On Women*, p. 217

When a woman gets this sort of integrated education she will become an ideal woman who will not simply consider being equal to the male or blind imitation of the West as her objective, but rather would be a great possession to the society. Spirituality, sacrifice and self-control will be their motto and *sevā* or service will be the vow of their lives. If the life of the ladies are moulded in such fashion, then alone will there be the reappearance of such ideal characters as Sītā, Sāvitrī and Gārgī. Even after marriage and entering into a family life, the girls educated in such manner will inspire their husbands with noble ideals and be the mothers of heroic sons. So in the eyes of Swami Vivekananda the ideal of female education was to bestow self-esteem among the women. To quote Sister Nivedita,

> The ideal of education . . . would be that which should best enable every woman, in time to come to resume into herself the greatness of all the women of the Indian past.
>
> — *The Master as I saw Him,* p. 239

Though Swamiji thought of the need of establishing a *maṭha* for the girls, he was not opposed to the ideals of marriage. He was only opposed to child-marriage, for marriage at a younger age will make both the mother and her children physically weak and will be the cause of their premature death. He argued for setting the age of marriage to be 16. He wanted to make it a rule for the guardians of the students of his proposed girl's school that they should not get their daughters married before the age of sixteen. Even when a girl attains this age, that is considered to be mature enough, she may be asked to give her opinion. If she gives consent for marriage, only then she can be got married, otherwise not. In other words, in Swamiji's opinion there was nothing wrong for a girl to remain unmarried throughout her life, being engaged in the occupation of teaching and learning. The ideal or greatness of Indian woman was not anything external — an ideal woman is she in whom we can find involvement in all her actions and loyalty to her husband in accordance with the tradition of India. If any woman fails to conform to that ideal, Swamiji would refuse to regard her as educated. How Swamiji used to look upon the ideal of modern woman gets clear from the following words of Sister Nivedita —

> A modernized Indian woman, on the other hand, in whom he saw the old-time intensity of trustful and devoted companionship to the husband, with the old-time loyalty to the wedded kindred, was still to him "the ideal Hindu wife." True womanhood, like true monkhood, was no matter of mere externals. And unless it held and developed the spirit of true womanhood, there could be no education of woman worthy of the name. — *The Master as I saw Him,* p. 239

The ideal of female education was for Swamiji a synthesis of modern science with the tradition of India.

Conclusion

While winding up the whole discussion, it may be pointed out that the main aim of Indian renaissance was to highlight before the countrymen suffering from the bondage of British domination, the glorious past of our own country. With this aim in view, Swami Vivekananda and Sri Aurobindo both tried to expalin the teachings of the Vedas and the Upaniṣads in a modern tone. Both of them realized that spirituality constituted the basis of Indian culture. So if anyone ignores this edifice and builds up the superstructure on something else, that structure is bound to fall to ground. As such the concepts of *sanātana dharma* (the traditional law) and spirituality have occurred again and again in their writings. That the traditional *dharma* was not opposed to women's enlightenment, rather reveals the true nature of feminity, has been exhibited through their views on the renaissance regarding women. The Indian woman was the first lady to write such a verse known as the *Devīsūkta*, considered to be the best verse written by a lady throughout the world, in such a period when there was no such advancement among the women of other countries. The woman in the *Ṛgveda* could realize the presence of the Supreme Reality in herself and declare —

> *aham rudrāya dhanurātanomi brahmadviṣe śarabe hantavā u* ।
> *aham janāya samadaṁ kṛṇomyahaṁ dyāvāpṛthivīā viveśa* ॥

> I have set the arrows of the self to the bow of Śiva, to destroy the eleven sense organs which constitute the hindrance to the path of obtaining knowledge of the Absolute and in this way I fight for the welfare of the whole universe. My presence is felt in the heaven as well as in the earth.

The women of this country had that courage to refuse the enjoyable wordly items for the attainment of the Ultimate Knowledge. The country which offered such a high position to the women, obviously, cannot tolerate any sort of degradation, any sort of humility shown towards their women. This was the basic spirit of the writings of both Swami Vivekananda and Sri Aurobindo regarding the revival of the position of Indian women. So what Sri Aurobindo thought of Indian renaissance as a whole holds true in the context of women also. We may conclude our discussion with the following quotation of Sri Aurobindo which would enable us to apprehend their spirit of renaissance properly —

> India of the ages is not dead nor has she spoken her last creative word; she lives and has still something to do for herself and the human peoples. And that which must now seek to awake is not an anglicized oriental people, docile pupil of the west, and doomed to repeat the cycle of the occident's success and failure, but still the ancient

immemorial *śakti* recovering her deepest self, lifting her head higher towards the supreme source of light and strength and turning to discover the complete meaning and a vaster form of her *dharma.*

Abrreviations

CWSV — Complete Works of Swami Vivekananda.

References

Gupta, Nolini Kanta, *About Women,* Pondicherry: Sri Aurobindo Centre for Advanced Research, 1999.

The Mother, *Words of Long Ago,* Pondicherry: Sri Aurobindo Society, India, 2001.

Sarma, G.N., *Sri Aurobindo and The Indian Renaissance,* Banglore: Ultra Publications, 1997.

Sister Nivedita, *The Master as I Saw Him,* Kolkata: Udbodhan Office, 2001.

Sri Aurobindo, *On Women,* Pondicherry: Sri Aurobindo Society, India, 2004.

Sri Aurobindo, *The Renaissance in India and Other Essays on Indian Culture,* Pondicherry: Sri Aurobindo Ashram, 2004.

Vivekananda, *The Complete Works of Swami Vivekananda,* vol. 7, Kolkata: Advaita Ashrama, 1979.

16

Raja Rammohan Roy

Forerunner of Women's Liberation Movement

Krishna Roy

NOWADAYS we are often hearing about feminist movement or women's liberation movement. Feminist studies and assertion of women's right are gaining more and more momentum all over the world. Social activists and intellectuals are acclaimed all over the world for their concern for the uplift of the womenfolk. Large amount of fund is being allocated by Governmental and Non-Governmental Organizations for doing such social work. In these days of organized feminist movement it is not easy to comprehend how difficult it was for one person to launch crusade against certain unjust social practices which were thoroughly detrimental to the condition of the womenfolk, and that too almost 200 years ago. But that had exactly happened in Bengal during the eighteenth century, when Raja Rammohan Roy started his fight against the prevailing evil practices of the society and tried to alter the fate of the Indian women both rationally and sympathetically. In order to understand the significance of Rammohan's contribution for the improvement of women's position in family and society — it is necessary to know the prevailing condition of women in the then society.

Rammohan flourished at a time which may be regarded as one of the darkest periods of our country. If we study the history of Indian society during the eighteenth century, we would find stories of conflicts and conspiracies. Corruption, cruelty and vices permeated the entire country. Being under the foreign subjugation, the onslaught of the West caused to fade the ancient glory and ideal of India. In those days of social degeneration and intellectual stagnation religion lost its spiritual value and was reduced to superstitious beliefs and malpractices. Economic disparity divided the society into two contending classes and the society was being controlled by the influential and the richer upper-castes, who proclaimed certain rites and customs which were mainly beneficial to that class only. All the customs prevailing at that time were advantageous to the upper-caste and classes and specially to the malefolk. As a result both the people belonging to poorer, lower classes and the so-called "weaker" section of the society, i.e. the womenfolk had to suffer immensely. In those days of ignorance and injustice appeared some great souls who wanted to dispel this gloom and tried to save the country from utter degeneration. Prominent among them was Raja Rammohan Roy, who may be regarded as the forerunner of the social, religious and cultural renaissance in India.

Rammohan Roy : A Many-faceted Social Reformer

Raja Rammohan Roy (1772–1833) was a many-splendoured personality, whose contribution to bring about reforms in Indian (specially Bengali) society was immense. The many-sided movement that Roy started was the total revolt against all sorts of irrational orthodoxy. He wanted to test all socio-religious practices by the light of reason. He launched a crusade against pseudo-religious rites and dogmas by offering fresh interpretations of the age-old Hindu Śāstras. It is difficult to enumerate the contributions of Rammohan Roy, as he wanted to infuse new spirit in the then social, economic, administrative, judicial and religious spheres. It was

Rammohan who wanted to save the country from bigotry and ritualism; he abolished the prevailing *satī* practice of widow-burning; he wanted to ascertain the need of the freedom of the press; he synthesized different religions; he felt the need of introducing English and Science teaching in this country. These are only a few of his many significant contributions. Since it is not possible to delineate all these varied contributions within a sort canvas, I would only focus in the present paper on his services for the improvement of the womenfolk of Indian society.

Being a sensitive, rational and broadminded person, Rammohan was deeply aggrieved by the miserable condition of the womenfolk in the then society. It was a completely male-dominated society, where women had no independent status and voice; their fate was entirely at the hands of the males and that too of the influential classes. There is a saying that women are being guided at their childhood by their parents, at their youth by their husbands and at the old age by their sons. That was exactly what used to happen in those days. If we read Simone de Beuvoir's famous book *The Second Sex* we would find that the condition of women in most of the societies of the world were more or less the same; the form of subjugation and suppression may vary but the overall condition of women all over the world was miserable. If we direct our attention to the condition of women in our own country we find reports and descriptions of women's torture which are both agonising and infuriating. The women of that period were totally helpless and unable even to open their mouth to narrate their own sufferings. Rammohan realized that irrational orthodoxy and blind superstitions were the main causes of such perverse attitude towards women and he tried his best to eradicate some of those evil practices which were detrimental to them.

Rammohan Against Satī

Rammohan's deep sense of concern, sympathy and respect for the womenfolk led him to launch a life-long struggle to end the most barbarous and shameful custom of widow-burning which was known as *satī*. *Satī* literally means pious or virtuous women and it was propagated by priests and social leaders that those widows who would accompany their dead husbands in their funeral pyres would be regarded as *satī* and this practice would free them from all sins incurred by them and their families. Rammohan started his first protest against such widow-burning as early as in 1812 but he began his direct movement against such practice since 1818. He published several articles not only condemning such practice but also challenging the pseudo arguments circulated in support of such custom.

Though from the early part of his life, Rammohan was against such inhuman practices like *satī* or widow-burning and protested by consolidating people's support, gradually he realized that this protest should be strengthened by both rational and legal arguments. In order to prove that the *satī* system was not sanctioned by religious texts, he thoroughly studied the scriptures of various religions. With his vast erudition and rational mind, Rammohan became convinced and propagated that the existing practice of *satī* or widow burning had no religious and Śāstric sanction. Among the various Dharmaśāstras, *Manu-Smṛti* has always been considered as very prominent and trustworthy. Quoting a *śloka* from *Manu-Smṛti*, Rammohan wanted to prove that such practice of self-immolation was never considered as one of the duties of a widow. Rather Manu directed the widow to lead an austere life. "She should continue till death performing harsh duties, avoiding all pleasures and willingly following the rules of virtue."[1]

1. English version of *śloka* number 158, section V, *Manu Saṁhitā*.

Rammohan pointed out that not only Manu but Yājñavalkya and many other important law givers prescribed virtuous and austere life for the widows rather than that of self-immolation. No rational person or authority, nor any religious scripture has ever supported the acts of murder and suicide as commendable; rather they always criticize and oppose such performances. Hence the acts by which widows were forcibly thrown into the funeral pyres of their dead husbands might be considered as murders and even if some widows voluntarily decide to terminate their lives, those acts would be regarded as acts of suicide and as such could never be supported. Rammohan wrote in this context: "Those who have no reliance on the Śāstras and those who take delight in the self-destruction of women, may well wonder that we should oppose that suicide which is forbidden by all Śāstras and by every race of man."[2]

Rammohan for Restoring Women-Rights

We all know that Rammohan wrote several thought-provoking articles, through which he wanted to convince the educated class of the society and the ruling government for prohibiting such inhuman practices as well as to assure the people of India and the British Government that such barbaric acts were not supported by Hindu Śāstras. In his second treatise on *satī* published in 1819, Rammohan declared:

> The practice, therefore, of forcibly tying down woman to the pile and burning her to death is inconsistent with the Śāstras, and highly sinful. It is of no consequence to affirm that this is customary in any particular country; (even) if it were universally practised the murders would still be

2. *Collected Works of Raja Rammohan Roy*, vol. II, p. 123; Quoted by N.C. Ganguly, *Raja Rammohan Roy*, Calcutta: YMCA Publishing House, 1934, pp. 108-09.

> criminal. The pretence that may be followed in matters where no particular rules are prescribed in the Śāstras, is not to be justified by the practices of a few.[3]

Thus, it becomes evident from all his writings and activities that Rammohan took it as a mission to restore certain basic rights to the women of India. We know that the right to live is one of the fundamental human rights and this fundamental right did not have any meaning and application in those days. It is the great service of Rammohan to fight for this basic right of women, to treat them with righteousness and respect.

Being a practical, sensitive and rational person, Rammohan realized that to restore to womenfolk the right to life was absolutely necessary but not sufficient; for life without property, possession, independence and dignity could be unbearable and disgraceful. Hence he also felt the need of restoring to women their right to inherit family property, which would enable them to live with dignity and confidence.

It is often said that the widows used to decide voluntarily to end their lives by joining their dead husbands but Rammohan's sensitive mind could realize the tacit reason behind such self-immolation. After the death of the husbands the widows were generally being treated by the family-members and neighbours in such a disrespectful way and in most cases they had to undergo severe tortuous practices that the helpless widows thought that it would be better to end their lives. Rammohan always insisted that this *satī* practice was not at all a religious practice and never had the sanction of the different Dharmaśāstras; it was only the result of some misinterpretation of the Śāstras with unjust ulterior motives. The tacit motive which possibly led to implement such inhuman

3. *English Works of J.C. Ghosh,* edited by J.C. Ghosh, Calcutta, 1901, vol. II, p. 137.

practice of widow-burning was to grab the property of the deceased person. Rammohan could realize that the root cause of this social evil lay in the economic system prevalent in the society. Consequently he also tried his best to eradicate this unjust practice of depriving of the women from their share in the family property.

Women and the Laws of Inheritance

As we try to look into the laws of inheritance, prevailing in the then society we notice that two different legal texts were being followed in different parts of India. One is Dāyabhāga by Jimutavāhana and the other is Mitākṣarā by Vijñāneśvara. It is noticed that the principles laid down in the Dāyabhāga was generally being followed in Bengal, whereas the principles of Mitākṣarā were being practised in many other States of India. If we look into the laws of inheritance, of the women specially, we notice that according to Dāyabhāga if a member of an undivided family dies, leaving no male issue, his widows shall inherit the property; but according to Mitākṣarā, the widow is not entitled to the property of the late husband. Thus it becomes clear that since the Dāyabhāga principles were being accepted in Bengali societies, the widows were entitled to get their husband's share after their demise. In order to debar a widow from getting and enjoying that property of her deceased husband, the male-dominated society tried to get rid of those widows by forcing them to the funeral pyre of their husbands. The death of the widow thus, would enable them to grab and enjoy the family property without taking the responsibility of supporting those widows. Thus under the pretext of social customs and religious practices the envious men and priests used to satisfy their greed without having any sympathy and compassion for the desolate widows. Being a benevolent person with a sensitive and sympathetic mind,

Rammohan could feel the agony and helplessness of those ill-fated widows.

Women in General Deprived of Property Rights

Rammohan further realized that not only the widows but the women in general were being deprived of their share in the family property. If we look through the economic condition of women in our society we notice that the male members of the society always have the tendency to deprive the women of their share in the family property; often they try to do so by citing "legal" grounds, giving somewhat motivated and malign interpretations of the legal texts. Jurisprudence is the subject where multiple interpretations are quite possible; one legal text or even one single legal principle may be interpreted differently by different advocates according to their requirement and intention. In the days of Rammohan such legal arguments were also being offered for alienating the women from their property rights. Rammohan thoroughly studied the ancient Hindu legal texts or Dharmaśāstras and tried his best to reveal the true message of those texts. He published two very significant treatises on this issue. In 1822 he published the essay entitled "Brief Remarks Regarding Modern Encroachments on the Ancient Rights of Females," where he proved that in ancient times the famous law givers of India like Yājñavalkya, Kātyāyana and Nārada unanimously supported the rights of women in the family property. Even a widow was entitled to have equal share with the son in the possessions of the deceased husband, so that the mother could live independently. It was only in the subsequent period that the Dāyabhāga laws deprived the mother of such share, making the mother totally dependent on her sons and daughters-in-law. Rammohan emphatically clarified that according to the ancient legal texts not only the mother but also the stepmothers were entitled to enjoy equal share with the sons. The ancient law givers also conferred certain property rights even to some unmarried sisters, while some later interpretations took away those rights.

Raja Rammohan Roy wrote another bigger treatise entitled *Essays on the Rights of Hindus Over Ancestral Property According to the Law of Bengal* in 1830. There we find his comparisons and clarifications regarding the Dāyabhāga and the Mitākṣarā laws on property. Giving authentic arguments from the ancient Dharmaśāstras, Rammohan tried to clarify that it was only due to wrong, motivated interpretations that women were debarred from enjoying their rights properly and it was only Rammohan's untiring effort and rational arguments that had helped the women to regain their lost rights.

Conclusion

It should be mentioned here that to change the existing socio-economic practices was not at all easy at that time. Rammohan and his followers had to face strong opposition from many quarters, but Rammohan faced all such challenges with strong determination and indomitable courage, for it was one of the missions of his life to save the women from bondage and suffering. Rammohan had great faith and respect for the women as he felt that women were in no way inferior to men. He wanted to reassure the women of their inherent strength and potentiality. He wanted to rekindle in them the sense of freedom and fight so that they could regain their basic rights to life and property.

Rammohan's attempt to abolish the *satī* practice and his efforts to restore the right to property to womenfolk were not two separate processes but were two allied and interconnected aspects of regenerating a new awareness amongst women to liberate them from death and dishonour. In order to fulfil such mission Rammohan further suggested some other changes in the social practice; he wanted to change the practices of child marriage, *kulinism* and polygamy. He felt that proper education, liberal attitude and organized effort would help to improve the condition of the women and to awaken them from inertia and passivity. Without going into the details of all his benevolent activities, we may mention that he wanted to instill the spirit of self-respect and aspiration amongst the women of India and as such Rammohan Roy can truly be considered as the forerunner of the women's liberation movement.

17

Violence or Non-violence

Interpretations by Sri Aurobindo and Mahatma Gandhi

Sushmita Bhowmik

THE mankind from the early period of human history has always desired and thereby put efforts towards the realization of a peaceful, harmonious, life and existence. But it has often failed to achieve its aspired goal due to the sudden intrusions of violent forces causing death and destruction. Nevertheless, human beings have been carrying on their struggle for existence. They have tried to seek solutions from such extinction of their life in this world. But the question which has repeatedly occurred to all of us is, what should be the right way to combat such violence? Is it violence itself or non-violence? It is quite difficult to give a precise and uniform answer to this very pertinent social and moral question.

Philosophers, social thinkers and social reformers in the different ages, in the various parts of the world, have tried to resolve such tension between war and peace, between violence and non-violence. Mahatma Gandhi and Sri Aurobindo — the two great thinkers of India, amongst others, may be said to have made such an attempt during the end of the nineteenth and the beginning of the twentieth century.

Gandhi, Aurobindo and Freedom Struggle

Both Mahatma Gandhi (1869–1948) and Sri Aurobindo (1872–1950) have played important roles as nationalist leaders during India's struggle for freedom against the British rule. Their aim has not been merely the freedom of their motherland, they have wanted to uplift the nation as a whole. Above all, they have been imbued with a sense of mission that the resurgence of not merely their own nation but the enrichment of the entire humanity is what they should try to bring about. For the regeneration of the entire human life and society they have tried to revive different human values among which there are love and peace, unity and harmony. Though they have common aims the ways towards their attainment have been different. One such difference that we find between Gandhi and Sri Aurobindo is that, both of them have wanted to free India as well as the entire world from all kinds of hatred and enmity, war and destruction and sought to re-establish love, unity, peace and harmony in our lives. In their efforts for the actualization of such goal while Gandhi has preached and practised non-violence, Sri Aurobindo has supported and even practised violence, though during the earlier part of his life.

Gandhi has been regarded as an apostle of peace and non-violence not only in India but also in the whole world. Non-violence has been for him the most potent force for fighting against all evils, injustice and violent forces in every sphere of life. It is primarily from this force that Gandhi derived his moral and spiritual strength in the struggle for the freedom of his motherland. To Gandhi, truth has been the end of life and non-violence has been the means to attain that end.

Unlike Gandhi, Sri Aurobindo's career in active politics has been a very brief one, i.e. from 1905 to 1910. During these five years he has created a powerful impression on the youths of India. Regarding his political technique he has rejected the mendicant policies of prayer, petition and protest which he has ascribed to the Moderates. His goal has been complete independence, for the achievement of which he has recommended direct revolutionary action, including terrorism and armed revolt. He has believed that, any means, including violence, were justified in bringing about the independence of the motherland. However, he has left politics in 1910 and retired to Pondicherry, where he has undertaken intense yogic meditation as a spiritual endeavour for gaining an inner power to uplift the entire humanity. These in short have been the two different approaches of violence and non-violence pursued by Gandhi and Sri Aurobindo.

Gandhi, Aurobindo and Violence and Non-Violence

Now, the question is, how Gandhi and Sri Aurobindo actually understood and interpreted violence and non-violence? According to Gandhi *ahiṁsā* or non-violence is the law of the human race and is infinitely greater than and superior to violence or the brute force. What then is the nature of non-violence to him? *Ahiṁsā* literally means non-killing. *Hiṁsā* or violence, as defined by Gandhi, is causing pain or killing any life out of anger, or with a selfish purpose, or with the intention of injuring anyone. Refraining from doing so is *ahiṁsā*. It is to be noted here that violence does not merely mean to cause physical harm to a person. If there is any bad intention or ill will even behind a thought or a word, or an act, that is an intention to do harm to other person, it would be considered as an act of violence. In other words, any kind of harm done to a person under the conditions of anger, pride, hatred, selfish considerations, bad intention and similar other considerations, is violence. But, harmlessness is only the negative meaning of non-violence.

According to Gandhi, in its positive aspect, non-violence means universal and unbounded love for the mankind. It also involves self-sacrifice and conscious-self-suffering. According to it, one must love even his enemy. But, then how can non-violence help to fight against enmity and hatred? Here the basic idea is that we should refuse to co-operate with what we consider to be the evil, but should continue to love the evil-doer; injustice can hardly exist when those on whom it is inflicted refuse to co-operate. By loving the wrong-doer and taking suffering upon his own self, the non-violent fighter would try to awaken the humanity of the evil-doer. This would enable the wrong-doer to realize his mistake and thereby to mend his ways. Thus non-violence helps to ward off the evil by effecting a change of the inner being of the evil-doer. It is to be noted in this connection that Gandhi has been primarily a social and moral reformer according to whom no reformation of the society can be effected unless there is a change of heart on the part of the individuals who constitute the society. He has thus always emphasized upon the self-purification of the individual beings of the society on the basis of moral values. That is why he is against violence as a method of combating wrong and injustice. The practice of violence, by coercing and humiliating the evil-doer, makes him more arrogant and violent. While violence or the brute force is a method of coercion, non-violence or the soul force is a method of conversion. Thus Gandhi has held that, in the adoption of non-violence lies the future of India and the world. It is the most harmless and yet equally effective way of dealing with the political and economic wrongs of the downtrodden portion of humanity. Though Gandhi has resorted to the method of non-violence, Sri Aurobindo has pursued a different path.

Strifes and Conflicts are rooted in our very existence : Aurobindo

Sri Aurobindo is of the view that if we really want to find a solution to this particular issue, namely, violence, which often threatens our existence, then we must try to understand what actually it is. And the answer is that there cannot be the origination, progression and continuation of our life and existence without the involvement of any violence and destruction. If we look into our life and the world around us, we would find that everything in this universe has been born from a clash of material and other forces. It is through a constant strife and conflict and by a struggle of forces, tendencies, principles that things take birth destroying the old and move forward towards higher and greater reality through the same process. Sri Aurobindo thus says that "this is certain that there will not only be no construction here without destruction, no harmony except for a poise of contending forces won out of many actual and potential discords, but also no continued existence of life except by a constant self-feeding and devouring of other life.[1] This truth has been realized not only by the Greek philosopher Heraclitus who said that war is the father of all things, but also by the old Upaniṣads. Darwinians have laid down that the struggle for life is the law of evolutionary existence. Even Nietzsche has insisted upon war as an aspect of life. Strife and conflict are therefore a fact of our life, rooted in our very existence.

Violence can be Won over through Violence alone : Aurobindo

But Apart from war and destruction, Sri Aurobindo has also recognized the principles of harmlessness and soul-force. How

1. Sri Aurobindo, *Essays on the Gita,* Pondicherry: Sri Aurobindo Ashram, 1922, p. 40.

does Sri Aurobindo evaluate the contribution of such soul-force towards the progress of mankind? According to Sri Aurobindo, it is not possible for a man or anybody as such to make progress if the principle of harmlessness is regarded as the only law of life. In every spheres of our social life — political, economic, religious or any other, there is always a struggle involved between two opposite forces which finally merge to give rise to a greater and higher existence than the remaining ones. Then, what should be the principle of an individual's action while dealing with the violent, evil forces? According to Sri Aurobindo, abstention from strife or being non-violent might be the highest and the best law of conduct, but when violent forces become too powerful and destructive, tending to shatter life and civilization, soul-force cannot then prove to be the most potent instrument against it. On the other hand, soul-force might then appear to be more terrible and destructive than the sword and the cannon.

According to Sri Aurobindo, to save mankind from such annihilation of existence what is needed is the very destruction of those destructive forces. He is of the view that "Evil cannot perish without the destruction of much that lives by the evil."[2] Thus, while according to Gandhi violence cannot be resolved except through non-violence, Sri Aurobindo holds that we can win over violence only through violence. According to Sri Aurobindo non-violence or soul-force implies immobility, inertia, or *tamas* which cannot help to rule out strife and destruction completely from the universe.

Violence cannot be the Law of Human Life and Action : Gandhi

Gandhi would object to this above view of Sri Aurobindo. He admits that to sustain our life, under certain circumstances,

2. Sri Aurobindo, *Essays on the Gita*, Pondicherry: Sri Aurobindo Ashram, 1922. p. 42.

himsā is unavoidable. He has also supported violence used for self-defence. He has argued that when the choice is between violence or cowardice, he would support the former. One who is unable to be brave and non-violent in the face of physical threat to his life, family, property, religion, etc. should use violence in order to defend them. Gandhi has even said that he would rather have India resort to arms in order to defend her honour instead of becoming or remaining a helpless witness to her own dishonour in a cowardly manner. But, he points out that when violence appears to do good, the good is only temporary, the evil it does is permanent.

Further, violence engenders violence and therefore cannot be won over through violence. Moreover, non-violence according to him does not mean submitting oneself totally to the will of the evil-doer, rather it means putting one's whole soul against the will of the tyrant. It does not imply any fear or cowardice on the part of the non-violent fighter for it is a conscious and deliberate restraint put upon one's desire for vengeance which is possible only when one fears no one on earth. Thus, in no way, according to Gandhi, non-violence implies *tamas* or darkness. In fact, it is more active than violence.

Gandhi, therefore, does not intend to deny that violence is a fact of our life, but according to him it cannot be the law of human life and action. He points out that if war and destruction had been the only reality, mankind would have ceased to exist.

However, Sri Aurobindo does not intend to say that strife and destruction are the only realities. He admits that just as there are dissociation and mutual strife in our life, similarly there are also the saving principles of association and mutual help. What is important is to see how these latter principles work. Association is not only an essential condition of mutual help, but at the same time it is required for defence and aggression, that is, when we need to strengthen ourselves and thereby resist other hostile powers. This means that the one and the same principle of association works in a positive as well as in a negative way. In this way everything in this world has a positive as well as a negative aspect, which are not totally different from one another, but are two aspects of the one and the same reality. According to Sri Aurobindo there is but one reality and everything is a manifestation of this one and the same truth. Thus what acts as a principle of non-violence in a particular situation, might turn out as a principle of violence in a situation different from the former.

Thus, we cannot separate the negative forces of war and destruction, strife and conflict, from the positive forces of peace and harmony. Our very existence reveals that the negative forces lie inseparably with the positive ones. Then, does it mean that mankind would consider strife and destruction as the end of its life? Should it not desire harmony instead of war as the goal of life? Should not the human race move towards the replacement of physical force by soul-force, of war by peace, of strife by union? Yes, mankind would certainly try to do away with all strife and suffering, death and destruction. And according to Sri Aurobindo it is by driving through all this clash, conflict and confusion that humanity should move ahead, transcending the present life and existence, towards a much higher and superior goal for which it is destined.

Conclusion

Thus, both Gandhi and Sri Aurobindo aspire for mankind a peaceful and harmonious life and existence, but the ways showed by them for its achievement have been different. The difference emanates from the ways they have interpreted violence and non-violence, which should be properly understood. While Gandhi has regarded them as two different and opposite forces, to Sri Aurobindo, they are but the two sides of the same coin, the difference consists in their applications only. Violence no doubt means conflict and destruction, but Sri Aurobindo looks at it from a positive point of view, that such conflict often implies the origination of a new life or the commencement of a new age. In other words, violence does not always mean the end of all existence, it can lead to the welfare of mankind if properly guided and controlled. But for Gandhi, except in some cases, violence is harmful and has to be avoided as far as possible. Non-violence, Gandhi holds, is a rule of conduct for social being in order to live in the society with harmony and dignity and make progress towards the attainment of peace of which men have been yearning for ages.

Now, the question is, what should be our interpretations of the thoughts of these two great thinkers? How should they be implemented in our life and practice? The increasing greed for power and wealth, selfish interests, dishonesty and disregard for others' life, have intensified the possibilities of strife and conflict not only in our personal life but also in our national as well as in the international affairs. Humanity has already witnessed their devastating effects. But it is a fact that as long as human civilization will be there, strife and destruction would continue to exist. Therefore, what we need is to control and prevent them from mastering our life and the world. If we turn towards our experiences of the practical life, we would find that it is not possible to reform each and every individual of the society and thereby make the society free from enmity and hatred. Sometimes the use of violent forces become inevitable and unavoidable and that is of course for the survival of the humanity itself. But, for that reason violence cannot be regarded as the sole or the ultimate means for fighting against all destructive and evil forces; it would, on the other hand, increase the possibilities of further death and destruction.

Therefore, if human society is to survive, what we needed is a method of controlling hostile powers which would work without threatening human life and causing destruction. We must find a non-violent alternative to war, whatever it may be, otherwise there can be no light and hope for human civilization. Probably this realization led Sri Aurobindo to forego the path of terrorism and armed revolt and in their place to engage himself in the search for a higher spiritual truth, a truth that would really help humanity to realize the strength of inner being and actualize the noble and lofty ideals of unity, peace and harmony in this life and the world.

References

Bose, Nirmal Kumar, 1948, *Selections from Gandhi*, Ahmedabad: Navajivan Publishing House.

Datta, Amlan, 1986, *The Gandhian Way*, Shillong: North-Eastern Hill University Publications.

Gandhi, M.K., 1961, *In Search of the Supreme*, vol. II, Ahmedabad: Navajivan Publishing House.

18

Sri Aurobindo, Mahatma Gandhi and India's Freedom Struggle

From Swadeshi to Non-Cooperation

Sujata Mukherjee

SRI AUROBINDO was the third son of Dr Krishnadhan Ghosh, a graduate of the Calcutta Medical College and a very successful civil surgeon, and Swarnalata Devi, the daughter of Rajnarain Bose, a famous leader of the Brahmo Samaj who was often called the "Grandfather of Indian Nationalism." Aurobindo was born on 15th August, 1872 in Calcutta. After three years' of study at Loreto Convent School, run by Irish nuns at Darjeeling, Aurobindo was taken to England in 1879 by his father along with his brothers Benoy Bhushan and Manomohan for education. Sri Aurobindo remained there till 1893. His interest in India's political situation started since his student days. After coming back to India, he became a guiding spirit of the new kind of nationalist political thoughts and activities which shaped in India since the 1890's as a new phase of the renaissance and which were essentially rooted in a deep sense of frustration and dissatisfaction with the political attitudes and methods of the moderate Congress leaders on the one hand and sense of glory and pride of India's past on the other. As has been pointed out by Sri Aurobindo's biographer:

> Sri Aurobindo's involvement in the evolution of India's destiny was, almost literally, a life-long process. His birth on 15 August 1872 could itself be viewed, in retrospect, as an augury of the coming of independence to India, exactly seventy-five years later, on 15 August 1947. In a narrower sense, however, Sri Aurobindo's active and open participation in Indian politics was of a much shorter duration: a period of no more than three and a half years, from August 1906 — when he joined the National College at Calcutta as it's Principal — to February 1910, when he left for Chandernagore in French India. Of this period, again a whole year (May 1908 to May 1909) was spent in jail at Alipur when Sri Aurobindo was an undertrial prisoner in connection with the Maniktolla Bomb case. Barely thirty months of active politics, yet Sri Aurobindo was destined to change the whole character of political activity in India and set the freedom movement firmly towards the goal of complete national independence.[1]

The clear formulation of a new trend in Indian political thoughts and activities emerged during the anti-partition or Swadeshi movement in 1905-06 which was influenced very strongly among others by Sri Aurobindo. It will not be incorrect to say that this trend was later developed to its fullest extent by another highly esteemed and world renowned leader of India's freedom struggle — Mohandas Karamchand Gandhi who led the Indian National Congress and the Indian masses into a full-fledged anti-imperialist struggle for Purna Swaraj.

---

1. K. R. Srinivasa Iyengar, *Sri Aurobindo — a biography and a history*, Pondicherry, 1972, p. 169. Among other important biographies of Sri Aurobindo are: A.B. Purani, *The Life of Sri Aurobindo*, Pondicherry, 1978; and Bina Mukhopadhyaya, *Sri Aurobindo* (in Bengali), Calcutta, 1988. Sri Aurobindo's political thoughts are discussed in Karan Singh, *Prophet of Indian Nationalism — Political Thought of Sri Aurobindo Ghosh* 1893–1910, London, 1963; and Haridas and Uma Mukherjee, *Sri Aurobindo's Political Thought*, Calcutta, 1958.

In this presentation I will seek to make a comparative analysis of the historical background, evolution, nature and impact of the political thoughts of Sri Aurobindo and Mahatma Gandhi as they shaped during the two great nationalist upheavals of twentieth century India, namely the anti-partition or the Swadeshi movement in the first decade of the twentieth century and the non-violent non-co-operation movement (1920-21) led by Mahatma Gandhi. My objective here is essentially to make an attempt to re-evaluate the contributions of two of the most important philosophers and thinkers of modern India towards India's struggle for freedom and their roles in shaping and reshaping Indian consciousness — which can be achieved by focusing on certain aspects of their thoughts and situating them in historical contexts.

Political Thought with Modern Concept Emerged

The growth of political consciousness among the educated class in Bengal is generally regarded as an essential component of the renaissance movement. It has been pointed out by historians that:

> Political thought, freed from the trammels of ancient śāstric conventions and shackles of medieval pattern and understood as a modern concept, is one of the several remarkable products of the revolutionary transformation, commonly known as the renaissance.[2]

Rammohan Roy, commonly called the "Father of the Indian Renaissance" has been credited with a pioneering role in initiating modern and systematic political thought in India. His thoughts largely derived from schools of Western political philosophy. It has been remarked: "His political ideas developed on the lines laid down by Montesquieu, Blackstone

---

2. Nisith Ranjan Ray, "Political Ideas 1833–1905" in N.K. Sinha, ed. *The History of Bengal* (1757–1905), University of Calcutta, 1996, p. 160.

and Bentham, with whose writings he appears to have been quite familiar."[3] Within the framework of sovereign rule of the British Raj he wanted assurance for enjoyment of full civil rights and individual liberty for Indians. He championed the cause of freedom of the press and protested against the Press Ordinance of 1823 which prescribed that no one should publish a newspaper or any other periodical without having previously obtained a licence from the Governor General-in-Council. In a memorial submitted to the Supreme Court in March 1823 Rammohan wrote:

> Every good ruler . . . must be conscious of the great liability to error in managing the affairs of a vast empire; and therefore he will be anxious to afford every individual the readiest means of bringing to his notice whatever many require his interference. To secure this important object, the unrestrained liberty of publication is the only effectual means that can be employed. And should it ever be abused, the established Law of the Land is very properly armed with sufficient powers to punish those who may be guilty of misrepresenting the conduct or character of government which are effectually guided by the same laws to which individuals must look for protection of their reputation and good name.[4]

He submitted an appeal to the King-in-Council George V, through the Board of Control in 1825, where he emphasized the effective role that a free press was expected to play as a link between the legislative body and the Indian people. In 1827, Rammohan declared the Jury Act as "unjust and oppressive" because it conferred on the Christians the right of being tried with the aid of a jury composed exclusively of

3. A.C. Banerjee, "Political Consciousness Before 1857" in J. Chakravorty, ed., *Studies in the Bengal Renaissance*, Jadavpur, 1977, p. 139.
4. Nitish Ranjan Roy, op. cit., p. 162.

their coreligionists. This right was denied to the Hindus and the Muslims who were also declared as ineligible for serving as Grand Jurors.

The Hindu College students and particularly those influenced by their teacher Henry Louis Vivian Derozio vehemently criticized different aspects of British rule and showed their intense patriotic sentiments through different organizations, speeches, and writings in periodicals. Derozio and his pupils started the Academic Association in 1828. Another famous organization was the Society for the Acquisition of General Knowledge launched in 1838. Derozio himself published a daily, the *East Indian*. Many of the Derozians or the members of the Young Bengal group brought out journals like the *Inquirer, Jnananveshan, Quill,* and *Bengal Spectator.* British policies were criticized in several other journals including *Tattvabodhini Patrika* (edited by Akshoy Kumar Datta from 1843 to 1855), *Reformer* (run by Prasanna Coomar Tagore), *India Gazette,* and *Bengal Harakaru* (partly owned by Dwarakanath Tagore). The Landholders' Society founded in 1837 has been described as "the first organization of Bengal with a distinct political object."[5] The Bengal British India Society was founded in April 1843 at the initiative of George Thompson, an eminent British liberal and orator, who came to India from England with Dwarakanath Tagore in January 1843. The two organizations merged in 1851 to form the British Indian Association. The latter Association took active interest in proposals of legislative and administrative measures, organized public meetings, encouraged the establishment of similar institutions in other parts of India as well as of branches in different districts of Bengal. The approach and attitude associated with it however were largely characterized by beliefs in British sense of justice and enlightenment.

5. A.C. Banerjee, op. cit.

In the late 1850s certain boldness was noticeable in the criticism of British attitudes when Harish Chandra Mukherjee wrote in the *Hindu Patriot* on 14 January 1858 in connection with the proposal for transferring the Government of India to the Crown:

> Can a revolution in the Indian Government be authorized by Parliament without consulting the wishes of the vast millions of men for whose benefit it is proposed to be made? The reply must be in the negative . . .. The time has nearly come when all Indian questions must be solved by Indians only.[6]

Anti-imperialist National Struggle Began

1860's, 1870's and 1880's are generally regarded as crucial years in the history of development of nationalist thoughts and ideas in Bengal. These years undoubtedly witnessed initiation of certain important trends which later on left an indelible impact on India's anti-imperialist nationalist struggle. There was, on the one hand, growth of certain activities and organizations which put emphasis on the idea of self-development and social reconstruction through self help — an idea which gradually grew extensively to reach climax during the Swadeshi era. The second half of the nineteenth century also witnessed the establishment of political association and organizations predominated by the educated middle class with the definite aims of uniting India on a political basis and also to pressurize the British Government to take into account the Indian public opinion.

The Brahmo Samaj started by Rammohan Roy and reorganized since the 1840s through the efforts of stalwarts like Debendranath Tagore and his associates including Rajnarain Bose, Akshoy Kumar Datta, young social reformers

6. Ibid., p. 150.

like Keshab Chandra Sen and Sivnath Sastri was no doubt successful in instilling a sense of pride among certain sections of educated Indians for their glorious heritage. The split-ridden Brahmo movement in 1866 between Debendranath and his associates on the one hand and Keshab Sen, Sivnath Sastri and others leading to the reorganizations of the former group under the banner of Adi Brahmo Samaj and the latter under the Sadharan Brahmo Samaj is often seen as manifestation of the division between the spirits of nationalism (represented by the Tagores, Rajnarain Bose and others belonging to the Adi Brahmo Samaj) and universalism (represented by the Keshabites).[7]

It has been pointed out that the *National Paper,* "which Debendranath commissioned Nabagopal Mitra to start in 1865, proved from 1867 onward to be the most effective means of propagating Hindu Brahmo nationalism against Keshabite universalism among the Western educated in Bengal."[8] Articles written by Dwijendranath Tagore and published in the newspaper during the first few years were brilliant expositions in defense of both the Adi Samaj and of the national culture. The *jatiya mela* which later came to be known as *Hindu mela,* started in 1867 by the combined initiatives of Rajnarain Bose, Dwijendranath Tagore and Nabagopal Mitra continued to be organized annually till 1880. Rabindranath Tagore wrote in his *Jībansmṛti* (Memoirs of his life):

> With the assistance of our family, a *mela* called the *Hindu mela* was begun. This was the first effort to realize with appropriate adulation, the notion of India as Swadesh, i.e. one's own nation.[9]

---

7. See David Kopf, *The Brahmo Samaj and the Shaping of the Modern Indian Mind,* Princeton, 1979.
8. J.C. Bagal, Hindu Melar Itibritta, Calcutta Maitri, 1968, p. 3, see David Kopf, ibid., p. 182.
9. *Jībansmṛti, Rabindra Racanabalī,* vol. X, Calcutta, 1989, p. 463.

Nationalist poems, songs and plays were written and performed, wrestling matches were also organized. The *mela* also exhibited agricultural produce, animals, birds, machinery and handicrafts items. It has been pointed out that "in promoting exhibition and display over economic transactions that were part of a traditional fair, the *Hindu mela* emphasized its desire to make visible a competent self-image. The *mela*'s display of competence at multiple levels in fact, attempted to challenge the power of the State to control all aspects of the colonial subject's life through law or trade regulations."[10]

The *Hindu mela* attempted to promote a Hindu identity which was thought to reflect ideally the Indian national identity. It also seemingly precipitated other nationalist activities like the National Society in 1870 and the National School in 1872.

British Policies Began to be Criticised

From the 1880's the intensification of British racism and cultural imperialism led to debilitating socio-economic policies in India. The British social and economic policies led to recurrent famines, drain of wealth to England and also adoption of notorious legal enactments which deprived Indians of their basic rights and liberties. The Dramatic Performances Act of 1876 entrusted the police commissioners with power to stop any performance they considered objectionable. The Arms Act and the Vernacular Press Act (1878) also curbed civil rights by denying the right of free expression. These acts as well as the organized opposition of the Europeans to the Ilbert Bill (1882-83) contributed to intensify the political opposition of the Indians. The widespread unemployment and under-employment among the educated youth and also the rising

10. Indira Chowdhury, *The Frail Hero and Virile History: Gender and Politics of Culture*, OUP, 1998, p. 12.

cost of living led to widespread dissatisfaction and frustration. According to one estimate, in the 1890s, the number of educated unemployed men rose to 40,000.[11]

While the objective conditions for rise of anti-British sentiments were thus prepared, the ideological basis for patriotic feelings was shaped by nineteenth century Bengali literature including poems, songs and dramas which expressed patriotic sentiments. Periodicals and dailies like *Hindu Patriot*, *Amrita Bazar Patrika*, and the *Bengalee*, under the editorship of Surendranath Banerji and published since 1 January 1879, became vocal organs of national opinion. When an Act of Parliament lowered the maximum age of a candidate for the Civil Service from 21 to 19, the *Indian Mirror* condemned the British for their injustice. The Indian Association, founded by S.N. Banerjea with the assistance of Anandamohan Bose, Dwarakanath Ganguly and others in 1876, organized all-India protest. The imprisonment of Surendranath Banerji, the celebrated nationalist leader — on the charge of contempt of court — also evoked a spontaneous protest from all over India. The Indian Association organized a National Conference in Calcutta in December 1883 which was attended by delegates from different parts of India. Soon after the second session of the National Conference, the Indian National Congress held its first session in 1885 in Bombay and was subsequently joined by the former.

Indian National Congress and British Policies

The leaders of the Indian National Congress showed unflinching faith in the British sense of justice during the first twenty years of its existence (1885–1905) and relied on constitutional methods of agitation for demanding reforms in

11. Amales Tripathi, *The Extremist Challenge: India between 1890–1910*, Calcutta, Orient Longmans, 1967, p. 145.

Indian administration. Most men of their generation received English education and enjoyed secure economic and social positions in the legal and other liberal professions or government services sometimes in addition to land and business activities. They also severely criticized British economic policies which remained standard throughout the later course of Indian nationalism.[12] Their social conservatism and political technique demanded little sustained mass work.

In his presidential address at the Benaras Congress of 1905, G.K. Gokhale asserted that the educated classes were the "natural leaders of the people" and that "political rights were being demanded not for the whole population, but for such portion of it as has been qualified by education to discharge properly the responsibilities of such association."

Forces critical of moderate attitudes and values had been building up in Maharashtra, Punjab and Bengal in the last two decades of the nineteenth century. The moderate method of appealing to the liberal British was criticized as "mendicancy" and instead of prayers and petitions self-help and constructive work became the new aims. Congress was condemned as a "three-day tamasha" by Aswini Kumar Datta in 1897. Writings of men like Bankim Chandra, Vivekananda and Rabindranath Tagore inspired the growth of a new spirit. Men like Bipin Chandra Pal contributed to the growth of the new political trend commonly known as extremism, which gradually became more and more powerful.

During his stay in England, Sri Aurobindo had been following the course of events in India by perusing the *Bengalee,* copies of which were sent to him regularly by his father with passages underlined that related to cases of British

12. Bipan Chandra, "The Rise and Growth of Economic Nationalism in India" in *Economic Policies of Indian National Leadership* (1880–1905), New Delhi, 1966.

misgovernment. While in Cambridge, Sri Aurobindo took an active part in the meetings of the Indian *Majlis,* and in London he joined a secret society, the "Lotus and Dagger," where probably for the first time Indian students in England had come together with a purpose that went beyond mendicancy and moderatism of most of the Congress leaders in India. Each member took a vow to work for the liberation of India generally and also to take up one particular line of work in furtherance of that aim. His interest in the Irish Liberation movement led by Parnell was perhaps, a reflection of Sri Aurobindo's increasing concern with the situation in India. It has been pointed out by his biographer that his rejection from the Indian Civil Service — partly manoeuvred by himself and partly provoked by his political activities at Cambridge — opened the way for him to engage in politics, first covertly and later openly, after his return to India in February 1893.

Aurobindo Arrives in India

On returning to India, Sri Aurobindo joined the Baroda State Service on 8 February 1893 and retained connection till 18 June 1907. He was first put in the Survey and Settlement Department and then in the Stamps and Revenue Departments and also worked for some time in the secretariat. From 1897 he became part-time lecturer in French at the Baroda College, and in 1900 was appointed as permanent Professor of English. Since 1904, he acted as Vice-Principal and was appointed Principal in March 1905.

Sri Aurobindo, soon after his arrival in India, was invited by his Cambridge friend K.G. Deshpande, who was then English editor of the journal *Indu Prakash* of Bombay, to write articles on the political situation in the country. Nine articles appeared serially and anonymously under the caption "New Lamps for the Old" between 7 August 1893 and 6 March 1894. These were followed by another series from the issue of 16 July to that of 27 August 1894 on the personality and achievements of Bankim Chandra Chatterjee. Introducing the series to the readers, K.G. Deshpande wrote in the issue on 7 August:

> Hypocrisy has been the besetting sin of our political agitation. Oblique vision is the fashion. True, matter of fact, honest criticism is very badly needed . . . The questions at issue are momentous. It is the making or the unmaking of a nation. We have, therefore, secured a gentleman of great literary talent, of liberal culture and of considerable English experience, well-versed in the art of writing and willing, at great personal inconvenience and probable misrepresentation, to give out his views in no uncertain voice, and . . . in a style and diction peculiarly his own. We . . . assure them (our readers) that they will find in those articles matter that will set them thinking and steel their patriotic souls.[13]

Sri Aurobindo's penetrating analysis and trenchant criticism of the contemporary political situation and role of Congress leaders reflected his burning patriotic spirit. In one article he wrote:

> I say, of the Congress, then, this that its aims are mistaken, that the spirit in which it proceeds towards their accomplishment is not a spirit of sincerity and wholeheartedness, and that the methods it has chosen are not the right methods, and the leaders in whom it trusts, are not the right sort of men to be leaders; in brief, that we are at present blind, led if not by the blind, at any rate by the one-eyed.[14]

According to historians his articles betrayed the "deep impression of French revolutionary thinking." Sri Aurobindo accused Pherozshah Mehta and other moderate Congress

---

13. A.B. Purani, *The Life of Sri Aurobindo*, Pondicherry, 1978, p. 41.
14. Sri Aurobindo, *Bande Mataram: Early Political Writings* I, Birth centenary Library, Pondicherry, 1972, p. 15.

leaders of ignoring the proletariat, and of "playing with bubbles" like the Legislative Council and simultaneous Civil Service examinations. He wrote:

> The proletariat is the real key of the situation. Torpid he is and immobile; he is nothing of an actual force, but he is a very great potential force, and whoever succeeds in understanding and eliciting his strength, becomes by the very fact master of the future. Our situation is indeed complex . . . but if there is one thing clear in it, it is that the right and fruitful policy for the burgess, the only policy that has any chance of eventual success, is to base his cause upon an adroit management of the proletariat. He must awaken and organize the entire power of the country and thus multiply infinitely his volume and significance."[15]

While at Baroda, Aurobindo came in touch with one Thakur Saheb (a noble of Udaipur) who was in overall charge of revolutionary activities in western India. Through his inspiration Aurobindo joined the revolutionary society of Bombay and in 1902 took up the task of propagating the society's objects in Bengal.[16] Sri Aurobindo's emissary Jatin Bandyopadhyay met P. Mitra, who was the president of a secret society called the Anusilan Samiti which had been founded by several students of the General Assemblies Institution and who were influenced by Bankim Chandra, Vivekananda and Jogendranath Vidyabhushan (the author of several books on Mazzini and Garibaldi).

---

15. Sri Aurobindo Birth Centenary Library, popular edition, vol. 1, Pondicherry, 1972, p. 54.
16. Amales Tripathi, op. cit., p. 63. He has referred in this connection to *Sri Aurobindo On Himself and On the Mother*, Pondicherry, 1953, pp. 30, 35. According to A. Tripathi, Dr B.B. Majumdar has misinterpreted the text to show that Aurobindo joined Thakur Saheb in 1902-03 after he had already started revolutionary work in Bengal in *Militant Nationalism in India*, Calcutta, 1966, p. 99.

In 1902, Sri Aurobindo went to Midnapore accompanied among others by his younger brother Barindranath Ghosh to initiate Hemchandra Kanungo, Satyen Basu and others of Midnapur.[17] In 1902, Sri Aurobindo also attended the Ahmedabad session of the Congress and here the famous Maharashtrian leader B.G. Tilak took Sri Aurobindo out of the pandal "and talked to him for an hour in the grounds, expressing his contempt for the Reformist movement and explaining his own line of action in Maharashtra."[18] Sri Aurobindo also attended the Bombay Congress (1904) and the Benares Congress (1905).

When the Bengal Partition Act of 1905 was passed by the Government, Sri Aurobindo said, "This is a very fine opportunity to carry on the anti partition agitation powerfully. We will get many workers for the movement."[19] Later Sri Aurobindo wrote a pamphlet entitled *No Compromise.*[20] Around this time he also wrote a famous revolutionary booklet *Bhawani Mandir* which was perhaps inspired by Bankim Chandra's *Ānandamaṭh.* The idea was that a temple of Mother India would be built somewhere in the forest or some mountain-top. Here workers would dedicate themselves to India's complete independence.

Achieving Complete Swaraj was the Target

According to modern researchers, the Swadeshi movement had four distinct trends within it — the moderate trend, the trend of constructive Swadeshi, political extremism using extended boycott or passive resistance in addition to development through self-help, and finally the trend of

17. Ibid.
18. K.R. Srinivasa Iyengar, op. cit., p. 175.
19. Purani, op. cit., p. 66.
20. Ibid.

terrorism.[21] The traditional moderate techniques of political agitation were tried during the first phase of the anti-partition movement, from December 1903 to July 1905. Numerous meetings, press campaigns, petitions and conferences were organized to protest against the plan of partition. The Town Hall meeting of 7 August passed the boycott resolution.[22] The moderates were however against educational boycott and this issue produced the first real split between the old and the new trends. Between 1905 and 1907, a distinct trend seemed to emerge in the political arena through anti-partition movement. Its aims as well as techniques were clearly different from old-style moderate politics. The main target was to achieve complete political independence or Swaraj — not mere constitutional reforms.

The word *swaraj* itself had first been used by Sakharam Ganesh Deuskar, in his biography of Shivaji in Bengali. The word was later popularized by the Bengali paper *Sandhya,* edited by Brahmabandhav Upadhyay. Sri Aurobindo advocated non-co-operation and passive resistance as the means to Swaraj. Sri Aurobindo's biographer wrote:

> Secret revolutionary propaganda and preparation; a more overt collaboration with nationalist leaders like Tilak and a behind-the-scene jostling with a view to converting the Congress to the new programme of Swaraj-Swadeshi-Boycott; and, finally, the nationwide mobilization of the people's idealism and energies through a movement of non-cooperation and passive resistance on the issue of immediate national independence, these were the three levels of Sri Aurobindo's political thinking and activity, at first distinct enough from one another, but really meant to coalesce sooner

21. Sumit Sarkar, *The Swadeshi Movement in Bengal* — 1903-08, New Delhi, 1973, p. 33.
22. Prithwis Chandra Roy, *The Case Against the Break-up of Bengal,* 1905, p. vi.

or later, into a single "Triveni," facilitating our baptism of rebirth as a new nation and a new people.

Sri Aurobindo's articles in *Bande Mataram* (9-23 April 1907) later reprinted as *Doctrine of Passive Resistance* (1948) clearly enunciated his ideas about the doctrine of passive resistance. According to him the term implied "an organized and relentless boycott" of British goods, officialized education, justice and executive administrations. This was to be supplemented by the positive development of national education, arbitration courts and leagues of mutual defence. The implementation of the doctrine of passive resistance also included in its agenda a programme of civil disobedience of unjust punitive laws and "social boycott" of traitors. We see here the blueprint of almost the whole programme of political action of later day Gandhian movement (except the latter's stress on non-violent methods). It should also be remembered that Aurobindo's suggestion in 1907 of a mass courting of arrest through violation of unjust laws had similarity with the Gandhian technique of flooding the prisons with volunteers.

Non-Violence, Satyagraha and Mahatma Gandhi

When India was witnessing the Swadeshi or anti-partition movement in the first decade of the twentieth century, Mohandas Karamchand Gandhi, a young Gujarati barrister, was busy organizing passive resistance among the Indian community in South Africa since 1907 against the discrimination expressed by the white population in laws and social conventions. As has been pointed out by historians, "the ideology behind Gandhi's passive resistance was a blend of the Hindu *Vaiṣṇava* tradition of *ahiṁsa,* non-violence, and a belief in suffering rather than fighting to overcome an opponent."[23] Gandhi himself mentioned about the influence

23. Judith M. Brown, *Gandhi's Rise to Power: Indian Politics* 1915-22, Cambridge, 1972, p. 6.

of Leo Tolstoy's writings on him in his early days in South Africa. He wrote: "I made . . . an intensive study of Tolstoy's books. *The Gospels in Brief, What to do?* and other books made a deep impression on me. I began to realize more and more the infinite possibilities of universal love."[24] Gandhi redefined passive resistance as *Satyagraha,* or "truth-force" meaning search for truth through non-violence and suffering. In his own words: "When in a meeting of Europeans I found that the term "passive resistance" was too narrowly construed, that it was supposed to be a weapon of the weak, that it could be characterized by hatred, and that it could finally manifest itself as violence, I had to demur to all these statements and explain the real nature of the Indian movement. It was clear that a new word must be coined by the Indians to designate their struggle."[25] Sri Aurobindo wrote about the success of the Transvaal *Satyagraha* led by Gandhi thus:

> There has been only one other instance of a victory as complete for passive resistance against the might of a great Government. We refer to the struggle in the Transvaal which was carried on with equal unity, perseverance and thoroughness to a success less absolutely unconditional but even more striking from the strength and stubbornness of the enemy it had to overcome.[26]

After returning to India, Gandhi set up the Sabarmati Ashram at Ahmedabad in May 1915 where some of the ideas spelt out in his book *Hind Swaraj* (1909) were sought to be pursued like the Swadeshi or use of things Indian, national education through vernacular media and so on. Both these Gandhian ideas of national education and Swadeshi had their precedence in the anti-partition movement as led by Sri Aurobindo and

24. Gandhi, *An Autobiography: The Story of My Experiments With Truth,* London, 1966, p. 133.
25. Ibid., p. 266.
26. Sri Aurobindo Birth Centenary Library, op. cit., p. 753.

others. The programme of boycott, Swadeshi as well as that of contacting the masses[27] were in the agenda of Gandhian movements as they developed between 1915 and 1921 and included Champaran, Kheda and Ahmedabad Satyagrahas during 1917-18, Rowlatt Satyagraha (1919), and the non-co-operation movement (1921-22).

Sri Aurobindo's Contemporary: Mahatma Gandhi

If one goes into a deeper analysis of the political thoughts of both these leaders of India's nationalist struggle, it is easy to see that both were trying to put India's political struggle on moral as well as ethical foundation. Both supported the ideal of constructive Swadeshi and Swaraj and attempted to give new meanings to these ideals through their activities. Both criticized British policy of education and experimented with new kind of education which would be truly national for the Indians. According to Sri Aurobindo, the system of Western education as introduced by the British was defective because

> of its calculated poverty and insufficiency, its anti-national character, its subordination to Government and the use made

---

27. Sri Aurobindo himself not only talked about arousing the proletariat who according to him was a great potential force, but tried to build up mass contact himself and through his brother Barin. Barin himself went to the villages of Bengal and organized a chain of *samitis* or youth organizations (during the early years of the first decade of the twentieth century) which would meet under all kinds of pretexts but with the real aim of providing a civic and political education and opening the eyes of the young to the affairs of the nation. After attending the Barisal conference on 14 April, 1906, Sri Aurobindo, along with B.C. Pal toured different places of East Bengal and addressed mammoth meetings against the Partition sometimes defying Government's prohibitory orders. Thus, he was taking political education to the people and was also educating himself by getting to know first hand the masses. It was by means of such tours and other forms of uninhibited mass contact that Sri Aurobindo attempted to penetrate the heart of the proletariat or the general people.

> of that subordination for the discouragement of patriotism and the inculcation of loyalty.[28]

The National Council of Education (founded in 1906) set up the Bengal National College in August 1906 with Sri Aurobindo as its first principal.[29] M.K. Gandhi wrote in *Hind Swaraj* (1909) that the foundation of English education laid by Macaulay (in 1835) "has enslaved us."[30] His remedy was national education

---

28. Sri Aurobindo, *Doctrine of Passive Resistance,* Calcutta, 1948, p. 37.
29. See Haridas Mukherjee and Uma Mukherjee, *The Origins of the National Education Movement,* Jadavpur University, 1957.
30. M.K. Gandhi, *Hind Swaraj and other Writings,* Cambridge University Press, 1997, p. 103. About the scheme of national education imparted in Bengal, Sri Aurobindo said in a speech delivered on 15 January 1908 at Girgaum, Bombay, "Nothing that is useful or important is neglected in the scheme, and instruction is, as far as possible, imparted in the vernacular. This is not the case with the education imparted in Government schools where the tender minds of students are uselessly burdened with Western ideas utterly antagonistic to their own modes of living and thinking. In profiting by our contact with Western civilization, we should be careful not to cut ourselves adrift from our original moorings, but should at the same time imitate the Japanese in taking the fullest advantage of modern scientific discoveries. In political matters we have much to learn from the Western nations, and we should also turn to them for lessons in popular Government. In our scheme of national education, we teach students how to take an active part in politics as we believe that without such training, their education will not be complete. As we teach them some handicrafts, they find it easy to obtain moderately remunerative employment on leaving our schools, which is not the case with the pupils attending Government institutions. Our seventh standard equals the intermediate course of the Indian Universities. Self-reliance forms the guiding principle of our scheme of education. We do not look to Government for help as we think that state assistance will destroy our national stamina. We challenge those who have been harping upon the alleged impracticability of imparting education "on national lines," to visit Bengal and see what is being done there in that direction." Vide *Sri Aurobindo Birth Centenary Library* — Popular Edition, vol. 27, Pondicherry, 1972, pp. 66-67.

as in his *ashram,* through vernacular media, stressing religious instruction and practical knowledge of agriculture and weaving, as well as more customary academic subjects. In the Calcutta Congress (Sept. 1920), Gandhi proposed his non-co-operation resolution which included among other things boycott of foreign goods and government schools and colleges. He also supported the idea of Swadeshi in the economic field, or the use of things belonging to one's own country. This would produce a mental revolution and would bring in true Swaraj.

Conclusion

After Mahatma Gandhi's tragic death on 30 January 1948, Sri Aurobindo wrote in a message (given in answer to a request from the All India Radio, Trichinopoly) on 5 February 1948:"

> I would have preferred silence in the face of these circumstances that surround us. For any words we can find will fall flat on such happenings. This much, however, I will say that the light which led us to freedom, though not yet to unity, still burns and will burn on till it conquers. I believe firmly that a great and united future is the destiny of this nation and its peoples. The Power that brought us through so much struggle and suffering to freedom, will achieve also, through whatever strife or trouble, the aim which so poignantly occupied the thoughts of the fallen leader at the time of his tragic ending; as it brought us freedom, it will bring us unity. A free and united India will be there and the mother will gather around her sons and hold them into a single national strength in the life of a great and united people.

The Contributors

Tirthanath Bandyopadhyay, PhD, is Professor in the Department of Philosophy, Jadavpur University, Kolkata. His publications include: *Man: An Essay in Philosophical Anthropology* (1988); *Man and Morality* (1991); *In Search of a Moral Criterion* (1994); *Human Action and Freedom* (1999); *Kant on Freedom* (2001); *Morality and Practice* (2002); and *Moral Normativeness* (2006). He is also the Co-editor of *Action: Explanation and Interpretation* (1990); *19th Century Thought in Bengal* (1998); and *Ethics: An Anthology* (2000) [address: Professor, Department of Philosophy, Jadavpur University, Kolkata].

Aparna Banerjee is presently Head of the Department of Philosophy at Maulana Azad College, Kolkata. She has written a book entitled *Explanation and Understanding in the Social Sciences,* and has done a Minor Research Project of the U.G.C. on "The Indian Caste Hierarchy". Besides, she has published several papers in reputed journals of Philosophy [**address:** Department of Philosophy, Maulana Azad College, KOLKATA].

Supriyo Bhattacharya has been on the teaching faculty of the Department of Economics, University of Kalyani, since 1984. First class MA in Economics from Calcutta University, he worked as Assistant Secretary in the Bengal National Chamber of Commerce and Industries, Kolkata. He is engaged in research on Sri Aurobindo and has been connected with research work that is being done at Kolkata Sri Aurobindo Bhavan and at Pondicherry. He received "Sri Aurobindo Puroskar", in 2006, from the Governor of West Bengal. He has been elected a Fellow of the Royal Asiatic Society of Great Britain and Ireland in June 2007 [**address**: Praity, HB Town, 1st Road, (Opposite Mother Dairy), 3rd Floor, P.O. Sodepur, North 24 Parganas, KOLKATA – 700 110].

Sushmita Bhowmik, presently Lecturer in Philosophy, Budge Budge College, Kolkata, passed MA from Jadavpur University in 2003 and is at present doing research on the topic "Regeneration of Values: A Comparison Between Mahatma Gandhi and Sri Aurobindo". She has written several articles for anthologies and journals [**address:** 23 A/4, R.K. Sarari, Behala, KOLKATA – 700 060; **e-mail:** <b_sushmita_79@yahoo.co.in>].

Manjula Bose, Director of Tagore Research Institute, Kolkata, did MA and PhD in Economics from Calcutta University and served as Professor and Head of the Department of Economics, Jadavpur University. Prof. Bose atttended many international conferences between 1979 and 1994. Books written by her include *Saumyandranath Tagore — Karma O Manane;* and *Rammohan Roy — O Bharater Arthaniti*. She has been the Editor of the bulletin *Tagore International* [**address:** 56/2A, Jubilee Park, CALCUTTA – 700 032].

Tara Chatterjea, presently attached to the Research Section of Ramakrishna Mission Institute of Culture, has completed D. Phil under the guidance of Professor J.N. Mohanty and taught in Lady Brabourne College, Kolkata and Jadavpur University as guest lecturer. An anthology has been published by Lexington Books, USA titled *Knowledge and Freedom in Indian Philosophy* and is currently editing a collection of essays by Prof. J.N. Mohanty [**address**: 7/1 Ballygunge Park, KOLKATA – 700 019; **e-mail:** <tarachatterjea@yahoo.com>].

Dilip Kumar Chatterjee (1952–) M.A., PhD, Reader and Head of the Department of English, Bangabasi College (Morning) and Guest Lecturer, Rabindra Bharati University, Kolkata, is now working on a research project on "Harindranath Chattopadhyay and Sri Aurobindo School of Indian English Poetry", approved by the UGC. His contribution to the Sri Aurobindo Number of the *Journal of South Asian Literature*, Asian Study Center, Michigan State University, USA deserves special mention. His pioneering research on James Henry Cousins as published from Delhi under the title *James Henry Cousins and the Theosophical Movement in India and the West* (1994) is widely acclaimed. He has edited with a long Introduction and Bibliographical note of Cousins' *The Renaissance in India* (2005), foreworded by Prof. R.K. Dasgupta, who called the edition "masterly". He gave the 23rd Annual Sri Aurobindo Memorial Lecture in Jadavpur University on "Sri Aurobindo's Concept of Nationalism" in 2006 [**address**: Indrani Apartments, 1st Floor-A/2, 129, Vivekananda Sarani, Kolkata – 700 078].

MADHUMITA CHATTOPADHYAY is a Professor in the Department of Philosophy, Jadavpur University. Her areas of research are Buddhist philosophy, logic and Indian ethics. She has published two books and several articles in national and international journals [**address:** Department of Philosophy, Jadavpur University, Jadavpur, KOLKATA – 700 032; **e-mail:** <c_madhumita@hotmail.com>].

D.P. CHATTOPADHYAYA (1933–) is MA, LL B, PhD, (Calcutta University), PhD (London School of Economics), D.Lit. (Hony. from different universities), studied Law, Ethics, Aesthetics and Philosophy; taught in various universities in India, Asia, Europe and the USA. Prof. Chattopadhyaya presently is Chairman, Centre for Studies in Civilizations; and also the Director, Project of History of Science, Philosophy and Culture in Indian Civilization (in 96 volumes). He was a former Chairman of the Indian Council of Philosophical Research, Delhi; and a former Chairman of the Indian Institute of Advanced Study, Shimla. His publications include 35 books — 18 authored and 17 edited and co-edited by him. He has also published over 300 papers in referred journals on Philosophy and related areas [**address:** Director, Centre for Studies in Civilization, 25 Park Mansion, 57-A, Park Street, KOLKATA – 700 016; **e-mail**: <dpc@cal.vsnl.net.in>].

AMAL KUMAR DE, Asst. General Secretary of the National Council of Education, Bengal (a parent body of Jadavpur University); Life Member of the World Union, Sri Aurobindo Ashram, Pondicherry, is now an advocate. Since childhood, he had profound respect for Sri Aurobindo and the Mother and felt an attraction towards their life and teachings. His works include, *Fate And Free-Will — A Sri Aurobindo Overview* (in English); *Sri Aurobinder Sonetsamagra* (in Bengali); among others [**address**: National Council of Education, Bengal, P.O. Jadavpur University, KOLKATA – 700 032; **e-mail:** <ibmnce@cal3.vsnl.net.in>].

Rama Prasad De is at present working as the Honorary Director, Rabisandhya Unit of Extension Lectures, National Council of Education, Bengal. He had been teaching Old and Middle English in the Department of English, Jadavpur University (1957–1991). He also taught (part-time) in the Rabindra Bharati University. He has written articles on "History of the English Language", and "Place Names and National Education Movement in our Country", among others [**address:** National Council of Education, Bengal, P.O. Jadavpur University, KOLKATA – 700 032; **e-mail**: <ibmnce@cal3.vsnl.net.in>].

Kireet Joshi (1931–), Editorial Fellow for the volume on "Synthesis of Yoga" under the hundred-volume project of History of Indian Philosophy, Science and Culture, New Delhi, and President of The Mother's Institute of Research, New Delhi, is MA, LL. B, recipient of D. Litt. (*honoris causa*) from four universities. He was selected for Indian Administrative Service in 1955. He resigned from the service in 1956 to join the Integral Yoga of Sri Aurobindo and the Mother at Pondicherry. He soon became (1958-75) the Registrar of the Sri Aurobindo International Centre of Education, Sri Aurobindo Ashram, Pondicherry. At the invitation of the Government of India, he joined the Ministry of Education in 1976 as its Chief Education Adviser. Between 1976 and 1988, he was concurrently the founder Member–Secretary of Indian Council of Philosophical Research. He remained Chairman of the Auroville Foundation (1999–2004). His works include: *Sri Aurobindo and the Mother; Philosophy and Yoga of Sri Aurobindo; Glimpses of Vedic Literature; Education for Character Development; Bhagavad-Gita and Contemporary Crisis; Philosophy of Education for the Contemporary Youth; Philosophy of Education for the Contemporary Teacher;* and *Philosophy of Evolution for the Contemporary Man,* among others [**address:** 192, Sukhdev Vihar, Ground Floor, NEW DELHI – 110 025; **e-mail:** <mothersinstitute@hotmail.com>].

Sujata Mukherjee, Professor of History and Director at the Centre for Gandhian Studies of Rabindra Bharati University, Kolkata, teaches Socio-cultural History of Modern India including History of Science, Technology and Medicine at Post-Graduate level. She has to her credit several research publications and articles on different aspects of socio-cultural and political history of modern India and on thoughts of Tagore and Gandhi [**address:** 256, B-block, Lake Town, KOLKATA – 700 050; **e-mail:** <suj_40@rediffmail.com>].

S.K. Nandi (1924–), Research Fellow at Calcutta University; Senior Fellow at Indian Institute of Advanced Study (Simla); and Fellow at the Asiatic Society (Kolkata), has worked as Professor of Philosophy and Aesthetics in Postgraduate Departments of Calcutta and Rabindra Bharati universities including the Presidency College, Kolkata for about thirty years. Dr Nandi's works include *Art and Aesthetics of Rabindaranath Tagore; Art and Aesthetics of Abanindranath Tagore; Studies in Modern Indian Aesthetics;* among others. He was awarded Rabindra Puruskar in 2000 and the Ashutosh Mukherjee Gold Medal in 1966 [**address:** 'Saucam', 18/10, Ballygunge Place East, KOLKATA – 700 019].

Rakhal Chandra Nath, MA, PhD, is formerly Professor and Head, Department of History, and Dean, Faculty of Arts and Commerce in the University of Kalyani. He has been writing on history and his published works include: *The New Hindu Movement; Bankim Chandra: A Historical Review; Unis Satak: Bhaba Sangata O Samanya* (in Bengali), *Mananer Aloke Bangalee* (in Bengali) [**address:** E/29, Central Road, Anandapuri, Barrackpore, KOLKATA – 700 122].

Dilip Kumar Roy was in West Bengal Educational Service and taught Philosophy in Presidency College, Kolkata, for a long period. His publications include *The Philosophy of George Santayana, The Comparative Study of Religions, The Dynamic Absolute — A Preface of Sri Aurobindo's Intergral Advaita,* "Sri Aurobindo's Integral Approach to the Concept of Evolution" — an article in *Understanding Thoughts of Sri Aurobindo* and *Upanisad Prasange Sri Aurobindo.* He is at present the Secretary of Sri Aurobindo Institute of Education, Salt Lake City, Kolkata [**address:** "Banabithi", KB-6, Flat-2, Sector-III, Salt Lake City, KOLKATA – 700 098; **e-mail:** <diluroy@yahoo.com>].

Krishna Roy, is associated with the Centre for Indological Study and Research at the Ramakrishna Mission Institute of Culture, Kolkata. She retired from the Department of Philosophy, Jadavpur University, Kolkata in 2006 as Head and Coordinator of the Centre of Advanced Study in Philosophy. Her areas of interest include

Phenomenology, Existentialism, Hermeneutics, Social and Political Philosophy. Shehasauthorededited *Hermeneutics: East and West* (1993); *Fusion of Horizons: Socio-Spiritual Heritage of India* (2000); and *Political Philosophy, East and West* (2003). She has also co-edited anthologies like *Language, Knowledge and Ontology* (1988); *Essays in Social and Political Philosophy* (1989); *Theory and Practice: A Collection of Essays* (2003); and *Understanding Thoughts of Sri Aurobindo* (2007) [**address:** 18, Jatin Bagchi Road, KOLKATA – 700 019].

INDRANI SANYAL is Professor of Philosophy at Centre of Advanced Study in Philosophy, Jadavpur University, Kolkata. She is also Co-ordinator, Centre for Sri Aurobindo Studies, Jadavpur University. Her areas of interest include Metaphysics, Philosophy of Language, Ethics: especially Indian Ethics, and Philosophy of Sri Aurobindo. Besides publishing many articles in anthologies and journals, she has authored *On Essentialist Claims*. She has co-edited *Wittgenstein: Jagat, Bhasa O Cintan; Siksaksetre Parasparika Samparka; Understanding Thoughts of Sri Aurobindo; Bharatiya Dharmanitir Bhittirupe Sruti;* among others [**address:** "Chirag", Flat 2, 56/4 Ballygunge Circular Road, KOLKATA – 700 019; **e-mail:** <indranisnyl@yahoo.co.in>].

Index